THE PROPHETS

THE PROPHETS

BY

ABRAHAM J. HESCHEL

VOLUME I

HARPER TORCHBOOKS
Harper & Row, Publishers
New York, Cambridge, Philadelphia, San Francisco
London, Mexico City, São Paulo, Sydney

The Revised Standard Version has been used throughout, interspersed occasionally with my own translation. Some paragraphs in this volume are taken from my book, *God in Search of Man*, Farrar, Straus & Cudahy, New York, 1955.

ISBN: 0-06-131421-8

First Harper paperback edition published 1969.

98 99 **RRD H** 40 39

To the martyrs of 1940-45

All this has come upon us,
Though we have not forgotten Thee,
Or been false to Thy covenant.
Our heart has not turned back,
Nor have our steps departed from Thy way . . .
. . . for Thy sake we are slain . . .
Why dost Thou hide Thy face?

—from Psalm 44.

ABBREVIATIONS USED IN
THE FOOTNOTES

AASOR	Annual of the American Schools of Oriental Research
ANET	J. B. Pritchard, ed., *Ancient Near Eastern Texts Relating to the Old Testament* (2nd ed.; Princeton, 1950)
ERE	J. Hastings, ed., *Encyclopedia of Religion and Ethics*
(H.)	Hebrew; used to denote verses in the Hebrew Bible when the numbering differs from RSV
HUCA	Hebrew Union College Annual, Cincinnati, Ohio
JBL	Journal of Biblical Literature
MGWJ	*Monatsschrift für die Geschichte und Wissenschaft des Judentums*
ThWBNT	*Theologisches Wörterbuch zum Neuen Testament*
ZAW	*Zeitschrift für die Alttestamentliche Wissenschaft*
ZDMG	*Zeitschrift der Deutschen Morgenländischen Gesellschaft*

CONTENTS

INTRODUCTION

This book is about some of the most disturbing people who have ever lived: the men whose inspiration brought the Bible into being—the men whose image is our refuge in distress, and whose voice and vision sustain our faith.

The significance of Israel's prophets lies not only in what they said but also in what they were. We cannot fully understand what they meant to say to us unless we have some degree of awareness of what happened to them. The moments that passed in their lives are not now available and cannot become the object of scientific analysis. All we have is the consciousness of those moments as preserved in words.

My aim therefore is to attain an understanding of the prophet through an analysis and description of his *consciousness*, to relate what came to pass in his life—facing man, being faced by God—as reflected and affirmed in his mind. By consciousness, in other words, I mean here not only the perception of particular moments of inspiration, but also the totality of impressions, thoughts, and feelings which make up the prophet's being.

By insisting on the absolutely objective and supernatural nature of prophecy, dogmatic theology has disregarded the prophet's part in the prophetic act. Stressing revelation, it has ignored the response; isolating inspiration, it has lost sight of the human situation. In contrast with what may be called "pan-theology," psychologists have sought to deduce prophecy entirely from the inner life of the prophets. Reducing it to a subjective personal phenomenon, they have disregarded the prophet's awareness of his confrontation with facts not derived from his own mind.

A rejection of both extremes must spring from the realization that the words of the prophets testify to a situation that defies both pan-theology and pan-psychology. Careful analysis shows that this situation is composed of revelation and response, of receptivity and spontaneity, of event and experience. I maintain, therefore, that the marks of the personal element are to be traced, not outside the prophet's act, but within it.

The prophet is a person, not a microphone. He is endowed with a mission, with the power of a word not his own that accounts for his greatness—but also with temperament, concern, character, and individuality. As there was no resisting the impact of divine inspiration, so at times there was no resisting the vortex of his own temperament. The word of God reverberated in the voice of man.

The prophet's task is to convey a divine view, yet as a person he *is* a point of view. He speaks from the perspective of God as perceived from the perspective of his own situation. We must seek to understand not only the views he expounded but also the attitudes he embodied: his own position, feeling, response—not only what he said but also what he lived; the private, the intimate dimension of the word, the subjective side of the message.

In the prophets of Israel we may trace similarities and parallels to personalities to be encountered elsewhere, since indeed the religion of the Hebrews shared much with other Semitic religions. It is therefore important to compare them with other types of men of ancient history who made similar claims. Yet the more difficult question is: What are the features that set the prophets of Israel apart? What constitutes their uniqueness?

The prophet is not only a prophet. He is also poet, preacher, patriot, statesman, social critic, moralist. There has been a tendency to see the essence and chief significance of prophecy in the display of one or another of these aspects. Yet this is a misapprehension of the intrinsic nature of prophecy.

The first objective of our inquiry should not be to see the prophet as an example of a species, but rather to ascertain the characteristics that set him apart as well as those he shares with others. In order to meet him truly as a prophet, the mind must shed certain habits of inquiry; traps and decoys of convenient patterns are to be avoided. The most assured way of missing the goal is an approach carried on with the preconceived certainty of being able to explain him. To explain the prophet in terms of a neat set of preconceived notions would be putting the cart before the horse. Explanation, when regarded as the only goal of inquiry, becomes a substitute for understanding. Imperceptibly it becomes the beginning rather than the end of perception.

The bias which so many scholars share and which may be defined as a principle—namely, that nothing is to be recognized as a datum unless it can be qualified *a priori* as capable of explanation—besides being pretentious and questionable, obstructs the view of much of reality and seriously affects our power to gain a pristine insight into what we face.

Confining attention to what is given in the literary sources, i.e., the prophetic books, I have sought to gain some insight into the minds of the prophets and to understand the decisive moments of their existence from that perspective.[1] It was not my intention in this study to pass judgment on the truth of their claim to have received revelation, nor to solve the enigma of prophecy by means of psychological or sociological explanations, nor yet to discover the conditions of its possibility or suggest means of its verification. The intention was to illumine the prophets' claim; not to explain their consciousness, but to understand it. By unveiling the decisive features of their awareness, the essential structure of experience as reflected in that consciousness may become manifest.

What I have aimed at is an understanding of what it means to think, feel, respond, and act as a prophet. It was not part of the task to go beyond his consciousness in order to explore the subconscious or reach out to the antecedent conditionings and experiences within the inner life of the individual. A surmise of what lies beyond and below the threshold of the prophet's consciousness can never be a substitute for the understanding of what is displayed in consciousness itself. Nor is it possible to confirm what he affirms. We may arrive at some knowledge of what stirred the prophet as a prophet—of the ideas by which he was moved at particular moments; we cannot prove the realities and events which preceded these moments.

The inquiry, then, was aimed, not at psychological motives to be looked for in the preprophetic background of the prophet's life, but at motives which are consciously given, even if not explicitly stated, and which constitute or at least reflect the decisive categories or the structural forms of prophetic thinking.

The procedure employed in an inquiry for gaining such insight was the method of pure reflection. Observation, inspection, tackling and probing, the sheer seeing of what we face, serve to introduce us to the realness of the phenomenon and sharpen our ability to formulate questions conducive to the discovery of what is unique about it. Indeed, it requires much effort to learn which questions should not be asked and which claims must not be entertained. What impairs our sight are habits of seeing as well as the mental concomitants of seeing. Our sight is suffused with knowing, instead of feeling painfully the lack of knowing what we see. The principle to be kept in mind is to know what we see rather than to see what we know.

---

[1] The destruction of Jerusalem in 587 marks the end of the classical era in the history of prophecy, and the understanding of the prophetic figures who emerged during the exile raises problems of a special kind. This book deals with the classical or literary prophets of the eighth and seventh centuries B.C.E. Of other prophets there is only occasional mention, with the exception of Second Isaiah, whose message illumines many of the enigmas in the words and intentions of his predecessors.

Rather than blame things for being obscure, we should blame ourselves for being biased and prisoners of self-induced repetitiveness. One must forget many clichés in order to behold a single image. Insight is the beginning of perceptions to come rather than the extension of perceptions gone by. Conventional seeing, operating as it does with patterns and coherences, is a way of seeing the present in the past tense. Insight is an attempt to think in the present.

Insight is a breakthrough, requiring much intellectual dismantling and dislocation. It begins with a mental interim, with the cultivation of a feeling for the unfamiliar, unparalleled, incredible. It is in being involved with a phenomenon, being intimately engaged to it, courting it, as it were, that after much perplexity and embarrassment we come upon *insight*— upon a way of seeing the phenomenon from within. Insight is accompanied by a sense of surprise. What has been closed is suddenly disclosed. It entails genuine perception, seeing anew. He who thinks that we can see the same object twice has never seen. Paradoxically, insight is knowledge at first sight.

Such an inquiry must suspend personal beliefs or even any intent to inquire—e.g., whether the event happened in fact as it did to their minds. It is my claim that, regardless of whether or not their experience was of the real, it is possible to analyze the form and content of that experience. The process and result of such an inquiry represent the essential part of this book as composed a good many years ago.[2] While I still maintain the soundness of the method described above, which in important aspects reflects the method of phenomenology, I have long since become wary of impartiality, which is itself a way of being partial. The prophet's existence is either irrelevant or relevant. If irrelevant, I cannot truly be involved in it; if relevant, then my impartiality is but a pretense. Reflection may succeed in isolating an object; reflection itself cannot be isolated. Reflection is part of a situation.

The situation of a person immersed in the prophets' words is one of being exposed to a ceaseless shattering of indifference, and one needs a skull of stone to remain callous to such blows.

I cannot remain indifferent to the question whether a decision I reach may prove fatal to my existence—whether to inhale the next breath in order to survive. Perhaps this is the issue that frightens the prophets. A people may be dying without being aware of it; a people may be able to survive, yet refuse to make use of their ability.

To comprehend what phenomena are, it is important to suspend judg-

---

[2] *Die Prophetie*, published by the Polish Academy of Sciences, Krakow, 1936 and by Erich Reiss, Berlin, 1936. For further details of the method employed, see the preface to that volume, pp. 1-6, as well as discussion throughout the present work.

ment and think in detachment; to comprehend what phenomena mean, it is necessary to suspend indifference and be involved. To examine their essence requires a process of reflection. Such reflection, however, sets up a gulf between the phenomena and ourselves. Reducing them to dead objects of the mind, it deprives them of the power to affect us, to speak to us, to transcend our attitudes and conceptions.

While the structure and the bare content of prophetic consciousness may be made accessible by an attitude of pure reflection, in which the concern for their truth and validity is suspended, the sheer force of what is disclosed in such reflection quietly corrodes the hardness of self-detachment. The magic of the process seems to be stronger than any asceticism of the intellect. Thus in the course of listening to their words one cannot long retain the security of a prudent, impartial observer. The prophets do not offer reflections about ideas in general. Their words are onslaughts, scuttling illusions of false security, challenging evasions, calling faith to account, questioning prudence and impartiality. One may be equally afraid to submit to their strange certainties and to resist their tremendous claims because of incredulity or impotence of spirit. Reflection about the prophets gives way to communion with the prophets.

Pure reflection may be sufficient for the clarification of what the prophet's consciousness asserts—but not for what his existence involves. For such understanding it is not enough to have the prophets in mind; we must think as if we were inside their minds. For them to be alive and present to us we must think, not *about,* but *in* the prophets, with their concern and their heart. Their existence involves us. Unless their concern strikes us, pains us, exalts us, we do not really sense it. Such involvement requires accord, receptivity, hearing, sheer surrender to their impact. Its intellectual rewards include moments in which the mind peels off, as it were, its not-knowing. Thought is like touch, comprehending by being comprehended.

In probing their consciousness we are not interested only in the inward life, in emotion and reflection as such. We are interested in restoring the world of the prophets: terrifying in its absurdity and defiance of its Maker, tottering at the brink of disaster, with the voice of God imploring man to turn to Him. It is not a world devoid of meaning that evokes the prophet's consternation, but a world deaf to meaning. And yet the consternation is but a prelude. He always begins with a message of doom and concludes with a message of hope and redemption. Does this mean that no human wickedness can prevail over God's almighty love? Does this mean that His stillness is stronger than the turmoil of human crimes, that His desire for peace is stronger than man's passion for violence?

Prophecy is not simply the application of timeless standards to particular human situations, but rather an interpretation of a particular moment in history, a divine understanding of a human situation. Prophecy, then, may be described as *exegesis of existence from a divine perspective*. Understanding prophecy is an understanding of an understanding rather than an understanding of knowledge; it is exegesis of exegesis. It involves sharing the perspective from which the original understanding is done. To interpret prophecy from any other perspective—such as sociology or psychology—is like interpreting poetry from the perspective of the economic interests of the poet.

The spirit of such exegesis makes it incongruous for our inquiry to take refuge in the personal question (however vital): What do the prophets mean to us? The only sensible way of asking the personal question is to be guided by another, more audacious question: What do the prophets mean to God? All other questions are absurd unless this one question is meaningful. For prophecy is a sham unless it is experienced as a word of God swooping down on man and converting him into a prophet.

Proper exegesis is an effort to understand the philosopher in terms and categories of philosophy, the poet in terms and categories of poetry, and the prophet in terms and categories of prophecy. Prophecy is a way of thinking as well as a way of living. It is upon the right understanding of the terms and categories of prophetic thinking that the success of our inquiry depends.

To rediscover some of these terms and categories requires careful exploration of the kinds of questions a prophet asks, and the sort of premises about God, the world, and man he takes for granted. Indeed, the most important outcome of the inquiry has been for me the discovery of the *intellectual relevance of the prophets*.

What drove me to study the prophets?

In the academic environment in which I spent my student years philosophy had become an isolated, self-subsisting, self-indulgent entity, a *Ding an sich*, encouraging suspicion instead of love of wisdom. The answers offered were unrelated to the problems, indifferent to the travail of a person who became aware of man's suspended sensitivity in the face of stupendous challenge, indifferent to a situation in which good and evil became irrelevant, in which man became increasingly callous to catastrophe and ready to suspend the principle of truth. I was slowly led to the realization that some of the terms, motivations, and concerns which dominate our thinking may prove destructive of the roots of human responsibility and treasonable to the ultimate ground of human solidarity. The challenge we are all exposed to, and the dreadful shame that shatters our capacity for inner peace, defy the ways and patterns of our thinking. One is forced to admit that some of the causes and motives of our thinking have led our existence astray, that speculative prosperity is no answer to spiritual bankruptcy. It was the realization that the right coins were not available in the common currency that drove me to study the thought of the prophets.

Every mind operates with presuppositions or premises as well as within a particular way of thinking. In the face of the tragic failure of the modern mind, incapable of preventing its own destruction, it became clear to me that the most important philosophical problem of the twentieth century was to find a new set of presuppositions or premises, a different way of thinking.

I have tried to elucidate some of the presuppositions that lie at the root of prophetic theology, the fundamental attitudes of prophetic religion, and to call attention to how they differ from certain presuppositions and attitudes that prevail in other systems of theology and religion. While stressing the centrality of pathos, a term which takes on major importance in the course of the discussion, I have tried not to lose sight of the ethos and logos in their teaching.

Disregarding derivative and subordinate circumstances and focusing attention upon the fundamental motives which give coherence and integral unity to the prophetic personality, I have been led to distinguish in the consciousness of the prophet between what happened *to* him and what happened *in* him—between the transcendent and the spontaneous—as well as between content and form. The structure of prophetic consciousness as ascertained in the analysis was disclosed as consisting, on the transcendent level, of pathos (content of inspiration) and event (form), and on the personal level, of sympathy (content of inner experience) and the sense of being overpowered (form of inner experience).

The prophet was an individual who said No to his society, condemning its habits and assumptions, its complacency, waywardness, and syncretism. He was often compelled to proclaim the very opposite of what his heart expected. His fundamental objective was to reconcile man and God. Why do the two need reconciliation? Perhaps it is due to man's false sense of sovereignty, to his abuse of freedom, to his aggressive, sprawling pride, resenting God's involvement in history.

Prophecy ceased; the prophets endure and can only be ignored at the risk of our own despair. It is for us to decide whether freedom is self-assertion or response to a demand; whether the ultimate situation is conflict or concern.

ABRAHAM J. HESCHEL

Jewish Theological Seminary
New York City
August, 1962

THE PROPHETS

1. WHAT MANNER OF MAN IS THE PROPHET?

SENSITIVITY TO EVIL

What manner of man is the prophet? A student of philosophy who turns from the discourses of the great metaphysicians to the orations of the prophets may feel as if he were going from the realm of the sublime to an area of trivialities. Instead of dealing with the timeless issues of being and becoming, of matter and form, of definitions and demonstrations, he is thrown into orations about widows and orphans, about the corruption of judges and affairs of the market place. Instead of showing us a way through the elegant mansions of the mind, the prophets take us to the slums. The world is a proud place, full of beauty, but the prophets are scandalized, and rave as if the whole world were a slum. They make much ado about paltry things, lavishing excessive language upon trifling subjects. What if somewhere in ancient Palestine poor people have not been treated properly by the rich? So what if some old women found pleasure and edification in worshiping "the Queen of Heaven"? Why such immoderate excitement? Why such intense indignation?

The things that horrified the prophets are even now daily occurrences all over the world. There is no society to which Amos' words would not apply.

> *Hear this, you who trample upon the needy,*
> *And bring the poor of the land to an end,*
> *Saying: When will the new moon be over*
> *That we may sell grain?*
> *And the Sabbath,*
> *That we may offer wheat for sale,*
> *That we may make the ephah small and the shekel great,*
> *And deal deceitfully with false balances,*
> *That we may buy the poor for silver,*
> *And the needy for a pair of sandals,*
> *And sell the refuse of the wheat?*
>
> *Amos 8:4-6*

Indeed, the sort of crimes and even the amount of delinquency that fill the prophets of Israel with dismay do not go beyond that which we regard as normal, as typical ingredients of social dynamics. To us a single act of injustice—cheating in business, exploitation of the poor—is slight; to the prophets, a disaster. To us injustice is injurious to the welfare of the people; to the prophets it is a deathblow to existence: to us, an episode; to them, a catastrophe, a threat to the world.

Their breathless impatience with injustice may strike us as hysteria. We ourselves witness continually acts of injustice, manifestations of hypocrisy, falsehood, outrage, misery, but we rarely grow indignant or overly excited. To the prophets even a minor injustice assumes cosmic proportions.

> *The Lord has sworn by the pride of Jacob:*
> *Surely I will never forget any of their deeds.*
> *Shall not the land tremble on this account,*
> *And every one mourn who dwells in it,*
> *And all of it rise like the Nile,*
> *Be tossed about and sink again, like the Nile of Egypt?*
> *Amos 8:7-8*

> *Be appalled, O heavens, at this,*
> *Be shocked, be utterly desolate, says the Lord.*
> *For My people have committed two evils:*
> *They have forsaken Me,*
> *The fountain of living waters,*
> *And hewed out cisterns for themselves,*
> *Broken cisterns,*
> *That can hold no water.*
> *Jeremiah 2:12-13*

They speak and act as if the sky were about to collapse because Israel has become unfaithful to God.

Is not the vastness of their indignation and the vastness of God's anger in disproportion to its cause? How should one explain such moral and religious excitability, such extreme impetuosity?

It seems incongruous and absurd that because of some minor acts of injustice inflicted on the insignificant, powerless poor, the glorious city of Jerusalem should be destroyed and the whole nation go to exile. Did not the prophet magnify the guilt?

The prophet's words are outbursts of violent emotions. His rebuke is harsh and relentless. But if such deep sensitivity to evil is to be called hysterical, what name should be given to the abysmal indifference to evil which the prophet bewails?

> They drink wine in bowls,
> And anoint themselves with the finest oils,
> But they are not grieved over the ruin of Joseph!
> *Amos 6:6*

The niggardliness of our moral comprehension, the incapacity to sense the depth of misery caused by our own failures, is a fact which no subterfuge can elude. Our eyes are witness to the callousness and cruelty of man, but our heart tries to obliterate the memories, to calm the nerves, and to silence our conscience.

The prophet is a man who feels fiercely. God has thrust a burden upon his soul, and he is bowed and stunned at man's fierce greed. Frightful is the agony of man; no human voice can convey its full terror. Prophecy is the voice that God has lent to the silent agony, a voice to the plundered poor, to the profaned riches of the world. It is a form of living, a crossing point of God and man. God is raging in the prophet's words.

THE IMPORTANCE OF TRIVIALITIES

"Human affairs are hardly worth considering in earnest, and yet we must be in earnest about them—a sad necessity constrains us," says Plato in a mood of melancholy. He apologizes later for his "low opinion of mankind" which, he explains, emerged from comparing men with the gods. "Let us grant, if you wish, that the human race is not to be despised, but is worthy of some consideration."[1]

"The gods attend to great matters; they neglect small ones," Cicero maintains.[2] According to Aristotle, the gods are not concerned at all with the dispensation of good and bad fortune or external things.[3] To the prophet, however, no subject is as worthy of consideration as the plight of man. Indeed, God Himself is described as reflecting over the plight of man rather than as contemplating eternal ideas. His mind is preoccupied with man, with the concrete actualities of history rather than with the timeless issues of thought. In the prophet's message nothing that has bearing upon good and evil is small or trite in the eyes of God (see pp. 363 f.)

Man is rebellious and full of iniquity, and yet so cherished is he that God, the Creator of heaven and earth, is saddened when forsaken by him. Pro-

---

[1] *Laws,* VII, 803.   [2] *De Natura Deorum,* II, 167.   [3] *Magna Moralia,* II, 8, 1207, 1208, 1209.

found and intimate is God's love for man, and yet harsh and dreadful can be His wrath. Of what paltry worth is human might—yet human compassion is divinely precious. Ugly though the behavior of man is, yet may man's return to God make of his way a highway of God.

LUMINOUS AND EXPLOSIVE

"Really great works," writes Flaubert, "have a serene look. Through small openings one perceives precipices; down at the bottom there is darkness, vertigo; but above the whole soars something singularly sweet. That is the ideal of light, the smiling of the sun; and how calm it is, calm and strong! ... The highest and hardest thing in art seems to me to be to create a state of reverie."[4]

The very opposite applies to the words of the prophet. They suggest a disquietude sometimes amounting to agony. Yet there are interludes when one perceives an eternity of love hovering over moments of anguish; at the bottom there is light, fascination, but above the whole soar thunder and lightning.

The prophet's use of emotional and imaginative language, concrete in diction, rhythmical in movement, artistic in form, marks his style as poetic. Yet it is not the sort of poetry that takes its origin, to use Wordsworth's phrase, "from emotion recollected in tranquility." Far from reflecting a state of inner harmony or poise, its style is charged with agitation, anguish, and a spirit of nonacceptance. The prophet's concern is not with nature but with history, and history is devoid of poise.

Authentic utterance derives from a moment of identification of a person and a word; its significance depends upon the urgency and magnitude of its theme. The prophet's theme is, first of all, the very life of a whole people, and his identification lasts more than a moment. He is one not only with what he says; he is involved with his people in what his words foreshadow. This is the secret of the prophet's style: his life and soul are at stake in what he says and in what is going to happen to what he says. It is an involvement that echoes on. What is more, both theme and identification are seen in three dimensions. Not only the prophet and the people, but God Himself is involved in what the words convey.

Prophetic utterance is rarely cryptic, suspended between God and man; it is urging, alarming, forcing onward, as if the words gushed forth from the

---

[4] Quoted by F. Kaufmann, *Thomas Mann, The World as Will and Representation* (Boston, 1957), p. 272.

heart of God, seeking entrance to the heart and mind of man, carrying a summons as well as an involvement. Grandeur, not dignity, is important. The language is luminous and explosive, firm and contingent, harsh and compassionate, a fusion of contradictions.

The prophet seldom tells a story, but casts events. He rarely sings, but castigates. He does more than translate reality into a poetic key: he is a preacher whose purpose is not self-expression or "the purgation of emotions," but communication. His images must not shine, they must burn.

The prophet is intent on intensifying responsibility, is impatient of excuse, contemptuous of pretense and self-pity. His tone, rarely sweet or caressing, is frequently consoling and disburdening; his words are often slashing, even horrid—designed to shock rather than to edify.

The mouth of the prophet is "a sharp sword." He is "a polished arrow" taken out of the quiver of God (Isa. 49:2).

> *Tremble, you women who are at ease,*
> *Shudder, you complacent ones;*
> *Strip, and make yourselves bare,*
> *Gird sackcloth upon your loins.*
> *Isaiah 32:11*

Reading the words of the prophets is a strain on the emotions, wrenching one's conscience from the state of suspended animation.

THE HIGHEST GOOD

Those who have a sense of beauty know that a stone sculptured by an artist's poetic hands has an air of loveliness; that a beam charmingly placed utters a song. The prophet's ear, however, is attuned to a cry imperceptible to others. A clean house or a city architecturally distinguished may yet fill the prophet with distress.

> *Woe to him who heaps up what is not his own, ...*
> *Woe to him who gets evil gain for his house, ...*
> *For the stone cries out from the wall,*
> *And the beam from the woodwork responds.*
> *Woe to him who builds a town with blood,*
> *And founds a city on iniquity!*
> *Habakkuk 2:6, 9, 11-12*

These words contradict most men's conceptions: the builders of great cities have always been envied and acclaimed; neither violence nor exploitation could dim the splendor of the metropolis. "Woe to him . . ."? Human justice will not exact its due, nor will pangs of conscience disturb intoxication with success, for deep in our hearts is the temptation to worship the imposing, the illustrious, the ostentatious. Had a poet come to Samaria, the capital of the Northern Kingdom, he would have written songs exalting its magnificent edifices, its beautiful temples and worldly monuments. But when Amos of Tekoa came to Samaria, he spoke not of the magnificence of palaces, but of moral confusion and oppression. Dismay filled the prophet:

> *I abhor the pride of Jacob,*
> *And hate his palaces,*

he cried out in the name of the Lord (Amos 6:8). Was Amos, then, not sensitive to beauty?

What is the highest good? Three things ancient society cherished above all else: wisdom, wealth, and might. To the prophets, such infatuation was ludicrous and idolatrous. Assyria would be punished for her arrogant boasting:

> *By the strength of my hand I have done it,*
> *And by my wisdom, for I have understanding; . . .*
> > *Isaiah 10:13*

And about their own people, because "their hearts are far from Me, . . . the wisdom of the wise men shall perish" (Isa. 29:13, 14).

> *The wise men shall be put to shame,*
> *They shall be dismayed and taken;*
> *Lo, they have rejected the word of the Lord,*
> *What wisdom is in them?*
> > *Jeremiah 8:9*

Ephraim has said,

> *Ah, but I am rich,*
> *I have gained wealth for myself;*
> *But all his riches can never offset*
> *The guilt he has incurred. . . .*
> *Because you have trusted in your chariots*
> *And in the multitude of your warriors,*
> *Therefore the tumult of war shall arise among your people,*
> *And all your fortresses shall be destroyed, . . .*
> > *Hosea 12:8; 10:13, 14*

Thus says the Lord: "Let not the wise man glory in his wisdom, let not the mighty man glory in his might, let not the rich man glory in his riches; but let him who glories, glory in this, that he understands and knows Me, that I am the Lord Who practice kindness, justice, and righteousness in the earth; for in these things I delight, says the Lord" (Jer. 9:23-24 [H. 9:22-23]).

This message was expressed with astounding finality by a later prophet: "This is the word of the Lord . . . : Not by might, nor by power, but by My spirit . . ." (Zech. 4:6).

ONE OCTAVE TOO HIGH

We and the prophet have no language in common. To us the moral state of society, for all its stains and spots, seems fair and trim; to the prophet it is dreadful. So many deeds of charity are done, so much decency radiates day and night; yet to the prophet satiety of the conscience is prudery and flight from responsibility. Our standards are modest; our sense of injustice tolerable, timid; our moral indignation impermanent; yet human violence is interminable, unbearable, permanent. To us life is often serene, in the prophet's eye the world reels in confusion. The prophet makes no concession to man's capacity. Exhibiting little understanding for human weakness, he seems unable to extenuate the culpability of man.

Who could bear living in a state of disgust day and night? The conscience builds its confines, is subject to fatigue, longs for comfort, lulling, soothing. Yet those who are hurt, and He Who inhabits eternity, neither slumber nor sleep.

The prophet is sleepless and grave. The frankincense of charity fails to sweeten cruelties. Pomp, the scent of piety, mixed with ruthlessness, is sickening to him who is sleepless and grave.

Perhaps the prophet knew more about the secret obscenity of sheer unfairness, about the unnoticed malignancy of established patterns of indifference, than men whose knowledge depends solely on intelligence and observation.

> *The Lord made it known to me and I knew;*
> *Then Thou didst show me their evil deeds.*
> *Jeremiah 11:18*

The prophet's ear perceives the silent sigh.

In the Upanishads the physical world is devoid of value—unreal, a sham, an illusion, a dream—but in the Bible the physical world is real, the creation of God. Power, offspring, wealth, prosperity—all are blessings to be cher-

ished, yet the thriving and boasting man, his triumphs and might, are
regarded as frothy, tawdry, devoid of substance.

> *Behold, the nations are like a drop from a bucket,*
> *And are accounted as the dust on the scales; ...*
> *All the nations are as nothing before Him,*
> *They are accounted by Him as less than nothing and emptiness.*
>
> > *Isaiah 40:15, 17*

Civilization may come to an end, and the human species disappear. This
world, no mere shadow of ideas in an upper sphere, is real, but not absolute;
the world's reality is contingent upon compatibility with God. While others
are intoxicated with the here and now, the prophet has a vision of an end.

> *I looked on the earth, and lo, it was waste and void;*
> *To the heavens, and they had no light.*
> *I looked on the mountains, and lo, they were quaking,*
> *All the hills moved to and fro.*
> *I looked, and lo, there was no man;*
> *All the birds of the air had fled.*
> *I looked, and lo the fruitful land was a desert;*
> *All its cities were laid in ruins*
> *Before the Lord, before His fierce anger.*
>
> > *Jeremiah 4:23-26*

The prophet is human, yet he employs notes one octave too high for our
ears. He experiences moments that defy our understanding. He is neither "a
singing saint" nor "a moralizing poet," but an assaulter of the mind. Often
his words begin to burn where conscience ends.

AN ICONOCLAST

The prophet is an iconoclast, challenging the apparently holy, revered,
and awesome. Beliefs cherished as certainties, institutions endowed with
supreme sanctity, he exposes as scandalous pretensions.

To many a devout believer Jeremiah's words must have sounded blasphemous.

> *To what purpose does frankincense come to Me from Sheba,*
> *Or sweet cane from a distant land?*
> *Your burnt offerings are not acceptable,*
> *Nor your sacrifices pleasing to Me.*
>
> > *Jeremiah 6:20*

Thus says the Lord of hosts, the God of Israel: Add your burnt offerings to your sacrifices, and eat the flesh. For in the day that I brought them out of the land of Egypt, I did not speak to your fathers or command them concerning burnt offerings and sacrifices. But this command I gave them: Obey My voice and I will be your God, and you shall be My people; and walk in all the way that I command you, that it may be well with you.

Jeremiah 7:21-23

The prophet knew that religion could distort what the Lord demanded of man, that priests themselves had committed perjury by bearing false witness, condoning violence, tolerating hatred, calling for ceremonies instead of bursting forth with wrath and indignation at cruelty, deceit, idolatry, and violence.

To the people, religion was Temple, priesthood, incense: "This is the Temple of the Lord, the Temple of the Lord, the Temple of the Lord" (Jer. 7:4). Such piety Jeremiah brands as fraud and illusion. "Behold you trust in deceptive words to no avail," he calls (Jer. 7:8). Worship preceded or followed by evil acts becomes an absurdity. The holy place is doomed when people indulge in unholy deeds.

Will you steal, murder, commit adultery, swear falsely, burn incense to Baal, and go after other gods that you have not known, and then come and stand before Me in this house, which is called by My name, and say, We are delivered!—only to go on doing all these abominations? Has this house, which is called by My name, become a den of robbers in your eyes? Behold, I Myself have seen it, says the Lord. Go now to My place that was in Shiloh, where I made My name dwell at first, and see what I did to it for the wickedness of My people Israel. And now, because you have done all these things, says the Lord, and when I spoke to you persistently you did not listen, and when I called you, you did not answer, therefore I will do to the house which is called by My name, and in which you trust, and to the place which I gave to you and to your fathers, as I did to Shiloh. And I will cast you out of My sight, as I cast out all your kinsmen, all the offspring of Ephraim.

Jeremiah, 7:9-15

The prophet's message sounds incredible. In the pagan world the greatness, power, and survival of a god depended upon the greatness, power, and survival of the people, upon the city and shrine dedicated to his cult. The more triumphs the king achieved or the more countries he conquered, the greater was the god. A god who would let enemies destroy his shrine or conquer the people who worshiped him would commit suicide.

A tribal god was petitioned to slay the tribe's enemies because he was conceived as the god of that tribe and not as the god of the enemies. When the Roman armies were defeated in battle, the people, indignant, did not hesitate to wreck the images of their gods.

The prophets of Israel proclaim that the enemy may be God's instrument in history. The God of Israel calls the archenemy of His people "Assyria, the rod of My anger" (Isa. 10:5; cf. 13:5; 5:26; 7:18; 8:7). "Nebuchadnezzar, the king of Babylon, My servant" whom I will bring "against this land and its inhabitants" (Jer. 25:9; 27:6; 43:10). Instead of cursing the enemy, the prophets condemn their own nation.

What gave them the strength to "demythologize" precious certainties, to attack what was holy, to hurl blasphemies at priest and king, to stand up against all in the name of God? The prophets must have been shattered by some cataclysmic experience in order to be able to shatter others.

AUSTERITY AND COMPASSION

The words of the prophet are stern, sour, stinging. But behind his austerity is love and compassion for mankind. Ezekiel sets forth what all other prophets imply: "Have I any pleasure in the death of the wicked, says the Lord God, and not rather that he should turn from his way and live?" (Ezek. 18:23.) Indeed, every prediction of disaster is in itself an exhortation to repentance. The prophet is sent not only to upbraid, but also to "strengthen the weak hands and make firm the feeble knees" (Isa. 35:3). Almost every prophet brings consolation, promise, and the hope of reconciliation along with censure and castigation. He begins with *a message of doom;* he concludes with *a message of hope.*[5]

The prominent theme is exhortation, not mere prediction. While it is true that foretelling is an important ingredient and may serve as a sign of the prophet's authority (Deut. 18:22; Isa. 41:22; 43:9), his essential task is to declare the word of God to the here and now; to disclose the future in order to illumine what is involved in the present.[6]

---

[5] See *Sifre Deuteronomy,* 342, beginning. Some modern scholars maintain that the pre-exilic prophets had no message except one of doom, that true prophecy is essentially prophecy of woe. Yet such a view can be maintained only by declaring, often on insufficient grounds, that numerous passages are interpolations. See H. H. Rowley, *The Servant of the Lord* (London, 1952), p. 125.

[6] See the divergent views of R. H. Charles, *Critical and Exegetical Commentary on the Book of Daniel* (Oxford, 1929), p. xxvi, and A. Guillaume, *Prophecy and Divination* (London, 1938), pp. 111 f. See also H. H. Rowley, *loc. cit.*

SWEEPING ALLEGATIONS

If justice means giving every person what he deserves, the scope and severity of the accusations by the prophets of Israel hardly confirmed that principle. The prophets were unfair to the people of Israel. Their sweeping allegations, overstatements, and generalizations defied standards of accuracy. Some of the exaggerations reach the unbelievable.

> *Run to and fro through the streets of Jerusalem,*
> *Look and take note!*
> *Search her squares to see*
> *If you can find a man,*
> *One who does justice*
> *And seeks truth; . . .*
> *But they all alike had broken the yoke,*
> *They had burst the bonds. . . .*
> *From the least to the greatest of them,*
> *Every one is greedy for unjust gain;*
> *And from prophet to priest,*
> *Every one deals falsely. . . .*
> *There is nothing but oppression within her.*
>
> *Jeremiah 5:1, 5; 6:13; 8:10; 6:6*

In contrast to Amos, whose main theme is condemnation of the rich for the oppression of the poor, Hosea does not single out a particular section of the community.

> *There is no truth, no love, and no knowledge of God in the land;*
> *Swearing and lying, killing and stealing, and committing adultery,*
> *They break all bonds, and blood touches blood.*
>
> *Hosea 4:1-2*

Isaiah calls Judah a "sinful nation, . . . laden with iniquity" (1:4), "rebellious children" (30:1), "a people of unclean lips" (6:5). Indeed, the prophets have occasionally limited the guilt to the elders, princes, and priests, implying the innocence of those not involved in leadership. The assurance given in the name of the Lord,

> *Tell the righteous that all shall be well with them, . . .*
> *Woe to the wicked! It shall be ill with him,*
> *For what his hands have done shall be done to him,*

is emphatically addressed to the righteous men in Israel, spoken of in the plural, as well as to the wicked individual in Israel, spoken of in the singu-

lar (Isa. 3:10-11) . The exclamation in the name of the Lord, "Wicked men
are found among My people!" (Jer. 5:26) , betrays, it seems, a more sober
appraisal of the situation and may be kept in mind as a modification of the
numerous extravagant qualifications uttered by the prophets *in their own
names*.[7]

Great orators in Rome had frequently manifested courage in publicly
condemning the abuse of power by individuals. But the prophets challenge
the whole country: kings, priests, false prophets, and the entire nation. The
historical accounts in the books of Kings would certainly have referred to
the moral corruption, had it been as grave as the prophets maintain.

In terms of statistics the prophets' statements are grossly inaccurate. Yet
their concern is not with facts, but with the meaning of facts. The significance of human deeds, the true image of man's existence, cannot be expressed by statistics. The rabbis were not guilty of exaggeration in asserting,
"Whoever destroys a single soul should be considered the same as one who
has destroyed a whole world. And whoever saves one single soul is to be
considered the same as one who has saved a whole world."

Extremely minute, yet vital entities formerly unknown to the mind were
suddenly disclosed by the microscope. What seems to be exaggeration is
often only a deeper penetration, for the prophets see the world from the
point of view of God, as transcendent, not immanent truth.

Modern thought tends to extenuate personal responsibility. Understanding the complexity of human nature, the interrelationship of individual and
society, of consciousness and the subconscious, we find it difficult to isolate
the deed from those circumstances in which it was done. But new insights
may obscure essential vision, and man's conscience grow scales: excuses,
pretense, self-pity. Guilt may disappear; no crime is absolute, no sin devoid
of apology. Within the limits of the human mind, relativity is true and
merciful. Yet the mind's scope embraces but a fragment of society, a few
instants of history; it thinks of what has happened, it is unable to imagine
what might have happened.

FEW ARE GUILTY, ALL ARE RESPONSIBLE

What was happening in Israel surpassed its intrinsic significance. Israel's
history comprised a drama of God and all men. God's kingship and man's

---

[7] Rhetorical exaggeration is a frequent mode of the biblical style of writing. Rabbi Simeon
ben Gamliel, who lived in Palestine in the first half of the second century A.D., asserted that

hope were at stake in Jerusalem. God was alone in the world, unknown or discarded. The countries of the world were full of abominations, violence, falsehood. Here was one land, one people, cherished and chosen for the purpose of transforming the world. *This* people's failure was most serious. The Beloved of God worshiped the Baalim (Hos. 11:1-2); the vineyard of the Lord yielded wild grapes (Isa. 5:2); Israel, holy to the Lord, "defiled My land, made My heritage an abomination" (Jer. 2:3, 7).

Defining truth as the conformity of assertion to facts, we may censure the prophets for being inaccurate, incongruous, even absurd; defining truth as reality reflected in a mind, we see *prophetic* truth as reality reflected in God's mind, the world *sub specie dei.*

Prophetic accusations are perhaps more easily understood in the light of the book of Job's thesis that men might judge a human being just and pure, whom God, Who finds angels imperfect, would not.[8]

> *Can mortal man be righteous before God?*
> *Can a man be pure before His Maker?*
> *Even in His servants He puts no trust,*
> *His angels He charges with error;*
> *How much more those who dwell in houses of clay,*
> *Whose foundation is in the dust,*
> *Who are crushed before the moth. . . .*
> *What is man, that he can be clean?*
> *Or he that is born of a woman, that he can be righteous?*
> *Behold God puts no trust in His holy ones,*
> *The heavens are not clean in His sight;*
> *How much less one who is abominable and corrupt,*
> *A man who drinks iniquity like water!*
>
> *Job 4:17-19; 15:14-16*

"For there is no man who does not sin" (I Kings 8:46). "Surely there is not a righteous man on earth who does good and never sins" (Eccles. 7:20). It is with a bitter sense of the tremendous contrast between God's righteousness and man's failure that the psalmist prays:

> *Enter not into judgment with Thy servant;*
> *For no man living is righteous before Thee.*
>
> *Psalm 143:2*

Scripture employs hyperbolic phrases, citing Deut. 1:28 as an example, *Sifre Deuteronomy,* p. 25. A similar view was expressed by Rabbi Ammi of the third century, *Tamid* 29a. Cf. also E. König, *Stilistik, Rhetorik, Poetik in Bezug auf die Biblische Literatur* (Leipzig, 1900), p. 69; C. Douglas, *Overstatement in the New Testament* (New York, 1931), pp. 3-36.
[8] Eliphaz' thesis is accepted by Job (9:2); see also 25:4.

Men are greatly praised when worthy of being reproved. Only a strong heart can bear bitter invectives.

Above all, the prophets remind us of the moral state of a people: Few are guilty, but all are responsible. If we admit that the individual is in some measure conditioned or affected by the spirit of society, an individual's crime discloses society's corruption. In a community not indifferent to suffering, uncompromisingly impatient with cruelty and falsehood, continually concerned for God and every man, crime would be infrequent rather than common.

THE BLAST FROM HEAVEN

To a person endowed with prophetic sight, everyone else appears blind; to a person whose ear perceives God's voice, everyone else appears deaf. No one is just; no knowing is strong enough, no trust complete enough. The prophet hates the approximate, he shuns the middle of the road. Man must live on the summit to avoid the abyss. There is nothing to hold to except God. Carried away by the challenge, the demand to straighten out man's ways, the prophet is strange, one-sided, an unbearable extremist.

Others may suffer from the terror of cosmic aloneness, the prophet is overwhelmed by the grandeur of divine presence. He is incapable of isolating the world. There is an interaction between man and God which to disregard is an act of insolence. Isolation is a fairy tale.

Where an idea is the father of faith, faith must conform to the ideas of the given system. In the Bible the realness of God came first, and the task was how to live in a way compatible with His presence. Man's coexistence with God determines the course of history.

The prophet disdains those for whom God's presence is comfort and security; to him it is a challenge, an incessant demand. God is compassion, not compromise; justice, though not inclemency. The prophet's predictions can always be proved wrong by a change in man's conduct, but never the certainty that God is full of compassion.

The prophet's word is a scream in the night. While the world is at ease and asleep, the prophet feels the blast from heaven.

THE COALITION OF CALLOUSNESS AND AUTHORITY

The prophet faces a coalition of callousness and established authority, and undertakes to stop a mighty stream with mere words. Had the purpose been to express great ideas, prophecy would have had to be acclaimed as a triumph. Yet the purpose of prophecy is to conquer callousness, to change the inner man as well as to revolutionize history.

It is embarrassing to be a prophet. There are so many pretenders, predicting peace and prosperity, offering cheerful words, adding strength to self-reliance, while the prophet predicts disaster, pestilence, agony, and destruction. People need exhortations to courage, endurance, confidence, fighting spirit, but Jeremiah proclaims: You are about to die if you do not have a change of heart and cease being callous to the word of God. He sends shudders over the whole city, at a time when the will to fight is most important.

By the standards of ancient religions, the great prophets were rather unimpressive. The paraphernalia of nimbus and evidence, such as miracles, were not at their disposal.[9]

LONELINESS AND MISERY

None of the prophets seems enamored with being a prophet nor proud of his attainment. What drove Jeremiah, for instance, to being a prophet?

> *Cursed be the day*
> *On which I was born! . . .*
> *Because He did not kill me in the womb;*
> *So my mother would have been my grave, . . .*
> *Why did I come forth out of the womb*
> *To see toil and sorrow,*
> *And spend my days in shame?*
> *Jeremiah 20:14, 17, 18*

Over the life of a prophet words are invisibly inscribed: All flattery abandon, ye who enter here. To be a prophet is both a distinction and an

---

[9] Very few miracles are ascribed to the prophets; see Isa. 38:7-8. Miracles have no probative value; see Deut. 13:1-3. What is offered to Ahaz (Isa. 7:11) is a sign rather than a miracle. On the meaning of this passage, see M. Buber, *The Prophetic Faith* (New York, 1949), p. 138.

Of Samuel it is reported that he called upon the Lord, and the Lord sent thunder and rain that day; and all the people greatly feared the Lord and Samuel (I Sam. 12:18). Gideon (Judg. 6:36-40) and Elijah (I Kings 18:36-38) implored God for miraculous signs. The miracle of the sundial (Isa. 38:1-8) was not performed for the purpose of verification. Miracles did not always have the power to put an end to uncertainty, since the magicians were able to duplicate them (see Exod. 8:7 [H. 7:11, 22]). The only medium of the prophet was the word or the symbolic act to illustrate its content. Even predictions of things to come did not always serve to verify the prophet's word.

affliction. The mission he performs is distasteful to him and repugnant to others; no reward is promised him and no reward could temper its bitterness. The prophet bears scorn and reproach (Jer. 15:15). He is stigmatized as a madman by his contemporaries, and, by some modern scholars, as abnormal.

> *They hate him who reproves in the gate,*
> *They abhor him who speaks the truth.*
>
> *Amos 5:10*

Loneliness and misery were only part of the reward that prophecy brought to Jeremiah: "I sat alone because Thy hand was upon me" (15:17). Mocked, reproached, and persecuted, he would think of casting away his task:

> *If I say, I will not mention Him,*
> *Or speak any more in His name,*
> *There is my heart as it were a burning fire*
> *Shut up in my bones,*
> *And I am weary with holding it in,*
> *And I cannot.*
>
> *Jeremiah 20:9*

Jeremiah, when chosen to become a prophet, was told by the Lord: "And I, behold, I make you this day a fortified city, an iron pillar, and bronze walls, against the whole land, against the kings of Judah, its princes, its priests, and the people of the land" (Jer. 1:18). And later he was reassured: "They will fight against you, but they shall not prevail over you" (Jer. 15:20).

The prophet is a lonely man. He alienates the wicked as well as the pious, the cynics as well as the believers, the priests and the princes, the judges and the false prophets. But to be a prophet means to challenge and to defy and to cast out fear.

The life of a prophet is not futile. People may remain deaf to a prophet's admonitions; they cannot remain callous to a prophet's existence. At the very beginning of his career, Ezekiel was told not to entertain any illusions about the effectiveness of his mission:

> *And you, son of man, be not afraid of them, nor be afraid of their words,*
> *though briers and thorns are with you and you sit upon scorpions; be not*
> *afraid of their words, nor be dismayed at their looks, . . . Behold, I have*
> *made your face hard against their faces, and your forehead hard against*
> *their foreheads. Like adamant harder than flint have I made your forehead;*
> *fear them not, nor be dismayed at their looks, . . . The people also are impu-*

*dent and stubborn: I send you to them; and you shall say to them, Thus says
the Lord God. And whether they hear or refuse to hear . . . they will know
that there has been a prophet among them.*

Ezekiel 2:6; 3:8-9; 2:4-5; cf. 3:27

The prophet's duty is to speak to the people, "whether they hear or refuse
to hear." A grave responsibility rests upon the prophet:

*If the watchman sees the sword coming and does not blow the trumpet,
so that the people are not warned, and the sword comes, and takes any one
of them; that man is taken away in his iniquity, but his blood I will require
at the watchman's hand. So you, son of man, I have made a watchman for
the house of Israel; whenever you hear a word from My mouth, you shall
give them warning from Me.*

Ezekiel 33:6-7; cf. 3:16-21

The main vocation of a prophet is "to declare to Jacob his transgression
and to Israel his sin" (Mic. 3:8), to let the people know "that it is evil and
bitter . . . to forsake . . . God" (Jer. 2:19), and to call upon them to return.
But do they attain their end? Publicly Jeremiah declared to the people:

*For twenty-three years . . . the word of the Lord has come to me, and I
have spoken persistently to you, but you have not listened. You have neither
listened nor inclined your ears to hear, although the Lord persistently sent
to you all his servants the prophets, saying, Turn now, every one of you,
from his evil way and wrong doings. . . . Yet you have not listened to Me,
says the Lord.*

Jeremiah 25:3-7

Yet being a prophet is also joy, elation, delight:

> *Thy words were found, and I ate them,*
> *Thy words became to me a joy*
> *The delight of my heart;*
> *For I am called by Thy name,*
> *O Lord, God of hosts.*
>
> *Jeremiah 15:16*

THE PEOPLE'S TOLERANCE

The striking surprise is that prophets of Israel were tolerated at all by
their people. To the patriots, they seemed pernicious; to the pious multitude, blasphemous; to the men in authority, seditious.

> *Cry aloud, spare not,*
> *Lift up your voice like a trumpet;*
> *Declare to My people their transgression,*
> *To the house of Jacob their sins.*
> *Isaiah 58:1*

In the language of Jeremiah, the prophet's word is fire, and the people wood, "and the fire shall devour them" (Jer. 5:14; cf. Hos. 6:5).

How could the people endure men who proclaimed in the name of God,

> *I will send a fire upon Judah,*
> *And it shall devour the strongholds of Jerusalem!*
> *Amos 2:5*

> *Zion shall be plowed as a field;*
> *Jerusalem shall become a heap of ruins,*
> *And the mountain of the house a wooded height!*
> *Jeremiah 26:18; cf. Micah 3:12*

It must have sounded like treason when Amos called upon the enemies of Israel to witness the wickedness of Samaria.

> *Proclaim to the strongholds in Assyria,*
> *And to the strongholds in the land of Egypt,*
> *And say: "Assemble yourselves upon the mountains of Samaria,*
> *And see the great tumults within her,*
> *And the oppressions in her midst!"*
> *Amos 3:9*

It is strange, indeed, that a people to whom the names of Sodom and Gomorrah were charged with extreme insult would brook a prophet who did not hesitate to address his audience as "you rulers of Sodom . . . you people of Gomorrah" (Isa. 1:10).

> *And on that day, says the Lord God,*
> *I will make the sun go down at noon,*
> *And darken the earth in broad daylight.*
> *I will turn your feasts into mourning,*
> *And all your songs into lamentation; I will bring sackcloth*
> *   upon all loins,*
> *And baldness on every head; I will make it like the mourning*
> *   for an only son,*
> *And the end of it like a bitter day.*
> *Amos 8:9-10*

AN ASSAYER, MESSENGER, WITNESS

The prophet is a watchman (Hos. 9:8), a servant (Amos 3:7; Jer. 25:4; 26:5), a messenger of God (Hag. 1:13), "an assayer and tester" of the people's ways (Jer. 6:27, RSV) ; "whenever you hear a word from My mouth, you shall give them warning from Me" (Ezek. 3:17) . The prophet's eye is directed to the contemporary scene; the society and its conduct are the main theme of his speeches. Yet his ear is inclined to God. He is a person struck by the glory and presence of God, overpowered by the hand of God. Yet his true greatness is his ability to hold God and man in a single thought.

The spiritual status of a diviner, not to be confused with a prophet, is higher than that of his fellow man; the diviner is regarded as more exalted than other members of his society. However, the measure of such superiority is that of individuality. In contrast, the prophet feels himself placed not only above other members of his own society; he is placed in a relationship transcending his own total community, and even the realm of other nations and kingdoms. The measure of his superiority is that of universality. This is why the essence of his eminence is not adequately described by the term *charisma*. Not the fact of his having been affected, but the fact of his having received a power to affect others is supreme in his existence. His sense of election and personal endowment is overshadowed by his sense of a history-shaping power. Jeremiah, for example, was appointed "a prophet to the nations" (1:5). He was told:

> *See, I have set you this day over nations and over kingdoms,*
> *To pluck up and to break down,*
> *To destroy and to overthrow,*
> *To build and to plant.*
>
> *Jeremiah 1:10*

It is common to characterize the prophet as a messenger of God, thus to differentiate him from the tellers of fortune, givers of oracles, seers, and ecstatics. Such a characterization expresses only one aspect of his consciousness. The prophet claims to be far more than a messenger. He is a person who stands in the presence of God (Jer. 15:19), who stands "in the council of the Lord" (Jer. 23:18), who is a participant, as it were, in the council of God, not a bearer of dispatches whose function is limited to being sent on errands. He is a counselor as well as a messenger.

> *Surely the Lord God does nothing*
> *Without revealing His secret*
> *To His servants the prophets,*
>
> *Amos 3:7*

When the secret revealed is one of woe, the prophet does not hesitate to challenge the intention of the Lord:

> *O Lord God, forgive, I beseech Thee!*
> *How can Jacob stand?*
> *He is so small!*
>
> *Amos 7:2*

When the lives of others are at stake, the prophet does not say, "Thy will be done!" but rather, "Thy will be changed."

> *The Lord repented concerning this;*
> *It shall not be, said the Lord.*
>
> *Amos 7:3*

It is impossible for us to intuit the grandeur of the prophetic consciousness. A person to whom the spirit of God comes, becomes radically transformed; he is "turned into another man" (I Sam. 10:6). The vastness and gravity of the power bestowed upon the prophet seem to burst the normal confines of human consciousness. The gift he is blessed with is not a skill, but rather the gift of being guided and restrained, of being moved and curbed. His mission is to speak, yet in the vision of consecration Ezekiel, for example, was forewarned of the inability to speak. "Cords will be placed upon you . . . and I will make your tongue cleave to the roof of your mouth, so that you shall be dumb and unable to reprove them; . . . But when I speak with you, I will open your mouth, and you shall say to them, Thus says the Lord God" (Ezek. 3:25-27).

As a witness, the prophet is more than a messenger. As a messenger, his task is to deliver the word; as a witness, he must bear testimony that the word is divine.

The words the prophet utters are not offered as souvenirs. His speech to the people is not a reminiscence, a report, hearsay. The prophet not only conveys; he reveals. He almost does unto others what God does unto him. In speaking, the prophet reveals God. This is the marvel of a prophet's work: in his words, *the invisible God becomes audible.* He does not prove or argue. The thought he has to convey is more than language can contain. Divine power bursts in the words. The authority of the prophet is in the Presence his words reveal.

There are no proofs for the existence of the God of Abraham. There are only witnesses. The greatness of the prophet lies not only in the ideas he expressed, but also in the moments he experienced. The prophet is a witness, and his words a testimony—to *His* power and judgment, to *His* justice and mercy.

The contradictions in the prophetic message seem perplexing. The book of Amos, out of which come the words, "The end has come upon My people Israel" (8:2) and "Fallen no more to rise is the virgin Israel" (5:2), concludes with the prediction:

> *I will restore the fortunes of My people Israel,*
> *And they shall rebuild the ruined cities and inhabit them;*
> *They shall plant vineyards and drink their wine,*
> *And they shall make gardens and eat their fruit.*
> *I will plant them upon their land,*
> *And they shall never again be plucked up*
> *Out of the land which I have given them,*
> *Says the Lord your God.*
>
> *Amos 9:14-15*

What hidden bond exists between the word of wrath and the word of compassion, between "consuming fire" and "everlasting love"?

Does the apparent contradiction within the assertions of a prophet destroy the validity of his message? It would if prophecy dealt only with laws or principles. But the prophet deals with relations between God and man, where contradiction is inevitable. Escape from God and return to Him are inextricable parts of man's existence. Conformity to logical standards is not characteristic of man's conduct, which is why contradiction is inherent in prophecy.

We will have to look for prophetic coherence, not *in what* the prophet says but *of Whom* he speaks. Indeed, not even the word of God is the ultimate object and theme of his consciousness. The ultimate object and theme of his consciousness is God, of Whom the prophet knows that above His judgment and above His anger stands His mercy.

The prophetic utterance has, therefore, no finality. It does not set forth a comprehensive law, but a single perspective. It is expressed *ad hoc,* often *ad hominem,* and must not be generalized.

THE PRIMARY CONTENT OF EXPERIENCE

What is the primary content of prophetic experience, the thought immediately felt, the motive directly present to the prophet's mind? What are the facts of consciousness that stirred him so deeply? Is it a sense of anxiety about the fate and future of the people or of the state? An impulse of patriotism? Is it personal irritation at the violation of moral laws and standards, a spontaneous reaction of the conscience against what is wrong or evil? Moral indignation?

In a stricken hour comes the word of the prophet. There is tension between God and man. What does the word say? What does the prophet feel? The prophet is not only a censurer and accuser, but also a defender and consoler. Indeed, the attitude he takes to the tension that obtains between God and the people is characterized by a dichotomy. In the presence of God he takes the part of the people. In the presence of the people he takes the part of God.

It would be wrong to maintain that the prophet is a person who plays the role of "the third party," offering his good offices to bring about reconciliation. His view is oblique. God is the focal point of his thought, and the world is seen as reflected in God. Indeed, the main task of prophetic thinking is to bring the world into divine focus. This, then, explains his way of thinking. He does not take a direct approach to things. It is not a straight line, spanning subject and object, but rather a triangle—through God to the object. An expression of a purely personal feeling betrays itself seldom, in isolated instances. The prophet is endowed with the insight that enables him to say, not I love or I condemn, but God loves or God condemns.

The prophet does not judge the people by timeless norms, but from the point of view of God. Prophecy proclaims what happened to God as well as what will happen to the people. In judging human affairs, it unfolds a divine situation. Sin is not only the violation of a law, it is as if sin were as much a loss to God as to man. God's role is not spectatorship but involvement. He and man meet mysteriously in the human deed. The prophet cannot say Man without thinking God.

Therefore, the prophetic speeches are not factual pronouncements. What we hear is not objective criticism or the cold proclamation of doom. The style of legal, objective utterance is alien to the prophet. He dwells upon God's inner motives, not only upon His historical decisions. He discloses *a divine pathos,* not just a divine judgment. The pages of the prophetic writings are filled with echoes of divine love and disappointment, mercy and indignation. The God of Israel is never impersonal.

This divine pathos is the key to inspired prophecy. God is involved in the life of man. A personal relationship binds Him to Israel; there is an interweaving of the divine in the affairs of the nation. The divine commandments are not mere recommendations for man, but express divine concern, which, realized or repudiated, is of personal importance to Him. The reaction of the divine self (Amos 6:8; Jer. 5:9; 51:14), its manifestations in the form of love, mercy, disappointment or anger convey the profound intensity of the divine inwardness.

From the descriptions later in this book of the part pathos plays in the lives and messages of the great prophets, we will discover its meaning as a conception and as an object of experience.[10]

THE PROPHET'S RESPONSE

In view of the insistence by the prophets of Israel upon the divine origin of their utterances, one inclines to agree with the ancient conception of the prophet as a mere mouthpiece of God. A careful analysis, however, compels us to reject the characterization of prophetic inspiration as a mere act of passive and unconscious receptivity (see pp. 357 f.). What, indeed, was the nature of the prophet's transmission of what he perceived? Was it an impersonal reproduction of an inspired message, a mere copy of the contents of inspiration, or did prophetic experience involve participation of the person in the act of transmission or even inspiration? Is prophecy to be thought of as a technical activity like divination? Is the prophet a person whose consciousness, in consequence of divine influence, utterly dissolves in surrender to the divine word, so that all spontaneous response and reaction is excluded?

The conception of the prophets as nothing but mouthpieces, the assumption that their hearts remain unaffected, would almost compel us to apply to them the words that Jeremiah used of the people:

> Thou art near in their mouth
> And far from their heart.
> Jeremiah 12:2

The prophet is not a mouthpiece, but a person; not an instrument, but a partner, an associate of God. Emotional detachment would be understandable only if there were a command which required the suppression of emotion, forbidding one to serve God "with all your heart, with all your soul, with all your might." God, we are told, asks not only for "works," for action, but above all for love, awe, and fear. We are called upon to "wash" our hearts (Jer. 4:14), to remove "the foreskin" of the heart (Jer. 4:4), to return with the whole heart (Jer. 3:10). "You will seek Me and find Me, when you seek Me with all your heart" (Jer. 29:13). The new covenant which the Lord will make with the house of Israel will be written upon their hearts (Jer. 31:31-34).

The prophet is no hireling who performs his duty in the employ of the Lord. The usual descriptions or definitions of prophecy fade to insignifi-

---

[10] See especially p. 231 and the Appendix: A Note on the Meaning of Pathos, p. 489.

cance when applied, for example, to Jeremiah. "A religious experience," "communion with God," "a perception of His voice"—such terms hardly convey what happened to his soul: the overwhelming impact of the divine pathos upon his mind and heart, completely involving and gripping his personality in its depths, and the unrelieved distress which sprang from his intimate involvement. The task of the prophet is to convey the word of God. Yet the word is aglow with the pathos. One cannot understand the word without sensing the pathos. And one could not impassion others and remain unstirred. The prophet should not be regarded as an ambassador who must be dispassionate in order to be effective.

An analysis of prophetic utterances shows that the fundamental experience of the prophet is a fellowship with the feelings of God, a *sympathy with the divine pathos,* a communion with the divine consciousness which comes about through the prophet's reflection of, or participation in, the divine pathos. The typical prophetic state of mind is one of being taken up into the heart of the divine pathos. Sympathy is the prophet's answer to inspiration, the correlative to revelation.

Prophetic sympathy is a response to transcendent sensibility. It is not, like love, an attraction to the divine Being, but the assimilation of the prophet's emotional life to the divine, an assimilation of function, not of being. The emotional experience of the prophet becomes the focal point for the prophet's understanding of God. He lives not only his personal life, but also the life of God. The prophet hears God's voice and feels His heart. He tries to impart the pathos of the message together with its logos. As an imparter his soul overflows, speaking as he does out of the fullness of his sympathy.

2. AMOS

AMOS AND HIS CONTEMPORARIES

Under the long and brilliant reign of Jeroboam II (*ca.* 786-746 B.C.E.) , the Northern Kingdom, also called the Kingdom of Israel, reached the summit of its material power and prosperity, expanding its territory northward at the expense of Hamath and Damascus, and southward at the expense of Judah. During this entire period Assyria was weak, and Syria on the decline; Jeroboam took advantage of the weakness of both to extend his dominion, foster commerce, and accumulate wealth.

When Amos appeared in the North there was pride (6:13-14), plenty, and splendor in the land, elegance in the cities, and might in the palaces. The rich had their summer and winter palaces adorned with costly ivory (3:15) , gorgeous couches with damask pillows (3:12) , on which they reclined at their sumptuous feasts. They planted pleasant vineyards, anointed themselves with precious oils (6:4-6; 5:11) ; their women, compared by Amos to the fat cows of Bashan, were addicted to wine (4:1) . At the same time there was no justice in the land (3:10) , the poor were afflicted, exploited, even

SELECTED BIBLIOGRAPHY: W. R. Harper, *A Critical and Exegetical Commentary on Amos and Hosea* ("The International Critical Commentary" [New York, 1915]) ; R. S. Cripps, *A Critical and Exegetical Commentary on the Book of Amos* (London, 1929) ; K. Cramer, *Amos, Versuch einer theologischen Interpretation* (Stuttgart, 1930) ; J. Morgenstern, *Amos Studies* (Cincinnati, 1941) ; A. Neher, *Amos: contribution à l'étude du prophétisme* (Paris, 1950) ; S. Spiegel, *Amos versus Amaziah* (New York, 1957) ; Y. Kaufmann, *The Religion of Israel*, VI (Heb.; Jerusalem, 1954) , 56-92; (Eng.; translated and abridged by M. Greenberg [Chicago, 1960]) , pp. 363 ff.; A. B. Ehrlich, *Randglossen zur Hebräischen Bibel*, vol. V. (Leipzig, 1912) . For the history of the period see A. T. Olmstead, *History of Assyria* (New York, 1923) , pp. 175 ff.; R. W. Rogers, *A History of Babylonia and Assyria*, II (New York, 1900) , 104 ff.; *Cambridge Modern History*, III (Cambridge, 1907 ff.) , 32-87; H. R. Hall, *The Ancient History of the Near East* (London, 1950) , pp. 461-494; G. Contenau, *Everyday Life in Babylon and Assyria* (London, 1954) ; L. W. King, *A History of Babylon* (New York, 1919) , pp. 270 ff.; M. Noth, *The History of Israel* (New York, 1958) ; J. Bright, *A History of Israel* (Philadelphia, 1959) ; W. F. Albright, "The Biblical Period," *The Jews*, vol. I, ed. by L. Finkelstein (New York, 1949) ; *idem*, *Archeology and the Religion of Israel* (Baltimore, 1953) ; *idem*, *From the Stone Age to Christianity* (2nd ed.; New York, 1957) .

sold into slavery (2:6-8; 5:11), and the judges were corrupt (5:12). In the midst of this atmosphere arose Amos, a shepherd, to exclaim:

> *Woe to those who are at ease in Zion,*
> *And to those who feel secure on the mountain of Samaria,*
> *The notable men of the first of the nations,*
> *To whom the house of Israel come!*
> *Pass over to Calneh, and see;*
> *And thence go to Hamath the great;*
> *Then go down to Gath of the Philistines.*
> *Are they better than these kingdoms?*
> *Or is their territory greater than your territory,*
> *O you who put far away the evil day,*
> *And bring near the seat of violence?*
> *Woe to those who lie upon beds of ivory,*
> *And stretch themselves upon their couches,*
> *And eat lambs from the flock,*
> *And calves from the midst of the stall;*
> *Who sing idle songs to the sound of the harp,*
> *And like David invent for themselves instruments of music;*
> *Who drink wine in bowls,*
> *And anoint themselves with the finest oils,*
> *But are not grieved over the ruin of Joseph!*
> *Therefore they shall now be the first of those to go into exile,*
> *And the revelry of those who stretch themselves shall pass away.*
>
> Amos 6:1-7

Amos was working as a shepherd and dresser of sycamore trees when he was suddenly overwhelmed by God and called to be a prophet.[1] Although his home was in Tekoa, a village southeast of Bethlehem in the Kingdom of Judah, his utterances were all directed against the Kingdom in the North, against Samaria, Bethel, and the rulers of the land.

> *Fallen, no more to rise,*
> *Is the virgin Israel;*
> *Forsaken on her land,*
> *With none to raise her up.*
>
> Amos 5:2

"The end has come upon My people Israel," the Lord said to him in a vision (8:2).

What is the nature of Him whose word overwhelmed the herdsman Amos? Is His grandeur like a towering mountain? Is His majesty comparable to an inscrutable constellation? Is He sublime as the morning and mysterious

---

[1] According to J. Morgenstern, *Amos Studies*, I (Cincinnati, 1941), 161-179, Amos began his prophetic activity in 752/1.

as darkness? All comparisons fade to insignificance when confronted with
what a person such as Amos asserted:

> For lo, He who forms the mountains, and creates the wind,
> And declares to man what is his thought;
> Who makes the morning darkness,
> And treads on the heights of the earth—
> The Lord, the God of hosts, is His name. . . .
> He who made the Pleiades and Orion,
> And turns deep darkness into the morning,
> And darkens the day into night,
> Who calls for the waters of the sea,
> And pours them out upon the surface of the earth,
> The Lord is His name,
> Who makes destruction flash forth against the strong,
> So that destruction comes upon the fortress.
>
> Amos 4:13; 5:8-9

When Amos called upon the people to "seek the Lord and live" (5:6),
he meant literally what he said. His words raged, proclaiming God's loathing for all men to know (6:8; 5:21).

GOD AND THE NATIONS

> The Lord roars from Zion,
> And utters His voice from Jerusalem;
> The pastures of the shepherds mourn,
> And the top of Carmel withers.
>
> Amos 1:2; cf. Joel 3:16 [H. 4:16][2]

These words are strange and inexplicable to us. Most of us who care for
the world bewail God's dreadful silence, while Amos appears smitten by
God's mighty voice. He did not hear a whisper, "a still small voice," but a
voice like a lion's roaring that drives shepherd and flock into panic.

What had provoked the anger of the Lord? What had happened to shatter
His silence? The answer is given in an account of events that happened in
the world of which Amos was a part. Two things stand out in the prophet's
condemnation: the absence of loyalty and the absence of pity. Tyre had
violated a treaty, "the covenant of brotherhood," and Edom had "pursued
his brother with the sword, and cast off all pity, and his anger tore per-
petually, and he kept his wrath for ever." Syria, ruled from its capital in
Damascus, had tortured and slaughtered the people of Gilead "with
threshing sledges of iron." Amos recalled how Philistia, ruled from Gaza, its
capital, had carried a whole people into captivity, selling them into slavery,

---

[2] On the voice of God as thunder, see Pss. 18:14; 29:3-9.

in order to make some money; how the Ammonites had ripped up women with child in Gilead in order to annex a strip of territory. He ended with Moab, how they had burned the bones of the king of Edom into lime. This act of vandalism had not even the poor excuse of being profitable: it brought nothing but the gratification of hate (1:3—2:3).

THE ANGER OF THE LORD

Yet the anger of the Lord was directed not only at the nations, but also at the people He had chosen. The people of Judah had rejected the Torah of the Lord, and had not kept His statutes (2:4). And the people of Israel, the Northern Kingdom (the creditors),

> . . . sell the righteous[3] for silver,
> And the needy for a pair of shoes—
> They that trample the head of the poor into the dust of the earth,
> And turn aside the way of the afflicted.
>
> Amos 2:6, 7; cf. 5:11

Man may remain callous, but God cannot keep silent. Terrible is His voice, because He has a heart.

> The Lord has sworn by the pride of Jacob:
> Surely I will never forget any of their deeds. . . .
> I will make the sun go down at noon,
> And darken the earth in broad daylight.
> I will turn your feasts into mourning,
> And all your songs into lamentation;
> I will bring sackcloth upon all loins,
> And baldness on every head;
> I will make it like the mourning for an only son,
> And the end of it like a bitter day.
>
> Amos 8:7, 9-10

It was not only iniquity that had aroused the anger of the Lord; it was also piety, upon which His words fell like a thunderbolt. Sacrifice and ritual were regarded as the way that leads to the Creator. The men and the institutions dedicated to sacrificial worship were powerful and revered. Came a "dresser of sycamores" from the wilderness of Judah and proclaimed the word of God:

> Even though you offer Me your burnt offerings and cereal offerings,
> I will not accept them,
> And the peace offerings of your fatted beasts

---

[3] Probably "the innocent." Debtors were sold into slavery because they could not pay some trifling debts.

I will not look upon.
Take away from Me the noise of your songs;
To the melody of your harps I will not listen.
But let justice well up as waters,
And righteousness as a mighty stream.

Amos 5:22-24

The juxtaposition of observing the laws of the Sabbath while waiting for the day to come to an end and of dealing "deceitfully with false balances" (8:5) strikes home a melancholy irony, easily lost on the modern reader. Man is waiting for the day of sanctity to come to an end so that cheating and exploitation can be resumed. This is a stunning condemnation. We are ready to judge a ritual act on its own merit. Properly performed, its value is undisputed. Yet, the prophet speaks with derision of those who combine ritual with iniquity.

The prophet's invectives could not be tolerated by his people. And when he went so far as to predict in public that the king of Israel would die by the sword and that the people of Israel would be led away captive, the outraged priest of Bethel, Amaziah, said to Amos: "Go, flee away to the land of Judah . . . ; never again prophesy at Bethel, for it is the king's sanctuary, and it is a temple of the kingdom" (7:12-13) .

But the prophet retorted:

I am no prophet, nor a prophet's son; but I am a herdsman, and a dresser of sycamore trees, and the Lord took me from following the flock, and the Lord said to me, Go, prophesy to my people Israel.

Now therefore hear the word of the Lord.
You say, Do not prophesy against Israel,
And do not preach against the house of Isaac.
Therefore thus says the Lord:
Your wife shall be a harlot in the city,
And your sons and your daughters shall fall by the sword,
And your land shall be parceled out by line;
You yourself shall die in an unclean land,
And Israel shall surely go into exile away from its land.

Amos 7:14-17

A REDEEMER PAINED BY THE PEOPLE'S FAILURE

What were the grounds on which Amos in the name of God doomed the nations? Judah was condemned

Because they have rejected the Torah of the Lord,
And have not kept His statutes.

Amos 2:4

Yet the nations were not, like Israel, condemned for internal transgressions, but for international crimes, although there was no law in existence governing international relations. Amos, however, presupposes the conception of a law which was not embodied in a contract, the conception of right and wrong which precedes every contract, since all contracts derive their validity from it. Here a conception of law was expressed which was binding for all men, though it was not formally proclaimed; and there was a Lawgiver capable of enforcing it and coercing transgressors.

Did Amos speak as a champion of ethics? Was it in the name of the moral law that the shepherd of Tekoa left his sheep to proclaim his message in Samaria? Amos insisted that it was God whose call he followed and whose living word he carried.

There *is* a living God who cares. Justice is more than an idea or a norm. Justice is a divine concern. What obtains between God and His people is not only a covenant of mutual obligations, but also a relationship of mutual concern. The message of God is not an impersonal accusation, but the utterance of a Redeemer who is pained by the misdeeds, the thanklessness of those whom He has redeemed. His words are plaintive and disconsolate.

> *I brought you up out of the land of Egypt,*
> *And led you forty years in the wilderness,*
> *To possess the land of the Amorite.*
> *And I raised up some of your sons for prophets,*
> *And some of your young men for Nazirites.*
> *Is it not indeed so, O people of Israel? . . .*
> *But you made the Nazirites drink wine,*
> *And commanded the prophets,*
> *Saying, You shall not prophesy.*
>
> *Amos 2:10-12*

ICONOCLASM

The most beautiful face lends itself to caricature, to a ludicrous exaggeration of some of its features. And the sublime ideas of biblical faith are equally subject to caricature. As examples may be cited the idea of "the people of the Lord" and the idea of "the day of the Lord."

From the beginnings of Israelite religion the belief that God had chosen this particular people to carry out His mission has been both a cornerstone of Hebrew faith and a refuge in moments of distress. And yet, the prophets felt that to many of their contemporaries this cornerstone was a stumbling block; this refuge, an escape. They had to remind the people that chosenness must not be mistaken as divine favoritism or immunity from chastisement, but, on the contrary, that it meant being more seriously exposed to divine judgment and chastisement.

Hear this word that the Lord has spoken against you, O people of Israel,
against the whole family which I brought up out of the land of Egypt:

> *You only have I known*[4]
> *Of all the families of the earth;*
> *Therefore I will punish you*
> *For all your iniquities.*
>   *Amos 3:1-2*

Does chosenness mean that God is exclusively concerned with Israel?
Does the Exodus from Egypt imply that God is involved only in the history
of Israel and is totally oblivious of the fate of other nations?

> *Are you not like the Ethiopians to Me,*
> *O people of Israel? says the Lord.*
> *Did I not bring up Israel from the land of Egypt,*
> *And the Philistines from Caphtor and the Syrians from Kir?*
>   *Amos 9:7*

The nations chosen for this comparison were not distinguished for might
and prestige—countries such as Egypt or Assyria—but rather, nations
which were despised and disliked. The color of the Ethiopians is black, and
in those days many of them were sold on the slave markets. The Philistines
were the archenemies of Israel, and the Syrians continued to be a menace to
the Northern Kingdom. The God of Israel is the God of all nations, and all
men's history is His concern.

There was a belief in the coming of "a day of the Lord," when God
would triumph over all His enemies and establish His rule in the world.
In the eyes of the multitude, that belief promised salvation for Israel, regardless of her conduct. The day of the Lord was seen as a day of punishment for pagans only rather than for all nations, Israel included.

> *Woe to you who desire the day of the Lord!*
> *Why would you have the day of the Lord?*
> *It is darkness, and not light;*
> *As if a man fled from a lion,*
> *And a bear met him;*
> *Or went into the house and leaned with his hand against the wall,*
> *And a serpent bit him.*
> *Is not the day of the Lord darkness, and not light,*
> *And gloom with no brightness in it?*
>
>   *Amos 5:18-20*

Amos tried to convey the sense of disappointment, God's aversion against
the people. Indeed, what God demands of man is expressed not only in
terms of action, but also in terms of passion. "I hate and abhor your

---

[4] On the meaning of the term in Hosea see pp. 57 ff.

feasts!" (5:21), says God. "Hate evil and love good" (5:15) is the great
demand.

Is it conceivable that the prophet set forth God's powerful pathos in inner
detachment? Does not the very fact of his conveying the pathos to the people
imply an inner identification with it? We know that standing before God,
Amos pleaded for the people. What, then, was his feeling when he stood
before the people?

> Does a lion roar in the forest,
> When he has no prey?
> Does a young lion cry out from his den
> If he has taken nothing?
> Does a bird fall in a snare on the earth,
> When there is no trap for it?
> Does a snare spring up from the ground,
> When it has taken nothing?
> Is a trumpet blown in a city,
> And the people are not afraid?
> Does evil befall a city,
> Unless the Lord has done it?
> Surely the Lord God does nothing,
> Without revealing His secret
> To His servants the prophets.
> The lion has roared;
> Who will not fear?
> The Lord God has spoken;
> Who can but prophesy?

> *Amos 3:4-8*

Amos, a prophet to whom the call of God came as a surprise and stayed
on as dismay, is startled. The voice of God is compared with the roar of a
lion about to fall upon its prey; Israel, God's chosen people, is the prey.
And no one hears, no one trembles. All save the prophet are deaf and complacent. Yet Amos' reaction is not fear[5] but the inner compulsion to convey
what the voice proclaims; not escape for shelter, but identification with the
voice.

It seems amazing that in the book of Amos, which proclaims that God's
supreme concern is righteousness and that His essential demand of man is to
establish justice, God is compared with a lion in search of its prey. To Amos
the good is not apart from God. At times God's call is, "Seek Me"; at other

---

[5] J. Wellhausen, *Die kleinen Propheten* (Berlin, 1892), and W. Nowack, *Die kleinen
Propheten* (Göttingen, 1897), emend the text "who can but prophesy" to "who shall not
fear." Sellin rejects this emendation as a remarkable misunderstanding of Amos' train of
thought.

times, "Seek the good." He who seeks a lion will end as a victim, but Amos hears that Israel can live only in seeking God.

> *For thus says the Lord to the house of Israel:*
> *Seek Me and live; ...*
> *Seek good, and not evil,*
> *That you may live; ...*
> *Hate evil, and love good,*
> *And establish justice in the gate; ...*
>   *Amos 5:4; 5:14, 15*

THE LORD REPENTED

The majority of scholars and theologians interpret the message of Amos as the application by the Deity of stern, mechanical justice.[6] Such a view disregards the powerful expression of divine inwardness in the message of the prophet.

Had the Lord been a God of stern, mechanical justice, then long ago He might have repudiated His covenant and cast Israel off. He had a deep affection for His people, and had known them more intimately than any of the other nations (3:2). Israel proved faithless, but again and again God had overlooked and forgiven, hoping that Israel might see the error of her way and repent. Again and again, He had sent into Israel warning portents, that Israel might take heed and return to Him. He sent upon them one calamity after another, "yet you did not return to Me."

The song of lament (see p. 36) concerning the obduracy of the people, with its recurrent refrain, five times repeated, "yet you did not return to Me," (4:6-13), is an expression of God's mercy and of His disappointment.

Harsh is God's intolerance of injustice, but the gate of repentance remains open. When shown in a vision the imminent destruction of Israel by locust or by fire, Amos has no arguments to offer in his attempt to save his people. He does not question God's justice; he appeals to God's mercy:

> *O Lord God, forgive, I beseech Thee!*
> *How can Jacob stand?*
> *He is so small!*
> *The Lord repented concerning this;*
> *It shall not be, said the Lord.*
>   *Amos 7:2-3; cf. 7:5-6*

"The Lord repented" not because the people are innocent, but because they are small. His judgment is never final. There is always a dimension of

---

[6] Morgenstern, *op. cit.*, pp. 418 f.

God's pervading affection where compassion prevails over justice, where
mercy is a perpetual possibility:

> It may be that the Lord, the God of hosts,
> Will be gracious to the remnant of Joseph.[7]
>
>   Amos 5:15

AN ENCOUNTER WILL SAVE

> I gave you cleanness of teeth in all your cities,
> And lack of bread in all your places,
> Yet you did not return to Me, says the Lord.
> And I also withheld the rain from you. . . .
> I would send rain upon one city,
> And send no rain upon another city; . . .
> Yet you did not return to Me, says the Lord.
> I smote you with blight and mildew; . . .
> Your fig trees and your olive trees the locust devoured;
> Yet you did not return to Me, says the Lord.
> I sent among you a pestilence after the manner of Egypt;
> I slew your young men with the sword; . . .
> Yet you did not return to Me, says the Lord.
> I overthrew some of you,
> As when God overthrew Sodom and Gomorrah,
> And you were as a brand plucked out of the burning;
> Yet you did not return to Me, says the Lord.
> Therefore thus I will do to you, O Israel;
> Because I will do this to you,
> Prepare to meet your God, O Israel!
> For lo, He Who forms the mountains, and creates the wind,
> And declares to man what is His thought;[8]
> Who makes the morning darkness,
> And treads on the heights of the earth—
> The Lord, the God of hosts, is His name!
>
>   Amos 4:6-13

Prepare to meet your God, O Israel. What will be the nature of that
meeting? The verse is generally understood by commentators as predicting
a punishment more severe than any of those which had been described.[9]
The long tale of infliction sets forth clearly the futility of chastisement.

---

[7] It is a striking fact that while God's aversion is expressed in the first person, the testimony
to His love is to be found only in the words of the prophet.

[8] Or "purpose," see I Kings 18:27. The Vulgate: *Et annuntians homini eloquium suum;*
cf. Amos 3:7.

[9] See, e.g., R. S. Cripps, *A Critical and Exegetical Commentary on the Book of Amos* (London, 1929) , pp. 176, 296 f. According to Rashi and Kimhi, in their *Commentaries, ad loc.,* it
is a call to repentance.

The soul is incapable of remorse. However, if hunger, drought, blight, locust, pestilence, slaying of sons, and destruction of cities have had no effect, what should the next action be? Another more bitter infliction would contradict the central thesis of the tale.

It could also mean a prediction of total destruction, and this would be consonant with other statements in Amos (7:8; 8:2). However, had this been his intention, the prophet would have said, "Prepare for the day of the Lord," signifying extreme disaster (5:18).

Moreover, according to the common interpretation, "to prepare" in this verse means "to prepare for disaster," and "to meet" means "to head for disaster." In biblical usage the Hebrew term "to meet" (*likrath*) denotes either to go to a place to receive favorably a person upon arrival, or to oppose someone in battle; it does not mean to head for disaster. The term "to prepare" denotes to prepare for war or for a constructive achievement, not to prepare for defeat.

Amos' primary mission is not to predict, but to exhort and to persuade (cf. 5:4, 6, 14). Israel has failed to seek Him, so He will go out to meet Israel. Indeed, both terms in this verse occur in the Hebrew Bible in connection with a divine encounter.

Prior to the theophany at Sinai, the people of Israel are told, *"Be prepared"* (Exod. 19:11, 15); Moses is told, *"Be prepared"* (Exod. 34:2). In the hope of receiving a word of God, Balaam said to Balak, "Perhaps the Lord will come *to meet* me" (Num. 23:3).[10] Significantly, the following verse in the Aramaic translation begins with the words: "For, lo, *He is revealing Himself* Who formed the mountains. . . ." Israel has a rendezvous with God. Castigation failed; an encounter will save.

This seems to be Amos' premise: God does not leave man in the dark; He communicates His thought to man.

> For lo, He Who forms the mountains, and creates the wind,
> And declares to man what is His thought; . . .
> The Lord, the God of hosts, is His name!
>
> *Amos 4:13*

Indeed, the prophecy of Amos that begins with a message of doom concludes with a vision of hope (9:11 ff.).[11]

Amos is so overwhelmed by his inspiration that there is little differentiation in his message between revelation and response. Conveying the word of

---

[10] In rabbinic literature, the necessity of preparation for prayer is derived from this verse; see *Tosefta Berachoth*, II, 18; *Bab. Berachoth*, 51b; *Shabbath* 10a.

[11] Amos' authorship of 9:8 ff. is maintained by Y. Kaufmann, *The Religion of Israel*, p. 368 (Heb.; vol. III, pt. I, pp. 88 f.).

God, he rarely (5:1-2, 15; 7:2, 5) adds his own word. There is no explicit statement of his sympathy, but only intimations of inner identifications and agreement.[12]

> *Do two walk together,*
> *Unless they have made an appointment? . . .*
> *Surely the Lord God does nothing,*
> *Without revealing His secret*
> *To His servants the prophets.*
>
> *Amos 3:3, 7*

These lines suggest a relation of *intimacy*, characteristic of those who are in close contact with one another and who have opened their hearts or their minds to such a degree that they deeply know and understand one another. Intimacy, however, never becomes familiarity. God is the Lord, and the prophets are His servants.

The prophet regards himself as one who walks together with God. God and he have agreed.

It is in the light of such sympathy, of such inner identification with the divine disappointment and aversion, that the spirit of Amos can be understood.

Amos' compassion for his people is profound. When beholding a vision of how "the Lord God was calling for a judgment by fire . . . it devoured the land," he prayed for mercy (7:4 ff.). And yet he also identified himself with God's threat of doom for the whole people. This is the burden of a prophet: compassion for man and sympathy for God.

---

[12] Cf. the correspondence between the divine exclamation "I hate your feasts" (5:21), and the prophetic admonition, "Hate the evil" (5:14).

3. HOSEA

HOSEA AND HIS TIMES

Hosea's prophecy dealt primarily with the Northern Kingdom of Israel—its religion, morals, and politics—and his favorite name for the land was Ephraim. "Hosea was the prophet of the decline and fall of the Northern Kingdom, and stood in the same relation to Ephraim in the eighth century as that in which Jeremiah stood to Judah a century and a half later."[1]

We know that Hosea was married, the father of three children, and well acquainted with agricultural life. From his use of certain striking figures of speech it has been suggested that he was a baker, lived as a farmer on the land, was associated with the priesthood and the sanctuaries, had a strongly developed sex instinct which he vigorously repressed. With the same right we could suggest that he was a lover of the desert and an expert on lions, panthers, and bears.

According to the superscription of his book, Hosea began his prophetic activity in the prosperous days of the reign of Jeroboam II (786-746 B.C.E.) and lived through the period of anarchy which followed Jeroboam's death. Some scholars assume that he ceased to prophesy before 734, the year of the Syro-Ephraimitic war against Judah, while others maintain that he continued to be active until after the fall of Samaria in 722 and that he predicted the return of the population from captivity (chs. 11 and 13).

For many generations Israel and Judah were not disturbed by any power greater than the small countries in the area. This relatively peaceful situation came to an end in the middle of the ninth century when Assyria

SELECTED BIBLIOGRAPHY: W. R. Harper, *A Critical and Exegetical Commentary on Amos and Hosea* (New York, 1915) ; E. Sellin, *Das Zwölfprophetenbuch* ("*Kommentar zum Alten Testament*" [2nd ed.; Leipzig, 1929]); S. L. Brown, *The Book of Hosea* ("Westminster Commentary" [London, 1932]) ; Y. Kaufmann, *The Religion of Israel* (Heb.; Jerusalem, 1954) , VI, 93-146; (Eng.; Chicago, 1960) , pp. 368 ff.; A. B. Ehrlich, *Randglossen zur Hebräischen Bibel,* vol. V (Leipzig, 1912) ; A. Wünsche, *Der Prophet Hosea* (Leipzig, 1868) ; H. L. Ginsberg, "Hosea's Ephraim, More Fool than Knave," *JBL,* LXXX (1961) , 339 f.

[1] S. L. Brown, *The Book of Hosea* (London, 1932) , p. xvi.

emerged as an empire and began to lead many expeditions across the Euphrates, compelling most of the states of Syria as well as the Northern Kingdom of Israel to submit to her sovereignty and to pay tribute. These expeditions, nightmares of extreme ruthlessness, enriched Assyria with plunder of gold, silver, and slaves.

The history of the following two centuries is but the story of the expansion of Assyria, and later of Babylonia, and the subjugation of western Asia. Subject states were spared complete extinction only on condition of submitting to severe terms of probation to test their fidelity to Assyria's rule. Such fidelity, however, was hard to bear. As soon as the invader departed, local kings would reassert themselves, and would seek to throw off the hated yoke.

The reign of Tiglath-pileser III (745-727 B.C.E.) saw the emergence of Assyria as a world empire. Tiglath-pileser resumed the policy of expansion toward the west, and by incessant wars subjugated peoples and countries, reducing them to vassals. He also introduced a new policy of conquest. Hitherto the westward incursions had ended in the exaction of booty, slaves, and annual tribute. Tiglath-pileser began the policy of deporting conquered populations from their homeland and of placing other exiles from distant areas in the evacuated territories, thus eliminating any effective rebellion. The record of the Assyrian policy is one of untold suffering and destruction, resulting in the downfall of the Kingdoms of Northern Syria (Arpad, Hamath, etc.), of Damascus (732), of the Northern Kingdom of Israel (721), of Judah (587), and even of Egypt (663). In 743, Tiglath-pileser embarked upon a campaign to subjugate the lands to the west. A coalition, according to conjecture headed by Uzziah, failed to stem the advance of the Assyrian army.

Assyria has been characterized as the nest of the bird of prey whence "set forth the most terrible expeditions which have ever flooded the world with blood. Ashur was its god, plunder its morality, cruelty and terror its means. No people was ever more abject than those of Ashur; no sovereigns were ever more despotic, more covetous, more vindictive, more pitiless, more proud of their crimes. Assyria sums up within herself all the vices. Aside from bravery, she offers not a single virtue."[2]

During the period of Tiglath-pileser, the Kingdom of Israel was in a state of anarchy. Within ten years following Jeroboam's death she had five kings, three of whom seized the throne by violence. The fall of Arpad in 740 was the signal for the prompt appearance of messengers from nearly all

[2] De Morgan, quoted by A. T. Olmstead, *History of Assyria* (New York, 1923), p. 645.

the neighboring states, including King Hiram of Tyre and King Rezin of Damascus, with presents of gold and silver, of ivory and purple robes. In the Northern Kingdom of Israel, Menahem (745-738 B.C.E.), who had usurped the throne, became a vassal of Assyria.[3]

The rulers felt relatively secure under Assyria's protection, but the hour of judgment was at hand. Hosea sounded an alarm, proclaiming the word of God:

> *Ephraim shall become a desolation*
> *In the day of punishment; . . .*
> *Upon them I will pour out*
> *My wrath like water.*
> *Ephraim is oppressed, crushed in judgment, . . .*
> *Therefore I am like a moth to Ephraim,*
> *And like dry rot to the house of Judah.*
>
> *Hosea 5:9-12*

Menahem remained king for six years, owing to the support of Assyria. Yet the pro-Assyrian policy evoked apparently strong opposition. Menahem's son, Pekahiah (*ca.* 738-737 B.C.E.) was murdered by Pekah (737-732 B.C.E.), son of Remaliah, who, after taking over the rule of the Kingdom, took part in the formation of an alliance between the small states of western Asia, directed against Assyria, and hoping for support from Egypt.[4]

POLITICAL PROMISCUITY

> *O Ephraim, you have played the harlot,*
> *Israel is defiled.*
>
> *Hosea 5:3; cf. 6:10; 9:1*

At times Hosea employed the term "harlot" in a figurative sense, in the sense of political promiscuity. The Northern Kingdom was in those days a hotbed of plots and intrigues, with constant military revolts and usurpations. King Zechariah, Jeroboam's son, had been slain by Shallum ben Jabesh; but the usurper had fallen a month later to Menahem, who only after much bloodshed had been able to establish his position. Hosea's horrified reaction was: "A vulture is over the house of the Lord!" (8:1.)

For Hosea, there was no legitimate king in the country at all. Kingship derived its prerogatives from a divine election; but of the kings who emerged from violence and rebellion, the word proclaims:

---

[3] *ANET*, p. 283.

[4] Referring apparently to Hoshea (732-724 B.C.E.), the last king of Samaria, who, though a vassal of Shalmaneser V, turned to Egypt for help (see II Kings 17:3-4); the prophet condemned him for mendacity and violence—they had made a treaty (*berith*) with Assyria, but they were taking oil to Egypt (12:1 [H. 12:2]).

> *They made kings, but not through Me,*
> *They set up princes, but without My knowledge.*
>
> *Hosea 8:4*

Nor was corruption only in high places. All the people engaged in the numerous conspiracies were practicing fraud: first acting furtively like thieves, then roaming abroad like bandits. Like an oven their hearts burned with intrigue:

> *All of them are hot as an oven,*
> *And they devour their rulers.*
> *All their kings have fallen;*
> *And none of them calls upon Me.*
>
> *Hosea 7:7*

In addition to multiplying "falsehood and violence" (12:1), the various political factions, pro-Egyptian or pro-Assyrian, seeking to gain power or protection with the aid of foreign states, made the country a ready prey for the appetites of Assyria and Egypt.

> *Ephraim is like a dove,*
> *Silly and without sense,*
> *Calling to Egypt, going to Assyria, . . .*
> *They make a bargain with Assyria,*
> *And oil is carried to Egypt.*
>
> *Hosea 7:11; 12:1 [H. 12:2];*
> *cf. 8:13; 9:3, 6*

The political game of hiring allies among the nations was both perilous and blasphemous, with Israel lying between the mighty Assyrian empire and an ambitious Egypt. Far from being a cure for Israel's weakness, taking advantage of the shifting political constellation could have had only the opposite effect.

> *For they sow the wind,*
> *And they shall reap the whirlwind.*
> *The standing grain has no heads,*
> *It shall yield no meal;*
> *If it were to yield,*
> *Aliens would devour it.*
> *Israel is swallowed up;*
> *Already they are among the nations*
> *As a useless vessel.*
>
> *Hosea 8:7-8*

In addition, an alliance with Assyria would have meant more than partnership in arms. It was Assyria's policy to require from her allies and tributaries recognition of her supreme god. Thus Israel was being led to the brink of the abyss.

Egypt, though not an abyss, could be like an earthquake. The central manifestation of the love and omnipotence of God, cherished and remembered in Israel, was the exodus from Egypt (11:1).

> *I am the Lord your God*
> *From the land of Egypt;*
> *You know no God but Me,*
> *And besides Me there is no savior.*
>   *Hosea 13:4*

But reliance on Assyria and Egypt would end in exile rather than security.

> *They shall return to the land of Egypt,*
> *And Assyria shall be their king,*
> *Because they have refused to return to Me.*
>   *Hosea 11:5; cf. 9:3, 6, 15; also 8:13*

Ephraim had given bitter provocation (12:14 [H. 12:15]); the judgment was inevitable and would not be long delayed. "Samaria shall bear her guilt, because she has rebelled against her God" (13:16 [H. 14:1]).

And yet the fall of Samaria was not the final phase in God's relationship to Israel. His love for Israel was ineradicable. He could not give up the people He loved (11:8). Hosea was sent primarily, not to announce doom, but to effect return and reconciliation.

> *Return, O Israel, to the Lord your God,*
> *For you have stumbled because of your iniquity.*
> *Take with you words*
> *And return to the Lord;*
> *Say to Him,*
> *Take away all iniquity;*
> *Accept that which is good,*
> *Our lips will replace the offering of bullocks.*
> *Assyria shall not save us,*
> *We will not ride upon horses;*
> *We will say no more, 'Our God,'*
> *To the work of our hands.*
> *In Thee the orphan finds mercy.*

The children of Israel shall return and seek the Lord their God, and David their king; and they shall come in fear to the Lord and to His goodness in the latter days.

> *I will be as the dew to Israel;*
> *He shall blossom as the lily, . . .*
> *His shoots shall spread out;*

His beauty shall be like the olive.
Hosea 14:1-4 [H. 14:2-4];
3:5; 14:5-6 [H. 14:6-7]

TENSION BETWEEN ANGER AND COMPASSION

What had Amos left undone, which Hosea must now do? Amos had proclaimed the righteousness of God, His iron will to let justice prevail. Hosea
came to spell out the astonishing fact of God's love for man. God is not only
the Lord who demands justice; He is also a God Who is in love with His
people.

There is a tone of divine nostalgia for the early days of God's relationship
with Israel.

Like grapes in the wilderness,
I found Israel;
Like the first fruit on the fig tree,
In its first season
I saw your fathers. . . .
When Israel was a child, I loved him,
And out of Egypt I called My son.
                Hosea 9:10; 11:1

Yet the more He called them, the more they went from Him.

It was I Who taught Ephraim to walk,
I took them up in My arms;
But they did not know that I healed them.
I led them with cords of compassion,
With the bands of love;
I became to them as One Who eases the yoke on their jaws,
I bent down to them and fed them gently.

                Hosea 11:3-4

In the face of God's passionate love, the prophet is haunted by the
scandal of Israel's desertion. "Israel has forgotten his Maker" (8:14). The
voice of God's offended majesty fills his whole being.

She did not know
That it was I Who gave her
The grain, the wine, and the oil,
And Who lavished upon her silver
And gold which they used for Baal.
        Hosea 2:8 [H. 2:10]

She went after the Baalim "and forgot Me, says the Lord" (2:13 [H. 2:15]).

The fertility of nature is an astounding wonder. To the non-Hebrew
population of Palestine, or Canaan, a land surrounded by desert, the mystery

of growth, the marvel of spring, remained a perpetual surprise. There were powers behind all this—the local gods of the land, called the Baalim, who were regarded as the givers of wool and flax, of oil and wine, of grain, vines, and fig trees (2:5, 12 [H. 2:7, 14]).

The conquest of Canaan by Israel was a process extending over several centuries. The Hebrews did not destroy the Canaanites (see Ps. 106:34), but merely occupied parts of the land, while other parts remained in the hands of the Canaanites. For some time there was constant warfare between the two groups, but gradually hostilities ceased, and the Hebrews began to mingle

> ... with the nations,
> And learned to do as they did.
> They served their idols,
> Which became a snare to them.
> They sacrificed their sons
> And their daughters to the demons;
> They poured out innocent blood,
> The blood of their sons and daughters,
> Whom they sacrificed to the idols of Canaan;
> And the land was polluted with blood.
> Thus they became unclean by their acts,
> And played the harlot in the doings.
>
> Psalm 106:35-39

Without abandoning the cult of the God of their Fathers, the Hebrews worshiped the gods of the land they had conquered, sacrificing on the tops of the mountains and making offerings "upon the hills, under oak, poplar, and terebinth, because their shade is good" (4:13). The rites included sacred prostitution (4:14) as well as intoxication. It was the worship of a god of the land rather than of the Creator of heaven and earth; a god who in return for the blessings of fertility demanded the gifts of incense and the excitements of the flesh rather than a God Who in return for all blessings demanded righteousness and justice, love and mercy, faithfulness and attachment, Who was the Lord of nature everywhere as well as the Master of history at all times.

"They . . . make for themselves molten images" and sacrifice to them (13:2 f.). They do not realize their stupidity. "Men kiss calves" (13:2). "A people without understanding shall come to ruin" (4:14).

> My people are destroyed for lack of knowledge;
> Because you have rejected knowledge,
> I reject you from being a priest to Me.
>
> Hosea 4:6

What fascination did the cult of Baal and Ashtoreth hold for the people? Pagan gods not only appeal to the imagination and are beloved by poets and painters alike; they are more comprehensible than the invisible God of Abraham. The conception of one God Who created heaven and earth is hard on the imagination. There is such multiplicity and variety of beings, there are thousands of communities, millions of human beings, countless numbers of days and nights—and only one God? Pagan gods, moreover, are more easily approached and appeased. "Men and gods are of one race: and both from the self-same mother we draw our breath; . . . in some measure we come near at least to the Immortals, either in respect of mind or our outward form."[5]

The serenity of the people, who felt safe in the enthusiastic worship of both God and the Baalim, was shattered by the prophet, whose words fell like the blows of a hammer over their heads:

> I am the Lord your God
> From the land of Egypt;
> You know no God but Me,
> And besides Me there is no savior.
> It was I who knew you in the wilderness,
> In the land of drought;
> But when they had fed to the full,
> They were filled, and their heart was lifted up;
> Therefore they forgot Me.
> So I will be to them like a lion,
> Like a leopard I will lurk beside the way.
> I will fall upon them like a bear robbed of her cubs,
> I will tear open their breast,
> And there I will devour them like a lion,
> As a wild beast would rend them.
>
>   *Hosea 13:4-8*

How deeply Hosea must have sensed the pathos of God to have been able to convey such dreadful words against his own people whom he loved so deeply. These words, however, were neither a final judgment nor an actual prediction. Their true intention was to impart the intensity of divine anger. And yet that anger did not express all that God felt about the people. Intense is His anger, but profound is His compassion. It is as if there were a dramatic tension in God.

---

[5] Pindar, *Nemean Odes*, VI, 1-2, 6-8. Despite long periods of eclipse, the pagan gods survived in Christian Europe during the Middle Ages. Jesus may become an Orpheus, "Jupiter may appear as one of the Evangelists, Perseus as a St. George, Saturn as God the Father." The glorification of the gods, particularly strong during the Renaissance, persisted in spite of protests and warnings of the Church against those who kept alive the memory of the gods. See J. Seznec, *The Survival of the Pagan Gods* (New York, 1961), pp. 213, 263.

Hosea describes a divine soliloquy in which the Lord considers with-holding the execution of His judgment, waiting for Israel to acknowledge her guilt and to return.

> *I will return again to My place,*
> *Until they acknowledge their guilt and seek My face,*
> *And in their distress they seek Me, saying,*
> *Come, let us return to the Lord;*
> *For He has torn, that He may heal us;*
> *He has stricken, and He will bind us up.*
> *After two days He will revive us;*
> *On the third day He will raise us up,*
> *That we may live before Him.*
> *Let us know, let us press on to know the Lord;*
> *His going forth is sure as the dawn;*
> *He will come to us as the showers,*
> *As the spring rains that water the earth.*
>
> *Hosea 5:15-6:3*

However, the soliloquy continues, there is little hope that such return will take place. Israel is erratic, and her love is fleeting. God's anxiety comes to expression:

> *What shall I do with you, O Ephraim?*
> *What shall I do with you, O Judah?*
> *Your love is like a morning cloud,*
> *Like the dew that goes early away.*
> *Therefore I have hewn them by the prophets,*
> *I have slain them by the words of My mouth, . . .*
>
> *Hosea 6:4-5*

HOSEA SEES A DRAMA

Amos knows God as the selfless and exalted Being Whose sensibilities and concern for justice are pained by the sinful transgressions of Israel. The emotions suggested in his prophecies are not spontaneous. Apart from the active emotion of disdain, these emotions are reactive, provoked by human deeds: resistance and abhorrence leading to rejection. The exciting cause of the divine intervention in the course of history is furnished by human conduct: the relationship between God and Israel is upset by the provoca-tions of man. We hear but sparingly of a positive spontaneous emotion welling up in the depths of the divine Being.

It is Hosea who flashes a glimpse into the inner life of God as He ponders His relationship to Israel. In parables and in lyrical outbursts the decisive motive behind God's strategy in history is declared. The decisive motive is love.

God is conceived, not as the self-detached Ruler, but as the sensitive Consort to Whom deception comes and Who nevertheless goes on pleading for loyalty, uttering a longing for a reunion, a passionate desire for reconciliation. Of all the prophets, only Jeremiah has sensed a wider scale of personal relations, a more intense subjectivity. Hosea has given us a supreme expression of the vision of the subjective God so typical for prophetic awareness.

> *How shall I give you up, O Ephraim!*
> *How shall I surrender you, O Israel!*
> *How can I make you like Admah!*
> *How can I treat you like Zeboiim!*
> *My heart is turned within Me,*
> *My compassion grows like a flame.*
> *I will not execute My fierce anger,*
> *I will not again destroy Ephraim;*
> *For I am God and not man,*
> *The Holy One in your midst,*
> *And I will not come to destroy.*
>   *Hosea 11:8-9*

Hosea centralizes the various incidental reactions. Where Amos sees episodes, Hosea sees a drama. Going beyond the description of momentary conditions, Hosea reaches an awareness of the basic feeling, of the latent subjective meaning in all individual announcements and decisions. We hear not merely of an incidental pathos, but also of the cardinal, fundamental emotion; not merely of particular attitudes, but also of the constitutive relationship between God and Israel. Over and above the immediate and contingent emotional reaction of the Lord we are informed about an eternal and basic disposition. The historically conditioned expressions of pathos and the immediate situation between God and man are set in the light of the eternal background. At the beginning "when Israel was a child I loved him" (11:1).

The traits of pathos announced by Amos recur verbally in the prophecies of Hosea. The pathos of repugnance receives important variations of tone. It is expressed as abhorrence ("My God will abhor them," 9:17), as hatred ("Every evil of theirs is in Gilgal; / There I began to hate them. / Because of the wickedness of their deeds . . . ," 9:15), as anger ("Upon them I will pour out / My wrath like water," 5:10; cf. 8:5; 13:11, 14). Also the detestation of the aristocracy and their palaces which we find in Amos is known to Hosea:

> *For Israel has forgotten his Maker,*
> *And built palaces; . . .*
>   *Hosea 8:14*

The modulation of the divine feelings toward repentance, found in Amos, is expressed most stirringly: "My heart is turned within me" (11:8; cf. 12:6). But it is also said: "Compassion remains hid from Me" (13:14).

A new factor not found in Amos is the sense of tenderness and mercy. Hosea is able to express as no other prophet the love of God for Israel in its most varied forms—as compassion (11:8), as a mother's tenderness (1:6-8; 2:3, 6, 21, 25; 11:1), as love between husband and wife (3:1 ff.).[6] From the perspective of the fundamental disposition of love, it is understandable that healing and reconciliation, not harm and destruction, finally prevail. The central idea put before the people is not a divine repugnance to cultic worship in general, but the provocation caused by idolatry as well as God's plea for a renewal of the covenant (2:16 ff [H. 2:18 ff.]).

EMOTIONAL SOLIDARITY

> Hear the word of the Lord, O people of Israel;
> For the Lord has a controversy with the inhabitants of the land.
> There is no truth or love, and no understanding for God in the land.
>
> Hosea 4:1

Whose part does the prophet take in the divine-human controversy?

The theme of Hosea's prophecy is apostasy. Most of his utterances are variations on the same theme. It is remarkable in his treatment that the subject of preoccupation is not the apostate, the backslider, but God the abandoned One. Hosea never tries to plead for the people or to dwell upon the reasons for the people's alienation from God. He has only one perspective: the divine partner. As a result there is little understanding on his part for the weakness of man. The words which Hosea flings at the people engaged in celebrating a harvest festival are stern and gloomy:

> Do not rejoice, Israel, like the peoples,
> For you have played the harlot, forsaking your God. . . .
> The days of visitation have come,
> The days of recompense have come.
>
> Hosea 9:1, 7

Hosea's emotional solidarity with God is apparent throughout the book. In a survey of the history of Israel (9:10-17), in which past and present are contrasted and the imminent catastrophe is depicted, Hosea does not implore mercy for the people; instead, his sympathy with divine wrath rings in the harsh words:

---

[6] A counterpart to the song of love (ch. 11) is the song of wrath (ch. 8; cf. 13:11), but again and again a cadence of reconciliation is heard (14:4 [H. 14:5]).

> *Give them, O Lord—*
> *What wilt Thou give?*
> *Give them a miscarrying womb*
> *And dry breasts.*
>
> *Hosea 9:14*

Hosea's prophecy, in which the essence of God's relationship to Israel is celebrated as love, tenderness, and nostalgia, contains also expressions of terrifying vehemence.

> *I will be like a lion to Ephraim,*
> *Like a young lion to the house of Judah.*
> *I, even I, will rend and go away,*
> *I will carry off, and none shall rescue.*
>
> *Hosea 5:14; cf. 13:7-8*

How does one reconcile the tenderness of divine love with the vehemence of divine punishment? Clearly it is not a love that is exclusive and that ignores the wickedness of the beloved, forgiving carelessly every fault. Here is a love grown bitter with the waywardness of man. The Lord is in love with Israel, but He also has a passionate love of right and a burning hatred of wrong.

LONGING FOR REUNION

God's relationship to Israel is most commonly described as a covenant. The word "covenant" conveys the permanence, steadfastness, and mutuality rather than the personal depth of that relationship. Is the covenant a tether, a chain, or is it a living intercourse?

In the domain of imagination the most powerful reality is love between man and woman. Man is even in love with an image of that love, but it is the image of a love spiced with temptation rather than a love phrased in service and depth-understanding; a love that happens rather than a love that continues; the image of tension rather than of peace; the image of a moment rather than of permanence; the image of fire rather than of light. But God said, "Let there be light."

To Hosea, marriage is the image for the relationship of God and Israel. This is one of the boldest conceptions of religious thinking. It may lack the excitement of adventure, but it has the aura of sublimity. It involves restraint, bringing with it duties and responsibilities, but it also endows with a nobility that is a synonym for eternity. Israel is the consort of God.[7]

---

[7] Hosea's conception of Israel as the consort of God represents one of the most important ideas in the history of Judaism (cf. Isa. 49:14-15; 62:5), and foreshadows the traditional interpretation of the Song of Songs.

Hosea's direct purpose, however, is not to celebrate the grandeur of that relationship, but rather to expose any implication of disturbance which that relationship may have for the life of God. Idolatry is adultery. More than objective falsehood, it is a betrayal of God; more than stupidity, it is lewdness. Israel is like a wanton wife, the Lord like a faithful, loving, but forsaken husband. The strain of disillusionment rings in the sharp and threatening words:

> *Plead with your mother, plead—*
> *For she is not my wife,*
> *And I am not her husband—*
> *That she put away her harlotry from her face,*
> *And her adultery from between her breasts; . . .*
> *Hosea 2:2 [H. 2:4]*

The prophet announces the intention of the Lord to repudiate the people, to devastate the land, to

> *. . . make her like a wilderness,*
> *And set her like a parched land,*
> *And slay her with thirst.*
> *Hosea 2:3 [H. 2:5]*

It is the utterance of a pathos—not a decree, not a decision.

Yet stronger than jealousy is God's longing for reunion and His hope for Israel's return. The day will come when "you will call Me 'my husband,' . . . and I will betroth you to Me for ever; I will betroth you to Me in righteousness and in justice, in love and in mercy. I will betroth you to Me in faithfulness, and you shall know the Lord" (2:16, 19-20 [H. 2:18, 21-22]). The reconciliation will take effect as a new betrothal. And these will be the gift and dowry for the bride: righteousness, justice, kindness, mercy. The pathos of love, expressed first in the bitterness of disillusionment, finds its climax in the hope of reconciliation. "I will heal their backsliding, I will love them freely, for Mine anger has turned from him" (14:4 [H. 14:5]).

HOW TO SHARE DISILLUSIONMENT

All images, parables, and symbols fade when applied to God. Even the description of God as the Consort of Israel fails to convey the love of God. A husband publicly betrayed by his wife is prevented by law and by emotion from renewing his marital life with her. But God's love is greater than law and emotion.

The pathos that moved the soul of Hosea possessed, in contrast to its elementary manifestations proclaimed by Amos, a complex structure. He was struck by the whole drama of God's relationship to Israel, a drama composed of various acts and stages. What would have made it possible for Hosea to attain an inner identification with all stages of the divine pathos? A mere knowledge of what has come to pass between God and Israel would have enabled him to have genuine sympathy for the present emotion, the disillusionment, but not for the whole gamut of experience, for all stages of the inner drama that preceded the present. The scope of sympathy is limited. One must share the experiences, or similar experiences, in order to share the emotional reactions to them. Moreover, disillusionment is a feeling the intensity of which is dependent upon the nature and depth of the emotional attitudes; one must have shared the love in order to share the disillusionment. Only a revival, one by one, of past happenings, together with the reactions they called forth, would enable the prophet to experience sympathy for the drama. For this purpose, the full story was re-enacted in the personal life of the prophet, and the variety of divine pathos experienced and shared in the privacy of his own destiny: love, frustration, reconciliation.

HOSEA'S MARRIAGE

Hosea was told by the Lord to marry a girl named Gomer, the daughter of Diblaim, whom he loved.[8] For a time they were happy in their mutual affection. Three children were born, to whom Hosea gave symbolic names.[9] Subsequently, however, he discovered that Gomer had been unfaithful and had given herself to many lovers. She could not remain his wife. She then left him, or was sent away by him. That was the legal way: to expel the woman who became an adulteress. The husband was not allowed to live with her. "No pity for the children, because they are children of harlotry; . . . she that conceived them had acted shamefully" (2:4 f.) .[10]

---

[8] The phrase *'esheth zenunim* does not connote a harlot, which is called *'ishah zonah* or simply *zonah*, but, as Ehrlich pointed out, a person who is disposed to become a harlot, a woman filled with the spirit of whoredom (*Randglossen zur Hebräischen Bibel*, V, 163). According to another view, the term denotes a woman who took part in the Canaanite fertility cult. See H. W. Wolff, "*Hoseas geistige Heimat*," *Theologische Literaturzeitung* (1956), pp. 83 ff. "In the course of the marriage Gomer's disposition revealed itself. Under the impression of this painful experience, Hosea describes his wife as she had become at the time of writing, i.e., after the birth of the three children mentioned in ch. 1." (H. Guthe in E. Kautzsch, *Die Heilige Schrift des Alten Testaments* [4th ed.; Tübingen, 1923-1924.]) The supposition that Hosea had married a harlot spoils the sense of the incident, which is meant to symbolize the historical relationship between God and Israel, the latter having been at the outset an obedient people.
[9] The first, a son, he called Yezreel, in token of the coming destruction of the dynasty of Jehu; the second, a daughter, and the third, another son, he named "Not-Pitied" and "Not-My-People," respectively, as signs of the Lord's rejection of Israel (1:2-9) .
[10] On the marriage of Hosea, cf. H. H. Rowley, *The Servant of the Lord* (London, 1952) , p. 115, n. 1; W. R. Harper, *Amos and Hosea*, pp. 208 f.; cf. also R. Gordis, "Hosea's Marriage and Message," *HUCA*, XXV (1954) , 9-34. Cf. H. L. Ginsberg, "Studies in Hosea 1-3," *Y. Kaufmann Jubilee Volume* (Jerusalem, 1960) , pp. 50 ff.

But God's way is higher than the legal way. The Lord said to Hosea: "Bring Gomer back to your home, renew your love for her, even as the Lord loves the people of Israel, though they turn to other gods" (3:1). Hosea did bring her from the slavery into which she had fallen; the marriage was renewed. God cannot abandon Israel. He will not forsake her in spite of her faithlessness.

The account of this strange incident has been a puzzle to commentators.[11] They have found it morally repugnant that God should have commanded a prophet to marry or even to remarry an adulterous woman. The suggestion has been made, therefore, that the incident took place in a vision or a dream and was never carried out in real life, or that the story was told as a parable or allegory. The first view is advanced by Ibn Ezra, Maimonides,[12] and Kimhi,[13] while the second view is expressed by the *Targum,* Rashi, and Hieronymus. Against these views and in favor of a literal understanding of the narrative, it is argued (a) that what is morally and religiously objectionable in actual practice becomes no more defensible by being presented as vision or parable; (b) that no indication is given by the prophet that this is vision or parable and not fact; (c) that the name Gomer bath Diblaim yields no symbolic significance; (d) that no symbolic significance can be attached to the fact that the second child is a girl rather than a boy; (e) that the literal view suits the realism of early prophecy better than the supposition that it is a product of literary imagination; (f) that the prophets were accustomed to giving symbolic names to real children; (g) that it would be strange for Hosea to tell such a story of his wife if false or, if he were unmarried, about himself; and (h) that a real experience such as this furnishes the best explanation of Hosea's message—it was the outcome of the sufferings of his own heart.[14] The nonliteral view has rightly been rejected by most modern scholars, who maintain that the narrative contains a report of actual events in the life of Hosea.

Some commentators question Hosea's claim that the marriage was concluded in obedience to a divine command. The prophet, they maintain, married Gomer under ordinary circumstances without suspecting what was to happen. Gomer went astray. As the prophet brooded over the tragedy in

---

[11] It is taken as a real event in Babylonian Talmud, *Pesahim* 87a-b; see also M. Friedmann, ed., *Seder Eliahu Rabba,* p. 187.

[12] *The Guide of the Perplexed,* II, 46.

[13] H. Cohen, ed., *Commentary on Hosea* (New York, 1929). Cf. *Midrash Agada,* ed. Buber (Wien, 1894), p. 40.

[14] See E. Sellin, *Einleitung in das Alte Testament* (4th ed.; Leipzig, 1910), p. 109. See also Allwohn, *Die Ehe des Propheten Hosea im psychoanalytischer Beleuchtung* (Gressen, 1926), pp. 35 ff.; K. Budde, "Der Abschnitt Hosea 1-3 und seine grundlegende religionsgeschichtliche Bedeutung," in *Alttestamentliche Forschungen, Sonderheft der theologischen Studien und Kritiken,* I (Stuttgart, 1925).

his own household, and wondered how God could bring such an experience upon him, he came to regard his marriage as having been ordained by divine Providence, and so proclaimed it to have taken place in fulfillment of a divine word which had gone forth to him.[15]

The idea behind this theory is that Hosea's claim to have been commanded by God originated in his own mind and that he never experienced a moment which would have entitled him to say, "And the Lord said to me, Go again, love a woman who is beloved of a paramour and is an adulteress" (3:10). Thus, what Hosea gave out as a divine call was due to his own impulse. But this theory reflects upon the integrity of the prophet. It imputes to Hosea a pretension with which false prophets are charged—the giving out as divine words the thoughts of their own mind—for Hosea proclaimed that in entering upon his marriage he was following a divine command. Apart from other objections, therefore, "this modern psychological theory is in any case to be rejected since it does not do justice to the integrality of the whole and arbitrarily changes the words of the prophet."[16] Our rationalistic prejudice gives us no right to maintain that what the prophet described as a divine call was actually pretension and the product of hindsight.

In addition to the historical and psychological problem, the question of the meaning of the marriage has often been discussed. Some scholars maintain that the purpose of the marriage was to teach through demonstration: to let the people recognize in this conjugal affair, played out before their gaze, a picture of their own conduct and fate. The impulse to this theory comes from the fact that the prophets of Israel often performed symbolic acts in order to demonstrate dramatically their message to the public.[17]

The facts to be dramatized were the following: betrayal by the wife, the naming of the children, the repudiation of the wife, the taking her back, and perhaps also the sorrow of the prophet. Publicly to dramatize a wife's adultery comes close to popularizing infidelity, and the moral didactic effect of such a dramatization would be highly questionable.

It is also unlikely that the prophet's repudiation of his wife was meant to demonstrate to the public God's actual rejection of the people. Hosea never proclaimed, but only threatened, the rejection of Israel; in that case the symbol would have been in contradiction to historical realities. Even the taking back of the wife cannot have been meant as an example. In Hosea's

---

[15] Wellhausen, Smith, *et al.* According to others Hosea's wife was corrupted by the immorality of the public cult. Then the prophet, as a result of his disillusionment in love, reached the position of fundamental world denial.

[16] See H. Gressmann in H. Schmidt, *Die Schriften des Alten Testaments*, II (1), 263.

[17] See G. Fohrer, *Die symbolischen Handlungen der Propheten* (Zurich, 1953).

view, the reconciliation of God and people was to be attained only through penitence and conversion (14:1 f. [H. 14:2 f.]). But nothing is said in the story about Gomer's conversion, and it is not to be supposed that the prophet would have offered the people a symbolic picture inconsistent with his own exhortations. Nor does it seem plausible that so emotional and sensitive a personality as Hosea's should have contracted a marriage which was meant purely for public instruction. To play for years that sort of theatrical role—and it should be remembered that he had three children by Gomer—would have been for Hosea a public vivisection of his own fate, a martyrdom, and something comparable with cultic prostitution. Nor is it likely that the sorrow of Hosea was meant to represent symbolically to the people the pain of God's deception.

It has been suggested that drama took its origin, not from the imitation of men, but from the desire to imitate the actions of divine beings. This theory seems to receive confirmation from the development of the drama in Egypt as well as among many American Indian tribes. The actors are masked to represent the appropriate deities. This implies, to the primitive mind, that the actor is, for the time being, the deity whom he represents. However, only those deities can be represented with whom the actor believes he can be identified. The Greek drama was closely connected with the cult of Dionysus. "Athene and Zeus and Poseidon have no drama because no one, in his wildest moments, believed he could become and be Athene or Zeus or Poseidon. It is indeed only in the orgiastic religions that these splendid moments of conviction could come, and, for Greece at least, only in an orgiastic religion did the drama take its rise."[18]

To the prophets of Israel the idea of a human being copying or imitating the inner life of God would have appeared as the height of absurdity. For man to play God, to believe himself to be God, would have been horrible blasphemy. Moreover, the purpose of symbolic acts was to anticipate or to forecast the future—such as the doom of the state, the captivity of the people, or their return to the land. In contrast, the symbolic function of Hosea's marriage would have been to re-enact the past. Yet the sins of the past were known. What purpose would be served by illustrating what was notorious?

THE MARRIAGE AN ACT OF SYMPATHY

It seems absurd to assume that the prophet's marriage was performed for effect, as a mere demonstration, as an action intended for public informa-

---

[18] J. Harrison, *Prolegomena to the Study of Greek Religion* (Cambridge, 1908), p. 568.

tion. One must not reduce the fullness of an act to its operational meaning. We cannot adequately understand a person by the impressions he produces in other people. A person is not a puppet, and martyrdom is not a masquerade. One thing is clear: the primarily given and immediate spiritual datum in the story of the marriage is the prophet's experience. The event stirred and shocked the life of Hosea regardless of its effect upon public opinion. It concerned him personally at the deepest level and had a meaning of the highest significance for his own life.

As time went by, Hosea became aware of the fact that his personal fate was a mirror of the divine pathos, that his sorrow echoed the sorrow of God. In this fellow suffering as an act of sympathy with the divine pathos the prophet probably saw the meaning of the marriage which he had contracted at the divine behest.

The marriage of Hosea was no symbolic representation of real facts, no act of recreating or repeating events in the history of Israel or experiences in the inner life of God. Its meaning was not objective, inherent in the marriage, but subjective, evocative. Only by living through in his own life what the divine Consort of Israel experienced, was the prophet able to attain sympathy for the divine situation. The marriage was a lesson, an illustration, rather than a symbol or a sacrament. Its purpose was not to demonstrate divine attitudes to the people, but to educate Hosea himself in the understanding of divine sensibility.

The tragic disturbance in the relationship between God and Israel must have determined decisively his attitude and outlook. Hosea, who again and again emphasized the unchanging devotion of God to Israel, was not simply an advocate of the people. His mind was powerfully affected by the embitterment of God, echoed in his own sympathetic experience.

A difference of opinion exists concerning the origin of the parable which expresses the relationship between God and Israel by the symbol of marriage. It has been sought in Canaanite religion, in the Baal and Ashtoreth cult.[19] However, "the idea of a marriage of Baal with the soil could not be conclusively shown to exist in Canaanite thought."[20] Although there are similarities in the God-Israel and Baal-land marriage symbolism, there are also unmistakable differences between the two ideas. In the first place, in Canaanite religion the relationship between the god and the land remains foremost, whereas in the religion of Israel, the people appear instead of the

[19] E. Sellin, *Das Zwölfprophetenbuch* (Leipzig, 1929), p. 24.
[20] J. Ziegler, *Die Liebe Gottes bei den Propheten* (Münster, 1930), p. 67.

land. In the second place, the Canaanite view emphasizes primarily the sensuous, naturalistic aspect, whereas the prophetic idea alludes to the emotional and legal bond.[21]

That the idea which lies behind this parable of marriage derives from the doctrine of the covenant between God and Israel is entirely plausible.

DAATH ELOHIM

Hosea's central complaint against the people is that they do not know God. He employs the verb "to know" with striking frequency, and coins the expression *daath elohim*, usually rendered as "knowledge of God." The verb *yada* does not always mean simply "to know," "to be acquainted with." In most Semitic languages it signifies sexual union as well as mental and spiritual activity. In Hebrew *yada* means more than the possession of abstract concepts. Knowledge compasses inner appropriation, feeling, a reception into the soul.[22] It involves both an intellectual and an emotional act.

An analysis of the usage of the verb in biblical Hebrew leads to the conclusion that it often, though not always, denotes an act involving concern, inner engagement, dedication, or attachment to a person. It also means to have sympathy, pity, or affection for someone. In a number of passages it is inaccurate to translate *yada* with "to know." Let us cite a few examples:

1. After relating that the people of Israel groaned under their bondage in Egypt and cried out for help, the book of Exodus says that "their cry under bondage came up to God. And God heard their groaning, and God remembered His covenant with Abraham, with Isaac, and with Jacob. And God saw the people of Israel and God *knew* their condition" (Exod. 2:24-25). What the text means is: and He *had pity*. In the same story we read: "Then the Lord said, I have seen the affliction of My people who are in Egypt, and have heard their cry because of their taskmasters; I *know* their sufferings" (Exod. 3:7). What the text means is: I *have sympathy for*, I *am affected by*, their sufferings.

2. Israel is told: "You shall not oppress a stranger; you *know* the heart of a stranger, for you were strangers in the land of Egypt" (Exod. 23:9). The correct meaning is: You *have sympathy*, or a *feeling*, for the heart of a

---

[21] *Ibid.*, p. 68.
[22] See the fine study by E. Baumann, "Yada *und seine Derivate*," *ZAW*, XXVIII (1908), 125, who justly remarks that "*daath hashem* in Hosea denotes especially the fulfilment of the conjugal intercourse between Israel and the Lord." See also S. Mowinckel, *Die Erkenntnis Gottes bei den alttestamentlichen Propheten* (Oslo, 1941), W. Reiss, "*Gott nicht kennen im Alten Testament*," *ZAW*, LVIII (1940-41), 70 f.; G. J. Botterweck, "*Gott erkennen*" im *Sprachgebrauch des Alten Testaments* (Bonn, 1951); W. Zimmerli, *Erkenntnis Gottes nach dem Buche Ezekiel* (Zurich, 1954). Cf. J. Pederson, *Israel*, I-II (London and Copenhagen, 1926), 109.

stranger. "A righteous man *has regard* for the life of his beast, but the mercy of the wicked is cruel" (Prov. 12:10). The correct meaning is: he *has a feeling* (or *sympathy*) for his beast.

> *Who can stand before His indignation?*
> *Who can endure the heat of His anger?*
> *His wrath is poured out like fire,*
> *And the rocks are broken asunder by Him.*
> *The Lord is good,*
> *A stronghold in the day of trouble;*
> *He knows those who take refuge in Him.*
> *But with an overflowing flood*
> *He will make a full end of His adversaries,*
> *And will pursue His enemies into darkness.*
>   *Nahum 1:6-8*

The correct meaning is: He *has pity on*.

> *I will rejoice and be glad for Thy steadfast love,*
> *Because Thou hast seen my affliction,*
> *Thou hast seen the troubles of my soul.*
>   *Psalm 31:7*

The true meaning is: Thou *hast a feeling* (or *pity*) for.

3. Joseph is viceroy over Egypt. He saves her people from starvation and changes the entire system of land tenure in the country. Such a position and such activities must have made him the most famous man in the country. Then, after Joseph died, we are told: "There arose a new king over Egypt, who did *not know* Joseph" (Exod. 1:8). In what sense is the verb used here? To have meant he *did not know* him personally would be a platitude; to have meant he *did not know of* him would be ludicrous. What is probably meant is that he *did not care* for Joseph; he disliked him.

4. Of the sons of Eli, the high priest at the central sanctuary of Shiloh and judge over Israel, I Sam. 2:12 records that "they were base men; they knew not the Lord." Knowledge in the sense of information they must have had; what they lacked was an inner commitment or an emotional attachment. "Adam *yada* Eve his wife, and she conceived and bore Cain" (Gen. 4:1). It is usually rendered "Adam *knew* Eve his wife." The word is used here as well as elsewhere in the Bible in a sense of intimate sexual relationship. It is, however, likely that the sense in which it is used here refers to a total relationship, emotional as well as sexual. A more accurate translation would be: "Adam *attached* himself to Eve his wife."[23]

---

[23] "The Lord knows the way of the righteous, but the way of the wicked will perish" (Ps. 1:6). The psalmist does not mean that the Lord knows the way topographically; he means

The relationship between God and Israel, conceived by Hosea in terms of marital love, desertion, and the hope of new betrothal, calls not only for right action, but also for a feeling for each other on the part of those involved. It implies not only legal obligations, but also inner attitudes. In the light of his own complete emotional solidarity with God, Hosea seems to have seized upon the idea of sympathy as the essential religious requirement. The words *daath elohim* mean *sympathy for God,* attachment of the whole person, his love as well as his knowledge; an act of involvement, attachment or commitment to God. The biblical man knew of no bifurcation of mind and heart, thought and emotion. He saw the whole person in a human situation. "For I desire steadfast love and not sacrifice, *daath* of God, rather than burnt offerings" (6:6) ; *daath* corresponds to *ḥesed,* or love. What is desired is an inner identification with God rather than a mere dedication to ceremonies. Thus the expression *daath elohim* must be understood in the framework of Hosea's thinking of the God-Israel relationship as one of engagement, marriage, betrayal, and remarriage.

> *Their deeds do not permit them*
> *To return to their God.*
> *For the spirit of harlotry is within them*
> *And they know not the Lord. . . .*
> *They have dealt faithlessly with the Lord,*
> *For they have borne alien children.*
>
> *Hosea 5:4, 7*

As an antithesis to "the spirit of harlotry," knowledge of God must mean an intimate relation to, or a feeling for, God.

According to the analogy of sexual union to which this verb points, this sympathy must be understood to imply an emotional experience that is reciprocal. Just as in sexual reciprocal emotion, where the feeling of one person is in no sense an object to the other, where rather both persons share the same feeling, the structure of the sympathy implied in Hosea's hypothesis is not compassion for one another, but a suffering together, the act of sharing an inner experience.

The word, then, as we have seen, has an intellectual as well as an emotional meaning. In most passages, the intellectual component of *daath* is stressed; in Hosea, the emotional component seems to be primary. His *daath*

---

that the Lord is concerned about every step the righteous man takes. "The heart knows its own bitterness, and no stranger shares its joy" (Prov. 14:10) . Here, too, "to know" means "to feel." What we know, a stranger can share; what we feel, no one can fully share. What we know is universal; what we feel is private. Cf. Ps. 131:2; Job 23:10; Isa. 43:2. See N. H. Snaith, *The Distinctive Ideas of the Old Testament* (London, 1947) , p. 135.

elohim does not connote a knowledge *about* God, but an awareness *of* God, a sensitivity for what concerns Him, a concern for the divine person, not only for the divine will[24]; a concern that involves inwardness as well as action.

That the word *daath* in Hosea denotes an act involving complete engagement of the person may be inferred from the words in which God predicts the new relationship with His people (2:19-20 [H. 2:21-22]) . Personal involvement, like the one that occurs when a man becomes engaged to a woman, seems to be regarded as the prerequisite for, or the essence of, the *daath* or "knowledge" of God. "I am the Lord your God from the land of Egypt; . . . It was I who *knew* you in the wilderness, in the land of drought" (13:4-5) . What the prophet means is "I *cared* for you" or "I was *attached* to you."

Unlike the prophetic sympathy which arises in response to a revelation and the pathos it discloses, the general sympathy which Hosea requires of man is a constant solidarity, an emotional identification with God. It is the central religious postulate. The loss of *daath* is the cause of man's undoing (4:6) .

The contrast between Amos and Hosea is seen both in what they condemn and in what they stress. To Amos, the principal sin is *injustice;* to Hosea, it is *idolatry.* Amos inveighs against evil *deeds;* Hosea attacks the absence of *inwardness.* In the words of Amos:

> *I hate, I despise your feasts, . . .*
> *I will not accept your* sacrifices. . . .
> *But let* justice *roll down like waters,*
> *And righteousness like a mighty stream.*
> *Amos 5:21-24*

In the words of Hosea:

> *For I desire* love [hesed] *and not sacrifice,*
> Attachment to God *rather than burnt offerings.*
> *Hosea 6:6*

In surveying the past, Amos dwells on what God has done (2:9 ff.) ; Hosea dwells on what God has felt for Israel (11:1-4). "You only have I known of all the families of the earth," in the words of Amos (3:2) . "When Israel was a child, I loved him," in the words of Hosea (11:1). And again from Hosea: "There is no loyalty (*'emeth*), no love (*hesed*), and no knowledge of God in the land" (4:1) .

---

[24] Baudissin, *Archiv für die Religionswissenschaft,* XVIII, 226, explains the term to mean "to be concerned about the divine will," but this does not render its peculiar meaning.

4. ISAIAH

(ISA. 1—39)

PROSPERITY AND POWER

Under the long reign of Uzziah (*ca.* 783-742 B.C.E.), in fame second only to Solomon's, Judah reached the summit of its power. Uzziah built up the economic resources of the country as well as its military strength. He conquered the Philistines and the Arabians, and received tribute from the Ammonites; he fortified the country, reorganized and re-equipped the army. "In Jerusalem he made engines, invented by skilful men, to be on the towers and the corners, to shoot arrows and great stones" (II Chron. 26:15). His success as king, administrator, and commander in chief of the army made him ruler over the largest realm of Judah since the disruption of the Kingdom.

Uzziah's strength became his weakness. "He grew proud, to his destruction," and attempted to usurp the power of the priesthood, even entering the Temple of the Lord to burn incense on the altar, a privilege reserved to the priest. Azariah, the chief priest, followed by eighty priests, "men of valor," pleaded with him:

"It is not for you, Uzziah, to burn incense to the Lord, but for the priests the sons of Aaron, who are consecrated to burn incense. Go out of the sanctuary; for you have done wrong, and it will bring you no honor from the Lord God." This angered Uzziah, and as his anger mounted, leprosy broke out on his forehead. "And King Uzziah was a leper to the day of his death, and being a leper dwelt in a separate house, for he was excluded from the house of the Lord" (II Chron. 26:18-21).[1]

SELECTED BIBLIOGRAPHY: B. Duhm, *Das Buch Jesaia* ("*Göttingen Handkommentar zum Alten Testament*" [9th ed.; Göttingen, 1922]) ; G. B. Gray, *A Critical and Exegetical Commentary on the Book of Isaiah* ("International Critical Commentary" [New York, 1912]) ; O. Procksch, *Isaia I* ("*Kommentar zum Alten Testament*" [Leipzig, 1930]) ; E. J. Kissane, *The Book of Isaiah*, vol. I (Dublin, 1941) ; Y. Kaufmann, *The Religion of Israel* (Heb.; Jerusalem, 1954), VI, 147-256; (Eng. trans., M. Greenberg [Chicago, 1960], pp. 378 ff.); A. B. Ehrlich, *Randglossen zur Hebräischen Bibel*, vol. IV (Leipzig, 1912) .

[1] Cf. II Kings 15:3-5; Josephus, *Antiquities*, IX, 10, 4; J. Morgenstern, "The Sin of Uzziah," *HUCA*, XII-XIII (1937-1939) , 1 ff.

It was about 750 B.C.E. when Uzziah was stricken with leprosy, and his place in public was taken over by his son Jotham, officially designated as regent, though actual power seems to have remained with Uzziah. Under Jotham (d. *ca.* 735), Judah continued to be the most stable, prosperous, and powerful state in the area. Her wealth and military power placed her in the forefront of the anti-Assyrian movement when Tiglath-pileser III of Assyria invaded Syria in 743.

The increasing prosperity of Judah "was not canalized for the exclusive benefit of the aristocracy and the wealthy merchants, as was apparently true of the Northern Kingdom in the eighth century. . . . All private houses so far excavated reflect a surprisingly narrow range of variation in the social scale. . . . In other words, there was no period in Judah during which was such concentration of wealth in the hands of individuals as to destroy the social order."[2] The people made good use of the opportunities for commercial and industrial expansion.

ISAIAH AND THE NORTHERN KINGDOM

The years in which Isaiah began his prophetic activity were the beginning of a most critical period for both Israel and Judah. He received his call to be a prophet in the year in which King Uzziah of Judah died (*ca.* 742), not long after the death of Jeroboam II of Israel (746) and the advent of Tiglath-pileser (745), under whom the Assyrians set themselves the tremendous task of conquering both Babylonia and Syria. Overpowering small states, plundering cities, deporting populations, the Assyrians became a menace that filled Syria and Palestine with terror. Soon Samaria in alliance with Damascus became involved in a treacherous adventure against Judah, which ended in their becoming prey to Assyria's aggression. The relative security of the preceding several centuries was rudely broken.

The future of Judah hung in the balance; Samaria was doomed. The message of Isaiah, particularly as received by him in his great vision, spelled the final judgment.

Amos and Hosea had devoted their ministries to trying to save the people of the Northern Kingdom. They had called for return, but met with no response. What was to be Isaiah's role in relation to Samaria?

Neither the words of the prophets nor the experience of disaster seemed to shake the self-reliance of the people of the Northern Kingdom. In pride and arrogance of heart they boasted:

---

[2] W. F. Albright, "The Biblical Period," in L. Finkelstein, ed., *The Jews* (New York, 1949), pp. 39 ff.

> *The bricks have fallen,*
> *But we will build with hewn stones;*
> *The sycamores have been cut down,*
> *But we will put cedars in their place.*
>   *Isaiah 9:10 [H. 9:9]*

All attempts to purify Samaria failed; its final destruction was proclaimed (17:1-11; 9:8-21 [H. 9:7-20]).

> *Through the wrath of the Lord of hosts*
> *The land is burned,*
> *And the people are like fuel for the fire; . . .*
>   *Isaiah 9:19 [H. 9:18]*

The judgment will be carried out at the decree of the Lord.

> *He will raise a signal for a nation afar off,*
> *And whistle for it from the ends of the earth;*
> *And lo, swiftly, speedily it comes!*
> *None is weary, none stumbles,*
> *None slumbers or sleeps,*
> *Not a waistcloth is loose,*
> *Not a sandal-thong is broken.*
> *Their arrows are sharp,*
> *All their bows bent,*
> *Their horses' hoofs seem like flint,*
> *And their wheels like the whirlwind.*
> *Their roaring is like a lion,*
> *Like young lions they roar;*
> *They growl and seize their prey,*
> *They carry it off, and none can rescue.*
>   *Isaiah 5:26-29*

The Northern Kingdom was doomed; Ephraim as a people would cease to exist (7:8); Isaiah had no role to play in its destiny (28:1-4). With few exceptions, his message was directed to Judah.

SURRENDER TO ASSYRIA

King Jotham died about 735 and was succeeded by his son Ahaz (735-715 B.C.E.), who at once found himself embroiled in a serious crisis. The western states had accepted the domination of Assyria only at the point of the sword. They hated the conquerors, and yielded only when crushed. The peoples hoped continually for an opportunity to free themselves from the bitter yoke, and the opposition did not long remain dormant. In the Kingdom of Israel a usurper named Pekah (737-732 B.C.E.), leader of an anti-Assyrian movement, came into power. Taking advantage of the Assyrian king's involvement in the east, Pekah together with Rezin of Damascus united against Assyria, and apparently they were joined by Askelon and Gaza, whose independence was threatened by Assyria. King Ahaz, who refused to join the anti-Assyrian coalition, found himself threatened by the allied kings whose combined forces subjected Jerusalem to a state of siege (II Kings 15:37; 16:5; Isa. 7:1 ff.). The object of this undertaking was to depose King Ahaz and to replace him by a friend of their own, probably an Aramaean, who would bring the Kingdom of Judah into the anti-Assyrian coalition. It would have meant the end of the dynasty of David.

The attack by the two superior enemies progressed well. The territory of Judah was devastated, Jerusalem was threatened; the Edomites and Philistines on the south, probably incited by the aggressors, annexed portions of Judah's territory (II Kings 10:5; II Chron. 28:16-18). King Ahaz as well as his people were in a state of panic. As Isaiah put it, "His heart and the heart of his people shook as the trees of the forest shake before the wind" (7:2). There seemed to be only one way to save the Kingdom: to implore powerful Assyria for aid. Assyria would save Jerusalem.

At that critical moment, probably in the year 735, while Jerusalem was besieged by the superior forces of the enemy, Isaiah conveyed the word of God to the king: "Take heed, be quiet, do not fear, and do not let your heart be faint, because of these two smoldering stumps of firebrands" who were planning to conquer Judah. "Thus says the Lord God: It shall not stand, it shall not come to pass." But Ahaz' fear was not allayed. In a final attempt to influence the king, Isaiah offered to confirm the divine authority of his words by a sign. "Ask a sign of the Lord your God; let it be deep as Sheol or high as heaven." But Ahaz said: "I will not ask, and I will not put the Lord to test" (7:1-12).

We have no right to question the king's sincerity. His refusal to ask for a sign was motivated by piety (cf. Deut. 6:16). Besieged and harassed by his enemies, he sent messengers to Tiglath-pileser III (745-727 B.C.E.), king of Assyria, saying: "I am your servant and your son. Come up, and rescue me from the hand of the king of Syria and from the hand of the king of Israel, who are attacking me" (II Kings 16:7).

No other ruler would have acted differently. The state was in peril, so he appealed to a great power for military aid. Isaiah offered words; Assyria had an army. To rely on God rather than on weapons would have been to subordinate political wisdom to faith. The issue was not to let faith in God be a guide in his personal life. The issue was to let faith be the guide in a public life: other people's lives were at stake, the future of the country was in peril. The king would have had to justify to his people a refusal to ask for help.

So Ahaz decided that it was more expedient to be "son and servant" to the king of Assyria than son and servant to the invisible God. He took refuge in a lie (cf. 28:15). The independence of Judah was surrendered to Assyria.

The appeal of Ahaz, accompanied by silver and gold from the treasuries of the Temple and the royal palace in Jerusalem, was accepted by Tiglath-pileser, though he hardly needed Ahaz' request for help as an incentive for his campaigns in Syria and Palestine. Having settled his difficulties in the east, he turned against the Kingdom of Israel and ravaged its northern territory. The whole of Galilee and Gilead together with a strip along the seacoast was made part of an Assyrian province, and the population deported. That was the first act in the Assyrian captivity. Samaria was left intact; the opposition, which presumably favored dependence upon Assyria, did away with Pekah and placed his assassin, Hoshea (732-724 B.C.E.), upon the throne. Hoshea paid tribute to Tiglath-pileser, and was recognized by him as a vassal king. Thereafter, according to his own account, Tiglath-pileser turned southward, capturing Askelon and Gaza, thus freeing Ahaz from the danger of his other enemies. In 734-732, he ravaged Syria and Palestine to the very borders of Egypt. Damascus was conquered, the king of Syria killed, his chief advisers impaled, his gardens and orchards hacked down, and the inhabitants deported. The whole west was turned into a series of Assyrian provinces.[3]

Ahaz, overawed by the triumphs of the Assyrian king, readily yielded to the glamour and prestige of the Assyrians in religion as well as in politics. In 732, he went to Damascus to pay homage to Tiglath-pileser. There he saw an altar, which he ordered copied and installed in the Temple at Jerusalem (II Kings 16:10 ff.). He also made changes in the arrangements and furniture of the Temple "because of the king of Assyria" (II Kings 16:18). The altar made after the Assyrian pattern carried, it seems, the acknowledgment of Assyria's greatness in the realm of religion and was a public recognition of the power of the alien god.

A COVENANT WITH DEATH

Isaiah asked Ahaz to believe that it was neither Pekah nor Rezin nor even the mighty Tiglath-pileser who governed history. The world was in the hands of God, and it was folly to be terrified by "these two smoldering stumps of firebrands"; those powers were destined for destruction, and even the might of Assyria would not last forever. The right policy was neither to join the coalition nor to rely upon Assyria. The judgment over Judah was inevitable, and it was not to be averted by alliances, arms or strategy. Accompanied by his son Shear-jashub—a symbolical name expressing the con-

---

[3] See *ANET*, pp. 281 f.; A. T. Olmstead, *History of Assyria* (New York, 1923), pp. 197 f.

viction that a remnant would turn to God and be saved—Isaiah appealed to
the king to be calm. He also announced that a young woman would have a
son and would call his name Immanuel—God is with us—and that before
the boy reached the age of two or three years, the allied kings would have
departed from the land. Then evil days would come upon Judah, such days
as she had not seen since the secession of the Northern Kingdom. Egypt and
Assyria would lay the land waste. But a remnant would return, and a reign
of everlasting peace and justice be inaugurated.

Ahaz and the court were feeling secure owing to the treaty with Assyria,
and were congratulating themselves on having so shrewdly frustrated their
enemies. Scoffingly they said:

> We have made a covenant with death,
> And with Sheol we have an agreement;
> When the overwhelming scourge passes through
> It will not come to us;
> For we have made lies our refuge,
> And in falsehood we have taken shelter.
>
> Isaiah 28:15

But Isaiah was distressed at their cynicism and folly. The Lord had warned
him "not to walk in the way of this people. . . . Do not call alliance[4] all
that this people call alliance, do not fear what they fear" (8:11-12). In the
name of God he proclaimed:

> I will make justice the line,
> And righteousness the plummet;
> Hail will sweep away the refuge of lies,
> Waters will overwhelm the shelter.
> Then your covenant with death will be annulled,
> Your agreement with Sheol will not stand;
> When the overwhelming scourge passes through,
> You will be beaten down by it.
>
> Isaiah 28:17-18

A gulf was separating prophet and king in their thinking and understanding. What seemed to be a terror to Ahaz was a trifle in Isaiah's eyes. The
king, seeking to come to terms with the greatest power in the world, was
ready to abandon religious principles in order to court the emperor's favor.
The prophet who saw history as the stage for God's work, where kingdoms
and empires rise for a time and vanish, perceived a design beyond the mists
and shadows of the moment.

While others acclaimed Ahaz for having gained the most powerful pro-

---

[4] See E. J. Kissane, *The Book of Isaiah,* I (Dublin, 1941), 103, and the reference to Neh. 4:2.

tection, Isaiah insisted that Assyria would bring disaster. "Because this people have refused the waters of Shiloah that flow gently, . . . the Lord is bringing up against them the waters of the River, mighty and many, the king of Assyria and all his glory; it will rise over all its channels and go over all its banks; it will sweep on into Judah, it will overflow and pass on, reaching even to the neck; its outspread wings will fill the breadth of your land, O Immanuel" (8:6-8).

When Tiglath-pileser died in 727, hopes of independence began to stir among the disgruntled vassals in the western part of the empire. Hoshea of Israel, after reaching an understanding with the Egyptian king, stopped payment of the annual tribute. In reprisal, Assyria sent her army against Samaria. Though Egypt failed to offer any aid, Samaria was able to hold out for three years. In 722, the city fell to Sargon II (722-705 B.C.E.); the Israelite monarch was overthrown and the population sent as captives to Assyria. The end of the Northern Kingdom filled the people of Judah with grief and consternation.

JERUSALEM REJOICES, ISAIAH IS DISTRESSED

Ahaz was succeeded by his son Hezekiah (ca. 715-687 B.C.E.) whose marvelous career was predicted by Isaiah when the child was still an infant. Hezekiah was the opposite of his father. No king of Judah among his predecessors or his successors could, it was said, be compared to him (II Kings 18:5). His first act was to repair and to purge the Temple and its vessels, to reorganize the services of the priests and Levites (II Chron. 29:3-36).

Hezekiah must have realized the prudence of Ahaz in refusing to be involved in intrigues against Assyria. To be sure, Judah was a vassal and was paying substantial tribute to the Assyrian overlord. Yet hateful as this condition was, Hezekiah seemed to realize that to throw off the yoke of Assyria would mean to court disaster, and in spite of strong pressure brought to bear upon him by the vassal states in Syria and Palestine to join them in rebellion, he held aloof. He took no part in the abortive revolt instigated by the king of Hamath.

Gradually, however, the people became impatient with the policy of submission to Assyria, which meant perpetual tribute and perpetual strain. In an inscription belonging to the year 711, Sargon II refers to the rulers of Palestine, Judah, Edom, Moab, and others, who had to bring tributes and presents to "my lord Ashur," but who meditated on hostility and plotted evil, and were sending their tokens of homage to the king of Egypt, "a potentate incapable to save them," seeking an alliance with him.[5] Indeed, it

---

[5] *ANET*, p. 287.

was Egypt that began in those years to play a fateful role in the political decisions of Judah.

For a long time Egypt had lapsed into relative stagnation, punctuated by civil war, and had broken up into numerous small states, independent of each other. Assyrian kings looked with desire upon Egypt, so rich and seemingly so defenseless, and Tiglath-pileser III advanced to her very border. Assyria was in control of Gaza, the gateway to the land of the Pharaohs. Around 720, conditions changed. A powerful state called Ethiopia, with its capital Napata, the biblical Noph, came into being, whose ruler Shabako invaded Egypt, seized the throne, set up a strong, unified government, and inaugurated the Twenty-second Dynasty. Egypt began to carry on intrigues in southern Palestine against the Assyrian conqueror and sought to encourage the subjugated states to rebel against the enemy.[6] It would appear that an ambitious plan was conceived, at the instigation of Egyptian agents, by which the Philistines, Moab, Edom, and Judah were to join Ashdod in a simultaneous attack on the Assyrians. Egyptian envoys arrived in Jerusalem to try to induce Judah to join the alliance, promising military support.

Egypt had set herself up as the champion of the subjugated nations, and while her envoys were entertained in Jerusalem they seem to have been greeted as deliverers from the Assyrian yoke. The poor, oppressed, helpless people were waiting for God to deliver them.

At that moment Isaiah again interfered, addressing his people with words of comfort and warning. God has not forgotten them. He is looking on from His abode in heaven, watching the events. The moment of deliverance from Assyria has not yet arrived, nor will Ethiopia be the agent to bring about the oppressor's end. Another nation is to be chosen for this act, which will come about at God's appointed time (18:1 ff.).[7]

To illustrate the futility of depending on Egypt (30:7) and the disaster to which the pro-Egyptian policy would lead, Isaiah walked about Jerusalem in the scanty garb of a slave—symbolic of what lay in store for the peoples of Egypt and Ethiopia. Not only would they fail to send effective aid to the rebel states of Palestine; they themselves would fall victims to the might of Assyria (ch. 20). It seems that Isaiah's advice was heeded. Judah did not take part in the battle of 711/713, led by Ashdod, which quickly collapsed.

As long as Sargon II reigned, no open break with Assyria was made. But when that king died and was succeeded by his greatly inferior son Sennacherib (705-681 B.C.E.), Hezekiah, evidently thinking the time propitious,

---

[6] J. H. Breasted, *A History of Egypt* (New York, 1912), pp. 547 f.
[7] The prophecy probably belongs to the early years of the Ethiopian dynasty, see Kissane, *op. cit.*, pp. 202 f.

formally refused tribute (II Kings 18:7), and took steps to defend his independence. Sargon had met his death in a battle that apparently ended in serious defeat for Assyria, and rebellion broke out at both extremities of the far-flung empire. In Babylon, Merodach-baladan rebelled, and with Elamite help, established himself as king (703). Looking for allies in his fight against Assyria, he sent envoys with letters and a gift to Hezekiah, ostensibly to congratulate him on his recovery from a serious illness. Hezekiah rejoiced over the distinguished visitors and showed them his treasure house and all his armory, trying to impress them with the wealth and strength of Judah. "There was nothing in his house nor in all his realm which Hezekiah did not show them." The object of this courtesy visit was to draw Judah into some compact against Assyria.

At that moment Isaiah appeared before Hezekiah, who seemed to be elated over the friendship of the Babylonian king, and denounced his enthusiasm for the new friend. He predicted that membership in the projected coalition would result in the destruction of the Kingdom and exile for the people. "Hear the word of the Lord of hosts: Behold, the days are coming, when all that is in your house, and that which your fathers have stored up till this day, shall be carried to Babylon; . . . Some of your own sons . . . shall be eunuchs in the palace of the king of Babylon . . ." (39:5-7).[8] Hezekiah again hesitated, but when the revolt spread throughout Palestine and Syria, and a powerful coalition of kingdoms was formed, Hezekiah not only joined the coalition, but seems to have become the leader of the insurrection. His envoys were dispatched to Egypt to negotiate a treaty (30:1-7; 31:1-3), carrying "their riches on the backs of asses, and their treasures on the humps of camels" (30:6). He was busy arranging his defences, providing arms, fortifying the walls of Jerusalem, and digging a tunnel through which water was brought underneath the hill of Jerusalem to a pool within the walls.

The decision to join the coalition against Assyria evoked

> . . . joy and gladness,
> Slaying oxen and killing sheep,
> Eating flesh and drinking wine.
> Isaiah 22:13

We can picture the scene. Jerusalem is tumultuous, exultant; the people are all on the housetops, shouting. The king speaks at a mass meeting in the square at the gate of the city. "Be strong and of good courage. Do not be afraid or dismayed before the king of Assyria and all the horde that is

---

[8] The date of this episode is uncertain, see J. Bright, *History of Israel* (Philadelphia, 1959), p. 269, n. 53; Albright, *op. cit.*, p. 43. It occurred either in 721-710 or in 704-703 B.C.E.

with him; for there is One greater with us than with him. With him is an arm of flesh; but with us is the Lord our God, to help us and to fight our battles" (II Chron. 32:7-8).

Jerusalem rejoices, and Isaiah is distressed. The people "looked to weapons" (22:8) as the source of security, rather than to Him Who is the true master of both nature and history. "You did not look to Him Who created it, or have regard for Him Who planned it long ago" (22:11).

Those who act as if there were no God, no divine order in history, are more foolish than one who would sow and plant, while completely disregarding the nature of the soil or the seasons of the year. They act as if man were alone, as if their deeds were carried out in the dark, as if there were no God Who saw, no God Who knew.

> Woe to those who hide deep from the Lord their counsel,
> Whose deeds are in the dark,
> And who say, Who sees us? Who knows us?
> You turn things upside down!
> Shall the potter be regarded as the clay;
> That the thing made should say of its maker,
> He did not make me;
> Or the thing formed say of him who formed it,
> He has no understanding?
>
> *Isaiah 29:15-16*

IF YOU WILL NOT BELIEVE, YOU WILL NOT ABIDE

The policy adopted by Hezekiah was tactically the same as the one employed by his father. He turned to Egypt for protection against Assyria, just as his father Ahaz had turned to Assyria for protection against the Northern Kingdom and Syria. My enemy's enemy is my friend, was his belief. The king put his trust in the art of politics, carrying out his plan, disregarding God's plan; entering an alliance, but not in God's spirit; taking refuge in the protection of Pharaoh, and assuming that man could be relied upon.

Isaiah's utter distrust of worldly power, his disgust for the military boots, for "every garment rolled in blood" (9:5 [H. 9:4]), for the scepter and the pomp of the wicked rulers (14:5, 11), for their arrogance, pride, and insolence, made it impossible for him to approve of any military alliance. And above all, reliance on the arms of Egypt meant denial of God's power over history.

> Turn away from man,
> In whose nostrils is breath,
> For of what account is he? . . .
> For the Lord is our Judge, the Lord is our Ruler,

The Lord is our King; He will save us. . . .
Woe to the rebellious children, says the Lord,
Who carry out a plan that is not from Me,
Who turn an alliance not of My spirit,
Adding sin to sin;[9]
Who set out to go down to Egypt,
Without asking for My counsel,
To take refuge in the protection of Pharaoh,
To seek shelter in the shadow of Egypt!
Therefore shall the protection of Pharaoh turn to your shame,
The shelter in the shadow of Egypt to your humiliation. . . .

Isaiah 2:22; 33:22; 30:1-2

Isaiah predicted that the alliance with Egypt would not only prove "worthless and empty" and bring "shame and disgrace" (30:7, 5); it would end in disaster (30:12 ff.). The soldiers, the chariots, and the horses, even if they should be superior in number to those of the enemy, would prove of no avail.

A thousand shall flee at the threat of one, . . .
Till you are left
Like a flagstaff on the top of a mountain,
Like a signal on a hill.

Isaiah 30:17

The efforts of those who try to oppose God's design are sinful and futile.

For He is wise and brings disaster,
He does not call back His words,
But will arise against the house of the evildoers,
Against the helpers of those who work iniquity. . . .
Return ye to Him from Whom you have deeply revolted,
O people of Israel.

Isaiah 31:2,6

AGAINST ALLIANCES

There were, we should like to suggest, three reasons for the prophet's opposition to any alliance with either Egypt or Assyria. (1) Reliance on a world power meant a demonstration of the belief that man rather than God, weapons rather than attachment to Him, determined the destiny of the nations. (2) Subservience to a nation such as Assyria meant accepting her gods and cults. (3) An alliance with Assyria meant an involvement in her military operations.

The history of Israel began in two acts of rejection: the rejection of Mesopotamia in the days of Abraham and the rejection of Egypt in the days

---

[9] See Kissane, *op. cit.*, p. 336.

of Moses. In both cases it was a rejection of political and spiritual sovereignty.[10] For many centuries the impact of both Mesopotamian and Egyptian
religion on the religion of western Asia had been prodigious. The names and
ideograms of Mesopotamian gods and goddesses were borrowed by Hurrians,
Hittites, Amorites, and Canaanites alike. The cult of Mesopotamian deities
like Dagan penetrated into southern Palestine. The cult of Ishtar of Nineveh
was carried into places as far removed from Assyria as Egypt and southwes-
tern Asia Minor.[11]

After settling in the land of Canaan, Israel had to face the political and
religious challenge of minor city-states and local cults. For generations
Israel remained secure from any direct involvement with either Mesopotamia or Egypt. The situation changed rapidly in the eighth century with the
emergence of Assyria as an empire, intent upon conquering the small states
in the Near East. In addition, Egypt, unwilling to permit the power of
Assyria to extend to her very borders, began to assert her political and
military influence in the same area. Caught in the contest between the two
powers, the kings of Judah and the Northern Kingdom of Israel would
turn either to Assyria for protection or, more often, to Egypt for protection
against Assyria. The hard-won emancipation from Mesopotamia and Egypt
that had been brought about in the days of Abraham and Moses faced a
dangerous test in the days of Hosea, Isaiah, and Jeremiah.

The Assyrians were fanatically devout. In military campaigns the king
assumed the role of the deputy of the god. The prowess and victories of the
army were thought to reflect the power of the god Ashur. Assyria imposed
the recognition of her gods as the overlords of the gods of the conquered
peoples. Political subservience involved acceptance of her religious institutions. It was nearly impossible for a small vassal state to keep from being
flooded with the idolatrous and superstitious practices under royal Assyrian
protection. This explains the infiltration into Judah of all sorts of foreign
cults and superstitions in the period in which she was a vassal of Assyria.

What did Isaiah propose in place of alliances?

> *In returning [to God] and in rest you shall be saved;*
> *In quietness and in trust shall be your strength.*
>   *Isaiah 30:15*

Isaiah's plea made little impression upon the government. Threatened as
the state was by the aggressive might of Assyria, was it not more prudent to
rely on Egyptian arms than to withdraw into quietness and trust in the
Lord? "No," was the answer to Isaiah's plea. "We will speed upon horses! . . .

---

[10] See E. A. Speiser, *New Horizons in Bible Study* (Baltimore, 1958) , pp. 8 f.
[11] W. F. Albright, *From the Stone Age to Christianity* (2nd ed.; Baltimore, 1957) , p. 212.

We will ride upon swift steeds!" (30:16). But Isaiah continued to insist: Do not rely on horses! Do not trust in chariots because they are many or on horsemen because they are very strong! (31:1.) Look to the Holy One of Israel; consult the Lord!

> *The Egyptians are men, and not God;*
> *And their horses are flesh, and not spirit.*
> *When the Lord stretches out His hand,*
> *The helper will stumble, and he who is helped will fall,*
> *And they will all perish together.*
>
> *Isaiah 31:3*

Isaiah could not accept politics as a solution, since politics itself, with its arrogance and disregard of justice, was a problem. When mankind is, as we would say, spiritually sick, something more radical than political sagacity is needed to solve the problem of security. For the moment a clever alignment of states may be of help. In the long run, it is bound to prove futile.

Is it realistic to expect that nations would discard their horses and look to the Lord instead? Indeed, it is hard to learn how to live by faith. But Isaiah insisted that one cannot live without faith. "If you will not believe, you will not abide" (7:9). Faith is not an easy or convenient path. There are frustrations in store for him who expects God to succeed at every turn in history. But "he who believes will not be in haste" (28:16). Enduring strength is not in the mighty rivers, but in "the waters of Shiloah that flow gently" (8:6).

Politics is based on the power of the sword. But Isaiah was waiting for the day when nations "shall beat their swords into plowshares and their spears into pruning hooks." Alliances involve preparation for war, but Isaiah was horrified by the brutalities and carnage which war entails. In his boundless yearning he had a vision of the day when "nation shall not lift up sword against nation, neither shall they learn war any more" (2:4). War spawns death. But Isaiah was looking to the time when the Lord "will swallow up death for ever, and the Lord God will wipe away tears from all faces" (25:8; see p. 183). Israel's security lies in the covenant with God, not in covenants with Egypt or other nations. The mysterious power of faith maintains: God alone is true protection. Such power will not collapse in the hour of disaster: "I will wait for the Lord, Who is hiding His face from the house of Jacob, and I will hope in Him" (8:17). Never must a calamity shake Israel's trust.

> *O Lord our God,*
> *Other lords besides Thee have imposed themselves upon us,*
> *But it is Thou alone upon Whom we call.*
>
> *Isaiah 26:13*

ASSYRIA SHALL FALL BY A SWORD NOT OF MAN

Assyria with all her might and triumph was but a tool in the hands of God for carrying out His work against sinful nations. But in her ruthlessness and arrogance she perpetrated dreadful crimes instead of manifesting justice.

> *Ah, Assyria, the rod of My anger,*
> *The staff of My Fury!*
> *Against a godless nation I send him,*
> *Against the people of My wrath I command him,*
> *To take spoil and seize plunder,*
> *To tread them down like the mire of the streets.*
> *But he does not so intend,*
> *His mind does not so think;*
> *To cut off nations not a few;*
> *For he says:*
> *Are not my commanders all kings?*
> *Is not Calno like Carchemish?*
> *Is not Hamath like Arpad?*
> *Is not Samaria like Damascus?*
> *As my hand has reached to the kingdoms of the idols*
> *Whose graven images were greater than those*
> *   of Jerusalem and Samaria,*
> *Shall I not do to Jerusalem and her idols*
> *As I have done to Samaria and her images?*
>
> *Isaiah 10:5-11*

While Assyria was at the height of her power, Isaiah proclaimed her downfall. His prediction was not the forecast of an isolated event, but part of a divine plan and purpose for Israel and all nations.

> *The Lord of hosts has sworn:*
> *As I have planned, so shall it be;*
> *As I have purposed, so shall it stand.*
> *I will break the Assyrian in My land,*
> *And upon My mountains trample him under foot;*
> *His yoke shall depart from them,*
> *And his burden from their shoulder.*
> *This is the purpose that is purposed*
> *Concerning the whole earth;*
> *This is the hand that is stretched out*
> *Over all nations.*
>
> *Isaiah 14:24-26*

The way in which the Lord carries out His plan remains inscrutable. But He employs human agents as well as "a sword not of man" to accomplish His designs.

Assyria shall fall by a sword, not of man;
A sword, not of man, shall devour him; . . .
His rock shall pass away through terror
And his princes in panic shall desert the standard,
Says the Lord Whose fire is in Zion,
And Whose furnace is in Jerusalem. . .

The Lord will cause His majestic voice to be heard and the descending blow of His arm to be seen, in furious anger and a flame of devouring fire, with a cloudburst and tempest and hailstones. The Assyrians will be terror-stricken at the voice of the Lord, when He smites with His rod.

Isaiah 31:8-9; 30:30-31[12]

Assyria's power was a phantom, "but the Lord of hosts, Him you shall regard as holy; let Him be your fear, let Him be your dread!" (8:13.) It was in such dread and fear that Isaiah proclaimed what the real problems were.

SENNACHERIB'S INVASION OF JUDAH

About 703, Sennacherib embarked on a series of campaigns, and with quick blows overwhelmed the rebels. He first smashed the resistance of Merodach-baladan and his Elamite ally, and, having secured his border east of the Tigris, launched an expedition in 701 against Syria and Palestine. The very presence of the mighty monarch, or, in his own words, "the terror-inspiring splendor of my lordship" stunned the petty kingdoms. Most rulers quickly surrendered by offering their tribute, while others were easily overrun. A large Egyptian and Ethiopian army dispatched to relieve the beleaguered town of Ekron was defeated. Important as it might have been to invade Egypt, Sennacherib's army instead turned against Judah, the chief enemy in this entire campaign. There was nothing to hinder their entrance into Judah. Soon her valleys were filled with Assyrian chariots and horse-men (22:7), the country ravaged, forty-six fortified cities turned over to the pro-Assyrian kings of the Philistine cities, and their population deported. Sennacherib set up his headquarters in Lachish, Judah's strong frontier fortress, where he awaited Hezekiah's surrender.

Facing the possibility of complete disaster, Hezekiah sent a message to the king of Assyria at Lachish. "I have done wrong; withdraw from me; what-ever you impose on me I will bear." An extremely heavy tribute was exacted, probably more than Jerusalem was able to bear (II Kings 18:14-16). Yet, Sennacherib apparently demanded still more: the surrender of Jerusalem.

---

[12] See also 17:12-14. "No serious argument has been advanced by those who deny" Isaiah's authorship of 30:27-33; see Kissane, *op. cit.*, p. 336.

This was impossible to accept. Hezekiah, encouraged by Isaiah who predicted that Sennacherib would never capture the city, refused to open its gates. Jerusalem was besieged; Hezekiah, Sennacherib boasted, was shut up in his capital "like a bird in a cage." But the powerful fortress, whose defences had been strengthened in preparation for the revolt, withstood the enemy's onslaught.

We can visualize the events. In order to force the city to capitulate by breaking down public morale, an Assyrian official, Rabshakeh, meets the representatives of Hezekiah and addresses them within the hearing of the people crowded on top of the city wall. He starts out by maintaining that Judah can rely neither on Egypt's aid nor on God's protection. Egypt is but "a broken reed," and the God of Israel is angry at Hezekiah for having closed the cultic shrines all over the country, thus forcing the people to come to the one shrine in Jerusalem. Moreover, "has any of the gods of the nations delivered his land out of the hand of the king of Assyria?" The God of Israel is just as powerless against the might of Assyria, as the gods of the conquered nations have been. Scoffingly Rabshakeh maintains that Judah has no horses, and if she had, she could not make use of them for lack of skilled horsemen. Apparently echoing statements made by the prophets, Rabshakeh then states that it is the Lord, the God of Israel, who ordered Sennacherib to destroy Judah (II Kings 18:17 ff.; Isa. 36:4 ff.) . Better to submit than to face defeat and deportation.

The plight of Jerusalem seemed desperate. All neighboring kingdoms either had surrendered or were crushed. The country was overrun by the enemy, Egyptian aid proved worthless. Jerusalem was alone. In that hour of distress and disgrace, Isaiah proclaimed the word that the Lord had spoken concerning Assyria.

> She despises you, she scorns you—
> The virgin daughter of Zion;
> She wags her head behind you—
> The daughter of Jerusalem.
> Whom have you mocked and reviled?
> Against whom have you raised your voice
> And haughtily lifted your eyes?
> Against the Holy One of Israel!
> By your servants you have mocked the Lord,
> And you have said, With my many chariots
> I have gone up the heights of the mountains,
> To the far recesses of Lebanon;
> I felled its tallest cedars,
> Its choicest cypresses;

I came to its remotest height,
Its densest forest.
I dug wells and drank waters,
And I dried up with the sole of my foot
All the streams of Egypt.
Have you not heard
That I determined it long ago?
I planned from days of old
What now I bring to pass,
That you should make fortified cities
Crash into heaps of ruins,
While their inhabitants, shorn of strength,
Are dismayed and confounded,
And have become like plants of the field
And like tender grass,
Like grass on the housetops,
Blighted before it is grown.
I know your sitting down
And your going out and coming in,
And your raging against Me.
Because you have raged against Me
And your arrogance has come to My ears,
I will put My hooks in your nose
And My bit in your mouth,
And I will turn you back on the way
By which you came.

Isaiah 37:22-29

Isaiah's prediction was vindicated by a miraculous event. A disastrous pestilence spread in the Assyrian camp, decimating the army. Sennacherib returned to Nineveh and was eventually murdered by his sons (II Kings 19:36-37).[13]

From 701 for about three-quarters of a century, until the downfall of the Assyrian empire, Judah continued to be a dependency of the Assyrian emperor, and was not involved in the political drama that took place close at hand. Under the reign of Sennacherib's son, Esarhaddon (681-669 B.C.E.), who conquered a great part of Egypt, and under Ashurbanipal (669-633?), Assyria reached the summit of her power.

CONFUSIONS

As we have seen, Isaiah's primary concern is not Judah's foreign policy, but rather the inner state of the nation. In the period in which he begins his activity, there is prosperity in the land.

---

[13] See *ANET*, pp. 287 f.; L. Honor, *Sennacherib's Invasion of Palestine* (New York, 1926).

The king is astute, the priests are proud, and the market place is busy.
Placid, happy, even gay, the people pursue their work and worship in their
own way, and life is fair. Then again appears a prophet, hurling bitter
words from the depth of a divine anguish. People buy, sell, celebrate, rejoice,
but Isaiah is consumed with distress. He cannot bear the sight of a people's
normal crimes: exploitation of the poor, worship of the gods. He, like the
prophets before him, has a message of doom and a bitter look. Even things
that are pretty are sickening to him.

> *Their land is filled with silver and gold,*
> *There is no end to their treasures;*
> *Their land is filled with horses,*
> *There is no end to their chariots.*
>   Isaiah 2:7

What is the issue that haunts the prophet's soul? It is not a question, but
a bitter exclamation: How marvelous is the world that God has created!
And how horrible is the world that man has made!

The essence of blasphemy is confusion, and in the eyes of the prophet
confusion is raging in the world.

The earth is full of the glory of God (6:3), but the land is filled with
idols (2:8). Men are haughty and full of pride (2:11), yet "they bow down
to the work of their hands, to what their own fingers have made" (2:8). They
regard themselves as wise and shrewd (5:21), but are devoid of the simple
insight with which even an animal is endowed—knowing whose he is (1:3).

Princes are scoundrels (1:23); judges are corrupt, acquitting the guilty
for a bribe and depriving the innocent of his right (5:23). They do not
defend the fatherless, and the widow's case does not come to them (1:23).
The people are being crushed by the elders and princes, while the mansions
of the wealthy contain the spoils of the poor (3:14 f.). And in spite of all
this, the knave is called noble, and the churl is said to be honorable (cf.
32:5).

Jerusalem—destined to be the place from which the word of God (2:3),
Him Who creates heaven and earth, went forth—even Jerusalem "the faithful city has become a harlot, she that was full of justice! Righteousness
lodged in her, but now murderers" (1:21), graven images, and idols (10:10
f.). Indeed, the land that the Lord has given to His people is "filled with
idols; they bow down to the work of their hands!" The house of Jacob is
"full of diviners from the east and of soothsayers like the Philistines"
(2:6-8).

The prophet is struck by man's interminable pride, by his soaring pretension. Things done by man are lofty, high, and brazen, even worshiped,
while the exaltation of God is but a hope.

You turn things upside down!
Shall the potter be regarded as the clay;
That the thing made should say of its maker:
"He did not make me";
Or that the thing formed say of him who formed it:
"He has no understanding"?

                                        Isaiah 29:16

THE ANGER OF THE LORD

The prophet knows that "the anger of the Lord is kindled against His people" (5:25). Visions of doom haunt the prophet's soul. The whole world is on the verge of disaster. The Lord is about to judge the nations, and His judgment will shake the world.

Behold, the name of the Lord comes from far,
Burning with His anger, and in thick rising smoke;
His lips are full of indignation,
And His tongue is like a devouring fire;
His breath is like an overflowing stream
That reaches up to the neck;
To sift the nations with the sieve of destruction,
And to place on the jaws of the peoples a bridle that leads astray....
I will punish the world for its evil,
And the wicked for their iniquity;
I will put an end to the pride of the arrogant,
And lay low the haughtiness of the ruthless.
I will make men more rare than fine gold,
And mankind than the gold of Ophir.
Therefore I will make the heavens tremble,
And the earth will be shaken out of its place,
At the wrath of the Lord of hosts
In the day of His fierce anger.

                          Isaiah 30:27-28; 13:11-13[14]

God when silent may be disregarded, but when He rises to terrify the earth, men will enter the caverns of the rocks and the clefts of the cliffs "before the terror of the Lord . . . and the glory of his majesty" (Isa. 2:19, 21).

Man shall be brought low, man shall be humbled,
And the eyes of the haughty shall be cast down.
But the Lord of hosts shall be exalted in justice,
And the Holy God show Himself holy in righteousness.

                                        Isaiah 5:15-16

---

[14] Some critics maintain that Isa. 13:1—14:2 was written on the occasion of the death of an Assyrian king (Sargon or Sennacherib) and that it was adapted by a later editor to the fall of Babylon.

Characteristic of the dreadful intensity of the divine anger is the phrase
used repeatedly by Isaiah, describing it when kindled against Ephraim:

> As the tongue of fire devours the stubble,
> As the dry grass sinks down in the flame,
> So their root will be rottenness,
> And their blossom go up like dust. . . .
> For all this His anger is not turned away
> And His hand is stretched out still. . . .
> So the Lord cut off from Israel head and tail,
> Palm branch and reed in one day, . . .
> The Lord . . . has no compassion on their fatherless and widows;
> For everyone is godless and an evildoer,
> And every mouth speaks folly. . . .
> Through the wrath of the Lord of hosts
> The land is burned,
> And the people are like fuel for the fire;
> No man spares his brother.
>
> Isaiah 5:24, 25; 9:14-19; cf. 9:20; 10:4

Grim, foreboding, relentless is the account of the anger in action.

Listening to the prophet's words about the grandeur of God's anger, even
the disparagers cannot dissemble their terror.

> The sinners in Zion are afraid;
> Trembling has seized the godless:
> Who among us can dwell with the devouring fire?
> Who among us can dwell with everlasting burnings?
>
> Isaiah 33:14

However, the destructiveness of God's power is not due to God's hostility
to man, but to His concern for righteousness, to His intolerance of injustice.
The human mind seems to have no sense for the true dimension of man's
cruelty to man. God's anger is fierce because man's cruelty is infernal.

DIVINE SORROW

Significantly, however, the speech that opens the book of Isaiah, and
which sets the tone for all the utterances by this prophet, deals not with the
anger, but with the sorrow of God. The prophet pleads with us to understand the plight of a father whom his children have abandoned.

> Hear, O heavens, and give ear, O earth;
> For the Lord has spoken:
> Sons have I reared and brought up,
> But they have rebelled against Me.
> The ox knows its owner

And the ass its master's crib;
But Israel does not know,
My people does not understand.
                    Isaiah 1:2-3

The prophet laments in his own words the children's desertion of their father:

They have forsaken the Lord,
They have despised the Holy One of Israel.
                    Isaiah 1:4

But the sympathy for God's injured love overwhelms his whole being. What he feels about the size of God's sorrow and the enormous scandal of man's desertion of God is expressed in the two lines quoted above which introduce God's lamentation. "Hear, then, O house of David! Is it too little for you to weary men, that you weary my God also?" (7:13.) In different words addressed to the king, the prophet conveys his impression of the mood of God: As happened in the time of Noah and as is happening again, God's patience and longsuffering are exhausted. He is tired of man. He hates man's homage, his festivals, his celebrations. Man has become a burden and a sorrow for God.

What to Me is the multitude of your sacrifices?
Says the Lord;
I have had enough of burnt offerings of rams
And the fat of fatted beasts;
I do not delight in the blood of bulls,
Or of lambs, or of he-goats.
When you come to appear before Me,
Who requires of you
This trampling of My courts?
Bring no more vain offerings;
Incense is an abomination to Me.
New moon and sabbath and the calling of assemblies—
I cannot endure iniquity and solemn assembly.
Your new moons and your appointed feasts
My soul hates;
They have become a burden to Me,
That I am weary to bear.
When you spread forth your hands,
I will hide My eyes from you;
Even though you make many prayers,
I will not listen;
Your hands are full of blood.

                    Isaiah 1:11-15

The weariness of God,[15] an important theological category in Isaiah's thinking, brings about a greater concealment of His personal involvement in history. It is a time in which divine anger becomes active in history.

> *I Myself have commanded My consecrated ones,*
> *Have summoned My mighty men to execute My anger.*
> *Isaiah 13:3*

There is a shift of emphasis from pathos as an emotion to pathos in action. Pathos is spoken of in Isaiah more frequently in an instrumental than in a personal sense. An important element in his thinking is the conception that the world's great powers are instruments of the divine will. Not the elements of nature, but primarily the powers of history carry out the designs of God. (Cf. 5:26; 7:18; 9:10 f.). The shift of emphasis comes to expression in phrases which characterize historic events as reflecting divine situations. "Ah, Assyria, the rod of My anger, the staff of My indignation" (10:5); "the weapons of My indignation" (13:5). Pathos becomes an attribute in action or a sign of judgment, as in the phrase, "Against the people of My wrath do I send him [Assyria]" (10:6).

THERE IS SORROW IN HIS ANGER

God's affection for Israel rings even in the denunciations. It is "My people" who do not understand (1:3). It is "My people" who are suppressed by "the elders and princes" (3:14). He is anxious to forgive, to wipe out their sins (1:18). They are His children (1:2), "rebellious children" (30:1).

God is more than Lord and Owner; He is Father (1:2-4; 30-1). But for all His love and compassion, He cannot tolerate the corruption of the leaders who succumb to bribes and run after gifts, who "do not defend the fatherless, and the widow's cause does not come to them" (1:23). "Your silver has become dross, your wine mixed with water" (1:22).

> *Therefore the Lord says,*
> *The Lord of hosts,*
> *The Mighty One of Israel:*
> *Ah, I will vent My wrath on My enemies,*
> *And avenge Myself on My foes.*
> *I will turn My hand against you*
> *And will smelt away your dross as with lye*
> *And remove all your alloy.*
> *And I will restore your judges as aforetime,*
> *And your counselors as at the beginning.*
> *Afterward you shall be called the city of righteousness,*

---

[15] The expression also occurs in Isa. 43:24.

The faithful city.
Zion shall be redeemed by justice,
And those in her who repent, by righteousness.

Isaiah 1:24-27

There is sorrow in God's anger. It is an instrument of purification, and its exercise will not last forever. "For the Lord will have compassion on Jacob and will again choose Israel, and settle them in their own land, and the stranger shall join himself to them, and will cleave to the house of Jacob" (14:1). His mercy is not discarded, merely suspended. His anger lasts a moment, it does not endure forever.

In a very little while My indignation will come to an end. . . .
Come, My people, enter your chambers,
And shut your doors behind you;
Hide yourselves for a little while
Until the indignation is past.

Isaiah 10:25; 26:20

Anger is not His disposition, but a state He waits to overcome.

Therefore the Lord waits to be gracious to you;
Therefore He exalts Himself to show mercy to you.
For the Lord is a God of justice
Blessed are all those who wait for Him.

Isaiah 30:18

Isaiah also stresses the quality of zeal, which to him seems to explain the miracle of "the surviving remnant." "For out of Jerusalem shall go forth a remnant, and out of Mount Zion a band of survivors. The zeal of the Lord of hosts will accomplish this" (37:32). The throne of David will be established "with justice and with righteousness. . . . The zeal of the Lord of hosts will accomplish this" (9:7 [H. 9:6]).[16]

SYMPATHY FOR GOD

Isaiah is animated by a sense of dread and the awareness of the transcendent mystery and exclusiveness of God, and only secondarily by a sense of intimacy, sympathy, and involvement in the divine situation.[17] He calls Him "the King" (6:13); *ha'adon* (1:24; 3:1; 10:16, 33; 19:4), "the Lord *tsebaoth*," but also *'abir Israel*, "the Mighty One of Israel"; "Rock of Israel" (30:29); "my God" (7:13); "my Beloved" (5:1). To Hosea, Israel is God's consort; to Isaiah, God's vineyard. Like Amos (1:2; 3:8, 12) and Hosea

---

[16] See Küchler, *"Der Gedanke des Eifers im Alten Testament," ZAW*, XXVIII, 42 ff.
[17] A comparison between the "prophetic marriages" of Hosea and Isaiah is instructive. Hosea finds its meaning in sympathy; Isaiah, in the realization of a divine decision (8:3 ff.; 9:5 ff.).

(5:14; 13:8), Isaiah uses the image of a lion to describe the might of the Lord.

> For thus said the Lord to me:
> As a lion or a young lion growls over his prey,
> And when a band of shepherds is called forth against him
> Is not terrified by their shouting,
> Or daunted at their noise,
> So the Lord of hosts will come down
> To fight upon Mount Zion and upon its hill.
>
> Isaiah 31:4

Isaiah's sympathy for God comes to expression in a parable describing the crisis in the relationship between God and Israel.

> I will sing of my Friend
> The song of this love for His vineyard:
> My Friend had a vineyard
> On a very fertile hill.
> He digged it, He cleared it of stones,
> And planted it with choice vines;
> He built a tower in the midst of it,
> And hewed out a wine press in it;
> He looked for it to yield grapes,
> But it yielded sour grapes.
> And now, O inhabitants of Jerusalem and men of Judah,
> Judge, I pray you, between Me and My vineyard.
> What more should I have done for My vineyard,
> That I have not done for it?
> Wherefore, when I looked for it to yield grapes,
> Why did it yield sour grapes?
> And now I will tell you
> What I will do to My vineyard.
> I will remove its hedge,
> And it shall be devoured;
> I will break down its wall,
> And it shall be trampled down.
> I will make it a waste;
> It shall not be pruned or hoed,
> It shall grow briers and thorns;
> I will also command the clouds
> That they rain no rain upon it.
> For the vineyard of the Lord of hosts
> Is the house of Israel,
> And the men of Judah
> Are His pleasant planting.
> He looked for justice,

> But behold, there is violence,
> For righteousness,
> There is outrage.
>
> Isaiah 5:1-7

In this song of the vineyard, the prophet speaks first in his own name (vss. 1-2), then as the voice of God (vss. 3-6), and again in his own name (vs. 7). What personal attitude is reflected in the prophet's words?

It is first the prophet's love of God, Who is called "my Friend" and for Whom he sings "a love song concerning His vineyard." He neither rebukes the people's ingratitude nor bewails their prospect of ruin and disgrace. The prophet's sympathy is for God Whose care for the vineyard had been of no avail. God's sorrow rather than the people's tragedy is the theme of this song.

The song contains a gentle allusion to the grief and the disappointment of God. He feels hurt at the thought of abandoning the vineyard He had rejoiced in, and in which He had placed so much hope and care. In another prophecy we hear the song of God's dream, in which is fondly conceived the preservation of the vineyard, and His joy at the thought of continuing to care for it.

> ... A precious vineyard—sing to it!
> I, the Lord, am its keeper;
> Every moment I water it.
> Lest any one harm it,
> I guard it night and day;
> I have no wrath.
> Would that I had thorns and briers to battle!
> I would set out against them,
> I would burn them up together.
> Or let them lay hold of My protection.
> Let them make peace with Me,
> Let them make peace with Me.
>
> Isaiah 27:2-5

AT ONE WITH HIS PEOPLE

What was the purpose of planting the vineyard (5:1-7), of choosing the people? The vineyard was planted to yield righteousness and justice. Yet the fruit it yielded was violence and outrage, affecting God, arousing His anger.

> Their speech and their deeds are against the Lord,
> Defying His glorious presence.
>
> Isaiah 3:8

Isaiah pleads for the meek and the poor, condemning the ruthless and the scoffers,

...all who watch to do evil,...
Who by a word make a man out to be an offender,
And lay a snare for him who reproves in the gate,
And with an empty plea turn aside him who is in the right.

Isaiah 29:20, 21

It is the moral corruption of the leaders that has shattered God's relationship to His people, and in a passage which seems to belong in the context of the parable of the vineyard we read:

The Lord shall enter into judgment
With the elders and princes of His people:
It is you who have devoured the vineyard;
The spoil of the poor is in your homes.
What do you mean by crushing My people,
By grinding the face of the poor?

Isaiah 3:14-15

However, it is not only the iniquity of others that upsets the prophet Isaiah. He feels polluted himself! "I am a man of unclean lips, and I dwell in the midst of a people of unclean lips" (6:5). Being unclean (literally: polluted) is a state of estrangement, a state in which one is kept away from the holy.

Isaiah, who flings bitter invectives against his contemporaries, identifies himself with his people (1:9) which are to be "my people" (3:12; cf. 8:10; 7:14). His castigation is an outcry of compassion. He sees his people all bruised and bleeding, with no one to dress their wounds.

The whole head is sick,
The whole heart is faint.
From the sole of the foot even to the head
There is no soundness in it,
But bruises and sores
And bleeding wounds;
They are not pressed out, or bound up,
Or softened with oil.

Isaiah 1:5-6

The Moabites, in the neighboring nation of Moab which had often been involved in hostilities with the Hebrews and entertained a contemptuous attitude toward them (Jer. 48:27; cf. Zeph. 2:8), are condemned by the prophets for their arrogance, boastfulness, and insolence (Isa. 16:6; cf. 25:10-12; Jer. 48:27).[18] And yet when Moab falls at the hands of the invader, Isaiah avers:

---

[18] At a later date, the Moabites mocked and scorned the fugitives from Judah (Ezek. 28:8-11).

> *My heart cries out for Moab....*
> *Let every one wail for Moab. Give counsel,*
> *Grant justice; make your shade like night*
> *At the height of noon;*
> *Hide the outcasts,*
> *Betray not the fugitive;*
> *Let the outcasts of Moab*
> *Sojourn among you;*
> *Be a refuge to them*
> *From the destroyer. . .*
> *I weep with the weeping of Jazer....*
> *I drench you with my tears.*
>
> Isaiah 15:5; 16:7; 16:3-4; 16:9[19]

A similar appeal is made by Isaiah on behalf of an Arabian tribe:

> *To the thirsty bring water,*
> *Meet the fugitive with bread. . . .*
> *For they have fled from the swords,*
> *From the drawn sword,*
> *From the bent bow,*
> *And from the press of battle.*
>
> Isaiah 21:14-15

However, in the face of idolatry and corruption, seeing that his people "have rejected the Torah of the Lord of hosts," and "despised the word of the Holy One of Israel" (5:24), the prophet seems to have lost his sense of compassion. In a moment of anger he utters the astounding words "forgive them not!" (2:9).

Is Isaiah's heart made of stone? Does he feel no pity for the people whose ruin he predicts? Indeed, two sympathies dwell in a prophet's soul: sympathy for God and sympathy for the people. Speaking to the people, he is emotionally at one with God; in the presence of God, beholding a vision, he is emotionally at one with the people. When told of the doom which threatens "this people," Isaiah exclaims with a voice of shock and protest, "How long, O Lord?" (6:11; cf. Jer. 4:14; Ps. 74:10).

Indeed, the stern visions of disaster which he beholds for Israel and other nations drive him into the depths of agony. This is how he describes what he felt when such a vision was told to him:

---

[19] Some commentators insist that Isa. 15—16 is no elegy on Moab, but was originally "a mocking song, sung by the enemies of the Moabites. The signs of sympathy with the Moabites are mere expressions of sarcasm." The mocking song, which "originated among Bedouins who had at some time or other invaded and partly conquered the land of Moab" was later used by a prophet from Judah, not Isaiah. See A. H. Van Zyl, *The Moabites* (Leiden, 1960), pp. 20 ff. Cf., however, the argument advanced by Y. Kaufmann, *The Religion of Israel* (Eng.; Chicago, 1960), p. 382.

A stern vision is told to me;
The plunderer plunders,
The destroyer destroys. . . .
My loins are filled with anguish,
Pangs have seized me,
Like the pangs of a woman in travail;
I am bowed down so that I cannot hear,
I am dismayed so that I cannot see.
My mind reels, horror has appalled me;
The twilight I longed for
Has been turned for me into trembling.
Isaiah 21:2-4

Nothing vitiates the impact of a prophet so much as mockery, and it is the incredibility of his message that encourages cynicism:

Let Him make haste,
Let Him speed His work
That we may see it;
Let the purpose of the Holy One of Israel draw near,
And let it come, that we may know it!
Isaiah 5:19

Isaiah's contemporaries are frivolous and gay, while the prophet is shattered by his vision of the day of the Lord: "a day of tumult and trumpeting and turmoil," "battering down of walls," famine, flight, captivity. The prophet's grief is more than he can bear.

Therefore I said:
Look away from me.
Let me weep bitter tears.
Do not labor to comfort me
For the ruin of my people.
Isaiah 22:4

Even though he sees ruin and disaster in the days to come, he does not cease to implore mercy:

O Lord, be gracious to us; we wait for Thee.
Be our arm every morning,
Be our help in time of trouble.
Isaiah 33:2

Israel has forsaken the Lord, but the Lord will not forsake Israel; He will not discard them. But in order to redeem, He must first smelt away the dross as with lye and remove the alloy (1:25). Grim and dreadful will be the process of purification. There is no redemption without affliction. When the Lord smites a people, He is both "smiting and healing" (19:22). This sort of knowledge cannot help but darken the heart.

THE VISION OF ISAIAH

In the year that King Uzziah died I saw the Lord sitting upon a throne, high and lifted up; and His train filled the temple. Above Him stood the seraphim; each had six wings: with two he covered his face, and with two he covered his feet, and with two he flew. And one called to another and said:

> *Holy, holy, holy is the Lord of hosts;*
> *The whole earth is full of His glory.*

And the foundations of the thresholds shook at the voice of him who called, and the house was filled with smoke. And I said: Woe is me! For I am lost; for I am a man of unclean lips, and I dwell in the midst of a people of unclean lips; for my eyes have seen the King, the Lord of hosts!

Then flew one of the seraphim to me, having in his hand a burning coal which he had taken with tongs from the altar. And he touched my mouth, and said: Behold, this has touched your lips; your guilt is taken away, and your sin forgiven. And I heard the voice of the Lord saying, Whom shall I send, and who will go for us? Then I said, Here I am! Send me. And he said, Go, and say to this people:

> *Hear and hear, but do not understand;*
> *See and see, but do not perceive.*
> *Make the heart of this people fat,*
> *And their ears heavy,*
> *And shut their eyes;*
> *Lest they see with their eyes,*
> *And hear with their ears,*
> *And understand with their hearts,*
> *And turn and be healed.*

Then I said, How long, O Lord? And He said:

> *Until cities lie waste without inhabitant,*
> *And houses without men,*
> *And the land is utterly desolate,*
> *And the Lord removes men far away,*
> *And the forsaken places are many in the midst of the land.*
> *And though a tenth remain in it,*
> *It will be burned again,*
> *Like a terebinth or an oak,*
> *Whose stump remains standing when it is felled.*
> *The holy seed is its stump.*

Isaiah 6

The mandate Isaiah receives is fraught with an appalling contradiction. He is told to be a prophet in order to thwart and to defeat the essential purpose of being a prophet. He is told to face his people while standing on his head. Did he not question his own faculties of seeing, hearing, and understanding when perceiving such a message? What gave him the certainty that it was God's voice speaking to him? It is generally assumed that the mission of a prophet is to open the people's hearts, to enhance their understanding, and to bring about rather than to prevent their turning to God.

Was not Isaiah's entire ministry devoted to persuading, to exhorting, and to influencing his people? I venture to advance a hypothesis: that this perplexing prophecy can be understood only if it be applied to the Northern Kingdom.[20]

Punishment described in the Bible is of two kinds: physical and spiritual. It is the second kind which Isaiah is told about. The people (of the Northern Kingdom?) are to be deprived of sensitivity to God and of the ability to repent.

Events burst forth in history which evoke man's sense of wonder. But history moves also in a way which drains one's faith, one's inner sight. It is as if God acted to deprive man of his sense of wonder, withholding his understanding, enhancing his callousness.

The haunting words which reached Isaiah seem not only to contain the intention to inflict insensitivity, but also to declare that the people already are afflicted by a lack of sensitivity. The punishment of spiritual deprivation will be but an intensification or an extension of what they themselves had done to their own souls. For hardening of the heart is either due to man himself (Jer. 5:3; Isa. 44:18; Zech. 7:11-13; Josh. 11:20; I Sam. 6:6; Ps. 95:8) or comes about as punishment from above. The Bible has several references to God hardening the heart of man. (See pp. 191 ff.)

UNCANNY INDIFFERENCE

Callousness is sovereign and smug; it clings to the soul and will not give in. The crack of doom is in the air, but the people, unperturbed, are carried away by a rage to be merry. *Carpe diem*—after all, death signifies merely the end of the opportunity to be merry.

> *In that day the Lord God of hosts*
> *Called for weeping and lamentation,*
> *And baldness and girding with sackcloth;*
> *And behold, joy and gladness,*
> *Slaying oxen and killing sheep,*
> *Eating flesh and drinking wine.*
> *Let us eat and drink*
> *For tomorrow we die!*

---

[20] On the whole problem, cf. F. Hesse, "*Das Verstockungsproblem im Alten Testament*," *BZAW*, LXXIV (Berlin, 1955), 44 ff.; M. Buber, *The Prophetic Faith* (New York, 1949), pp. 130 f.; G. von Rad, *Theologie des Alten Testaments*, II (München, 1961), 162 ff.; M. M. Kaplan, "Isaiah 6:1-11," *JBL*, XLV (1926), 251-259.

The Lord of hosts has revealed in my ears:
Verily, this iniquity shall not be pardoned till you die,
Says the Lord God of hosts.

Isaiah 22:12-14

The threat of scourge and doom does not frighten the scoffers, nor does the prophet's condemnation of their cherished beliefs as lies and falsehood shake their self-assurance. Frivolously they boast: "Evil shall not overtake or meet us" (Amos 9:10).

We have made a covenant with death,
We have made a pact with Sheol.
The overwhelming scourge, when it passes,
Shall not come upon us.
For we have made lies our refuge,
We have taken shelter in falsehood.

Isaiah 28:15

Obstinacy in an hour of imminent disaster is uncanny, irrational. Can a people whose plight is so grave remain deaf to the redeeming word of God? How shall one explain such a disposition?

In His effort to bring Israel back to His way, the Lord had tried to call upon the people, to confer favors upon them. Yet, "the more I called them, the more they went away from Me" (Hos. 11:2). "When the wicked is spared, he does not learn righteousness; in the land of uprightness he deals perversely and does not regard the majesty of the Lord" (Isa. 26:10). So He chastised them in order to make them repent, and chastisement proved to be no cure. The people were smitten and continued to rebel (1:5); they did not stop to ponder about the meaning of their suffering nor to "turn to Him who smote them, nor seek the Lord of hosts" (9:12; cf. 10:20).[21] How did the inhabitants of Samaria explain the calamity that overtook their land? They thought it was due to an error in politics rather than to a failure in their relation to God.

In pride and in arrogance of heart [they boasted]:
The bricks have fallen,
But we will build with dressed stones;
The sycamores have been cut down,
But we will replace them with cedars.

Isaiah 9:9-10 [H. 9:8-9]

Moved by compassion for his people, the prophet does not suppress his cry of anguish: "How long, O Lord?" (6:11). And yet, he could not fail to carry out his sad mission.

---

[21] See Rashi and Kimhi, *Commentaries, ad loc.*

> *Stupefy yourselves and be in a stupor,*
> *Blind yourselves and be blind!*
> *Be drunk, but not with wine;*
> *Stagger, but not with strong drink!*
> *For the Lord has poured out upon you*
> *A spirit of deep sleep,*
> *And has closed your eyes, the prophets,*
> *And covered your heads, the seers.*
>
> *Isaiah 29:9-10*

How else could the prophet perform such a fateful task if not in overwhelming sympathy with the divine pathos? The prophet in speaking, as it seems, of what is supremely important, says to the people: "The vision of all this has become to you like the words of a book that is sealed. When men give it to one who can read, saying, Read this, he says, I cannot, for it is sealed. And when they give the book to one who cannot read, saying, Read this, he says, I cannot read" (29:11-12).

On another occasion, however, Isaiah in beseeching the Lord for mercy describes the people's sobbing words to their God:

> *O Lord, in distress they sought Thee,*
> *They poured out a prayer*
> *When Thy chastening was upon them.*
> *Like a woman with child,*
> *Who writhes and cries out in her pangs,*
> *When she is near her time,*
> *So have we been because of Thee, O Lord.*
> *We are with child, we writhe,*
> *We have, as it were, brought forth wind.*
>
> *Isaiah 26:16-18*

MY PEOPLE GO INTO EXILE FOR WANT OF KNOWLEDGE

Isaiah's primary mission is to his own people. Unlike the nations of the world, Israel is reprimanded not only for arrogance and moral iniquity, but also for idolatry and the abandonment of God. The Creator of heaven and earth is called by Isaiah "the Holy One of Israel." There is a unique and intimate relationship between God and His people, yet the people have gone astray.

A factual description of the state of religion in the time of Isaiah, based upon the data cited in his accusation, would speak of disregard and deviation, of disobedience and evasion. Yet Isaiah speaks of rebellion, rejection, and disdain.

> *Ah, sinful nation,*
> *A people laden with iniquity,*
> *Offspring of evildoers,*

> *Sons who deal corruptly!*
> *They have forsaken the Lord,*
> *They have despised the Holy One of Israel,*
> *They are utterly estranged...*
> *They have despised the Torah of the Lord of hosts,*
> *They have contemned the word of the Holy One of Israel.*
>
> *Isaiah 1:4; 5:24*

There is no contrition, no compunction, no regret. Instead there is pride, conceit, and complacency (32:9 ff.).

"Israel does not know, My people does not understand" (1:3) is, we have seen, the divine complaint with which the book of Isaiah begins. We are told again what Hosea had proclaimed: *"My people go into exile for want of knowledge"* (5:13). The sort of knowledge they lack is alluded to in:

> *They do not regard the deeds of the Lord,*
> *Or see the work of His hands.*
>
> *Isaiah 5:12*

The people do not know how sick they are. Their leaders are "wise in their own eyes and shrewd in their own sight" (5:21). Does the wisdom of their leaders keep them from complete confusion?

> *Woe to those who call evil good*
> *And good evil,*
> *Who put darkness for light*
> *And light for darkness,*
> *Who put bitter for sweet*
> *And sweet for bitter!*
>
> *Isaiah 5:20*

Human wisdom and understanding have failed to save man from pride, presumption, and arrogance. It is in the face of such failure that Isaiah proclaims the intention of the Lord to discredit man's wisdom and shatter his understanding.

> *Therefore, behold I will again*
> *Do marvelous things with this people,*
> *Wonderful and marvelous;*
> *The wisdom of their wise shall perish,*
> *The understanding of their prudent men shall be hid.*
>
> *Isaiah 29:14*

What, then, is the hope? What will take the place of human wisdom?

A REMNANT WILL RETURN

Neither words of persuasion nor threats of castigation will have any effect. Something greater than prophetic words, namely, an eschatological event, will be necessary to silence the arrogance of man.

Behold the day of the Lord comes,
Cruel, with wrath and fierce anger,
To make the earth a desolation,
And to destroy its sinners from it. . . .
I will punish the world for its evil,
And the wicked for their iniquity;
I will put an end to the pride of the arrogant,
And lay low the haughtiness of the ruthless.

                                    Isaiah 13:9, 11

If mankind's basic malady is callousness, will the extermination of arrogance bring about a cure? The extinction of evil is, indeed, but a part of the eschatological vision. Suffering does not redeem; it only makes one worthy of redemption; for the purpose of redemption is to initiate an age in which "those who err in spirit will come to understanding, and those who murmur will accept instruction" (29:24).

There is "a screen that is cast over all peoples, a veil that veils all nations." That screen, that veil, will be destroyed at the eschatological feast which the Lord of hosts will make for all peoples on Mt. Zion (25:6-7). Something new, an outburst of the Spirit, will initiate redemption.

For the palace will be forsaken,
The populous city deserted;
The hill and the watchtower
Will become dens for ever,
A joy of wild asses,
A pasture of flocks;
Until the Spirit is poured upon us from on high. . . .

                                    Isaiah 32:14-15

Isaiah holds out two hopes for mankind. One is immediate, partial, historical: "A remnant will return!" The other is distant, final, eschatological: the transformation of the world *at the end of days.*

Isaiah had named one of his sons *Shear-jashub,* which means "a remnant will return," as God's living sign for a supreme hope (cf. 8:18). "A remnant will return, the remnant of Jacob, to the mighty God. For though your people Israel be as the sand of the sea, only a remnant of them will return" (10:21-22).

The type of man who will survive the ordeals of history is described by Isaiah as one

. . . who walks righteously and speaks uprightly;
He who despises the gain of oppressions;
Who shakes his hands, lest they hold a bribe;

Who stops his ears from hearing of bloodshed,
And shuts his eyes from looking upon evil.

Isaiah 33:15

But beyond the hope that a remnant will return lies the ultimate hope that the whole world will be transformed.

ZION

Isaiah knew that disaster was bound to come, but also that a remnant would survive, that Zion would endure, and that through Israel and out of Zion redemption for all nations would flow. Unlike Jeremiah, Isaiah never predicted the destruction of Jerusalem.[22]

Over and above all the threats and denunciations uttered by Isaiah rises the more powerful certainty of God's lasting, indestructible attachment to His people and to Zion. His disengagement from Israel is inconceivable. Anger passes; His attachment will never pass. Prophetic messages of doom are ambivalent. He is "smiting and healing" (19:22). Prophecy always moves in a polarity, yet the tension of yes and no, of anger and love, of doom and redemption, is often dissolved in the certainty of God's eternal attachment, as, for example, in the words of a postexilic prophet: "For thus said the Lord of hosts, after His glory sent me to the nations who plundered you, for he who touches you touches the apple of His eye" (Zech. 2:8 [H. 2:12]).

There are words spoken by Isaiah which are unrelated to any historic situation and which allude to that attachment not contingent upon human merit or conduct:

Ah, the thunder of many peoples,
They thunder like the thundering of the sea!
Ah, the roar of nations,
They roar like the roaring of mighty waters!
The nations roar like the roaring of many waters,
But He will rebuke them, and they will flee far away,
Chased like chaff on the mountains before the wind
And whirling dust before the storm.
At evening time, behold, terror!
Before morning, they are no more!
This is the portion of those who despoil us,
And the lot of those who plunder us.

Isaiah 17:12-14

The covenant is not only with the people, but also with the land, with

---

[22] See G. von Rad, *op. cit.*, pp. 166 ff.

Jerusalem, with Zion. All hopes and visions of things to come are connected with these places.

> *Like birds hovering, so the Lord of hosts*
> *Will protect Jerusalem;*
> *He will protect and deliver it,*
> *He will spare and rescue it.*
>
> Isaiah 31:5

Zion is not only His chosen place, founded by the Lord, "and in her the afflicted of His people find refuge" (14:32); His design for the history of the nations is to be finished on Mt. Zion and in Jerusalem (10:12).

Zion is where at the end of days all the nations shall go to learn the ways of God.

> *For out of Zion shall go forth Torah*
> *And the word of the Lord from Jerusalem.*
>
> Isaiah 2:3; see also 4:5; 33:20;
> cf. Micah 4:14; Isaiah 40;
> 65:18; Zechariah 2

> *Thus says the Lord God:*
> *Behold, I have laid a foundation in Zion:*
> *A stone, a tested stone,*
> *A precious cornerstone,*
> *An indestructible foundation:*
> *He who believes will not be in haste.*
>
> Isaiah 28:16

Judah will succumb before the invaders, but when the period of oppression is ended Zion will be restored (16:4).

> *Then a throne shall be established in mercy,*
> *And there shall sit on it in truth,*
> *In the tent of David,*
> *A judge who seeks justice,*
> *And excels in righteousness.*
>
> Isaiah 16:5

And yet, God is above all a God of justice, not a mere patron. Thoughts that savor of content, the combination of iniquity and reliance on God, "Is not the Lord in the midst of us? No evil shall come upon us" (Mic. 3:11), the certainty that Jerusalem is indestructible, which Isaiah's contemporaries entertain, are, in his eyes, a refuge in a lie (28:15). "I have heard a decree of destruction from the Lord God of hosts upon the whole land" (28:22). The Lord Himself will fight His people.

> *I will distress Ariel. . . .*
> *I will encamp against you round about. . . .*

Then deep from the earth you shall speak,
From low in the dust your word shall come;
Your voice shall come from the ground like the voice of a ghost,
Your speech shall whisper out of the dust.

Isaiah 29:2-4

Israel is surrounded by enemies. Nations conspire and take counsel together to destroy her. Yet,

He Who sits in the heavens laughs; . . .
Then He will speak to them in His wrath,
And terrify them in His fury, saying:
I have set My king
On Zion, My holy hill.

Psalm 2:4-6

The divine sarcasm expressed by the psalmist rings in Isaiah's words:

Take note, you peoples, and be dismayed;
Give ear, all you far countries;
Gird yourselves and be dismayed;
Gird yourselves and be dismayed.
Take counsel together, but it will come to nought;
Speak a word, but it will not stand,
For God is with us.

Isaiah 8:9-10; cf. 18:4

5. MICAH

Micah, a contemporary of Isaiah, apparently regarded the purpose of his mission to be "to declare to Jacob his transgression and to Israel his sin" (3:8). He was the first prophet to predict the destruction of Jerusalem. It was in the days of Hezekiah (cf. Jer. 20:17 f.) that Micah expressed the dreadful words:

> The Lord is coming forth out of His place,
> And will come down and tread upon the high places of the earth.
> The mountains will melt under Him
> And the valleys will be cleft,
> Like wax before the fire,
> Like waters poured down a steep place.
> All this for the transgression of Jacob.
> And for the sins of the house of Israel. . . .
> Zion shall be plowed as a field;
> Jerusalem shall become a heap of ruins,
> And the mountain of the house a wooded height.
>
> Micah 1:3-5; 3:12

Micah refers only by implication to the sin of idolatry, to the people who bow down to the work of their own hands, to the sorcerers and soothsayers. In his eyes the fatal sin is the sin of moral corruption. The rich men are full of violence, and the inhabitants speak lies: "Their tongue is deceitful in their mouth" (6:12).

The prophet directs his rebuke particularly against the "heads of the house of Jacob and the rulers of the house of Israel, who abhor justice and pervert all equity." It is because "they build Zion with blood and Jerusalem with wrong" (3:9-10) that Zion and Jerusalem will be destroyed.

Again and again he hurls bitter words at the leaders:

SELECTED BIBLIOGRAPHY: A. J. Tait, *The Prophecy of Micah* (New York, 1917); P. Haupt, *The Book of Micah* (Chicago, 1910).

It is not for you to know justice?—
You who hate the good and love the evil,
Who tear the skin from off My people,
And their flesh from off their bones;
Who eat the flesh of My people,
And flay their skin from off them.
Micah 3:1-3

Here, amidst a people who walk haughtily (2:3), stands a prophet who relentlessly predicts disaster and disgrace for the leaders as well as for the nation, maintaining that "her wound is incurable" (1:9), that the Lord is "devising evil" against the people: "It will be an evil time" (2:3). The heads of the people, he exclaims,

... give judgment for a bribe,
Its priests teach for hire,
Its prophets divine for money.
Yet they lean upon the Lord and say,
Is not the Lord in the midst of us?
No evil shall come upon us.
Micah 3:11

"Do not preach," the prophet is told, "one should not preach of such things; disgrace will not overtake us" (2:6). But the prophet spells out his message:

You shall eat, but not be satisfied. ...
You shall sow, but not reap ...
That I may make you a desolation, ...
And you shall bear the reproach of My people.
Micah 6:14, 15, 16

To the soul of Micah, the taste of God's word is bitter. In his love for Zion and his people, he is tormented by the vision of the things to come:

For this I will lament and wail;
I will go stripped and naked;
I will make lamentation like the jackals,
And mourning like the ostriches. ...
Because evil has come down from the Lord
To the gate of Jerusalem.
Micah 1:8, 12

Micah does not question the justice of the severe punishment which he predicts for his people. Yet it is not in the name of justice that he speaks, but in the name of a God who "delights in steadfast love," "pardoning iniquity and passing over transgression" (7:18). In the name of the Lord he proclaims:

In anger and wrath I will execute judgment
Upon the nations that did not obey.

Micah 5:15

Yet, there is reluctance and sorrow in that anger. It is as if God were apologizing for His severity, for His refusal to be complacent to iniquity. This is God's apology to Israel. He cannot forget "the treasures of wickedness in the house of the wicked" or "acquit the man with wicked scales and with a bag of deceitful weights" (6:10, 11).

God's sorrow and disappointment are set forth before the people.

> *Hear what the Lord says:*
> *Arise, plead your case before the mountains,*
> *And let the hills hear your voice.*
> *Hear, you mountains, the controversy of the Lord,*
> *And you enduring foundations of the earth;*
> *For the Lord has a controversy with His people,*
> *And He will plead with Israel.*
> *O My people, what have I done to you?*
> *And in what have I wearied you? Answer Me!*
> *For I brought you up from the land of Egypt,*
> *And redeemed you from the house of bondage,*
> *And I sent before you Moses, Aaron, and Miriam.*
> *O My people, remember what Balak king of Moab devised,*
> *And what Balaam the son of Beor answered him;*
> *And what happened from Shittim unto Gilgal,*
> *That you may know the righteous acts of the Lord.*
>
> *Micah 6:1-5*

"Answer Me!" calls the voice of God. But who hears the call? "The voice of the Lord cries to the city" (6:9), but the city is complacent.

The prophet is a lonely man. His standards are too high, his stature too great, and his concern too intense for other men to share. Living on the highest peak, he has no company except God.

> *Woe is me! For I have become*
> *As when the summer fruit has been gathered,*
> *As when the vintage has been gleaned:*
> *There is no cluster to eat,*
> *No first-ripe fig which my soul desires,*
> *The godly man has perished from the earth,*
> *And there is none upright among men;*
> *They all lie in wait for blood,*
> *And each hunts his brother with a net.*
> *Their hands are upon what is evil, to do it diligently;*
> *The prince and the judge ask for a bribe,*
> *And the great man utters the evil desire of his soul;*

Thus they weave it together.
The best of them is like a brier,
The most upright of them a thorn hedge.
The day of their watchmen, of their punishment, has come;
Now their confusion is at hand.
Put no trust in a neighbor,
Have no confidence in a friend;
Guard the doors of your mouth
From her who lies in your bosom;
For the son treats the father with contempt,
The daughter rises up against her mother,
The daughter-in-law against her mother-in-law;
A man's enemies are the men of his own house.
But as for me, I will look to the Lord,
I will wait for the God of my salvation;
My God will hear me.

Micah 7:1-7

In spite of the gloom of his predictions, Micah insists that his message is for the good of his people. Though not openly calling for a repentance that would avert God's judgment, his words imply such a call. To those who oppose him, saying, "Do not preach," Micah responds:

Should this be said, O house of Jacob?
Is the Spirit of the Lord impatient?
Are these His doings?
Do not my words do good to him who walks uprightly?

Micah 2:7

Together with the word of doom, Micah proclaims the vision of redemption. God will forgive "the remnant of His inheritance," and will cast all their sins "into the depths of the sea" (7:18 f.), and every man shall sit "under his vine and under his fig tree, and none shall make them afraid" (4:4).

Among the great insights Micah has bequeathed to us is how to accept and to bear the anger of God. The strength of acceptance comes from the awareness that we have sinned against Him and from the certainty that anger does not mean God's abandonment of man forever. His anger passes, His faithfulness goes on forever. There is compassion in His anger; when we fall, we rise. Darkness is not dismal. When we sit in the darkness, God is our light.

Rejoice not over me, O my enemy;
When I fall, I shall rise;
When I sit in darkness,
The Lord will be a light to me.

> *I will bear the indignation of the Lord,*
> *Because I have sinned against Him,*
> *Until He pleads my cause*
> *And executes judgment for me.*
>
> *Micah 7:8-9*

In another great insight the prophet, speaking as an individual and in the first person singular, poses the most urgent question of religious existence: What is the way of true worship?

> *With what shall I come before the Lord,*
> *And bow myself before God on high?*
> *Shall I come before Him with burnt offerings,*
> *With calves a year old?*
> *Will the Lord be pleased with thousands of rams,*
> *With ten thousands of rivers of oil?*
> *Shall I give my first-born for my transgression,*
> *The fruit of my body for the sin of my soul?*
> *He has showed you, O man, what is good;*
> *And what does the Lord require of you*
> *But to do justice, and to love kindness,*
> *And to walk humbly with your God?*
>
> *Micah 6:6-8*

6. JEREMIAH

O land, land, land,
Hear the word of the Lord!

Jeremiah 22:29

The call to be a prophet came to Jeremiah in the year 625 B.C.E., and he was active during the reigns of the last kings of Judah—Josiah (640-609 B.C.E.), Jehoiakim (609-598 B.C.E.), Jehoiachin (598-597 B.C.E.), Zedekiah (597-587 B.C.E.)—and continued for some time after the fall of Jerusalem in 587 B.C.E.

The word of the Lord came to me saying,

> *Before I formed you in the womb I knew you,*
> *And before you were born I consecrated you;*
> *I appointed you a prophet to the nations.*

Then I said, Ah, Lord God! Behold, I do not know how to speak, for I am only a youth. But the Lord said to me,

> *Do not say, I am only a youth;*
> *For to all to whom I send you, you shall go,*
> *And whatever I command you, you shall speak.*
> *Be not afraid of them,*
> *For I am with you to deliver you, says the Lord.*

Then the Lord put forth His hand and touched my mouth; and the Lord said to me,

> *Behold, I have put My words in your mouth,*
> *See, I have set you this day over nations and over kingdoms,*

SELECTED BIBLIOGRAPHY: P. Volz, *Der Prophet Jeremia* ("Kommentar zum Alten Testament" [Leipzig, 1922]) ; W. Rudolph, *Jeremia* ("Handbuch zum Alten Testament" [Tübingen, 1947]) ; E. A. Leslie, *Jeremiah Chronologically Arranged, Translated, and Interpreted* (New York, 1954) ; A. C. Welch, *Jeremiah, His Time and His Work* (Oxford, 1954) ; *The Book of Jeremiah* ("The Expositor's Bible"), exegesis by J. P. Hyatt, exposition by S. R. Hopper (New York, 1956) ; S. D. Luzzatto, *Commentary on Jeremiah* (Heb.; Lemberg, 1876) ; Y. Kaufmann, *The Religion of Israel* (Heb.; Jerusalem, 1954) , VII, 393-474: (Eng. trans., M. Greenberg [Chicago, 1960]) , pp. 409 ff.; A. B. Ehrlich, *Randglossen zur Hebräischen Bibel*, vol. IV (Leipzig, 1912) ; J. Skinner, *Prophecy and Religion* (Cambridge, 1922) ; A. Malamat, "Jeremiah and the Last Two Kings of Judah," *Palestine Exploration Quarterly*, I (1951) , 81-87.

> *To pluck up and to break down,*
> *To destroy and to overthrow,*
> *To build and to plant.*

And the word of the Lord came to me, saying, Jeremiah, what do you see?
And I said, I see a rod of almond. Then the Lord said to me, You have seen
well, for I am watching over My word to perform it.

The word of the Lord came to me a second time, saying, What do you see?
And I said, I see a boiling pot, facing away from the north. Then the Lord
said to me, Out of the north evil shall break forth upon all the inhabitants
of the land. For, lo, I am calling all the tribes of the kingdoms of the north,
says the Lord; and they shall come and every one shall set his throne at the
entrance of the gates of Jerusalem, against all its walls around about, and
against all the cities of Judah. And I will utter My judgments against them,
for all their wickedness in forsaking Me; they have burned incense to other
gods, and worshiped the works of their own hands. But you, gird up your
loins; arise, and say to them everything that I command you. Do not be dis-
mayed by them, lest I dismay you before them. And I, behold, I make you
this day a fortified city, an iron pillar, and bronze walls, against the whole
land, against the kings of Judah, its princes, its priests, and the people of the
land. They will fight against you; but they shall not prevail against you, for
I am with you, says the Lord, to deliver you.

Jeremiah 1: 4-19

COMPLACENCY AND DISTRESS

Although Isaiah had insisted that Jerusalem would withstand the onslaught of her enemies, Jeremiah, like Micah, was told that the enemies
would overwhelm Jerusalem and all the fortified cities of Judah: "Out of
the north evil shall break forth" (1:14). They maintained that the state of
Judah had forfeited the privilege of God's protection.

And yet, Jeremiah did not think that evil was inevitable. Over and above
man's blindness stood the wonder of repentance, the open gateway through
which man could enter if he would. Jeremiah's call was addressed to Israel
as a whole as well as to every member of the people (18:11):

> *Return, faithless Israel, says the Lord,*
> *I will not look on you in anger,*
> *For I am merciful, says the Lord.*
>> *Jeremiah 3:12 [H. 3:11];*
>> *cf. 4:1; 25:5; 35:15[1]*

> *Like a basket full of birds,*
> *Their houses are full of treachery;*
> *Therefore they have become great and rich,*

---

[1] On the refusal to return, see 5:3; 8:5; 22:27; 44:5.

They have grown fat and sleek.
They know no bounds in deeds of wickedness;
They judge not with justice
The cause of the fatherless, . .
They do not defend the rights of the needy.
Jeremiah 5:27-28

Jeremiah, looking upon the garishness of Jerusalem, felt hurt by the people's guilt and by the knowledge that they had a dreadful debt to pay. The Lord's severe judgment would be meted out; He would not swerve aside. It was hard for God to deal harshly with His beloved people. Rather than inflict a penalty on the whole people, the Lord had tried to purify them:

Behold, I will refine them and test them,
For what else can I do, because of My dear people?
Jeremiah 9:7 [H. 9:6]

Yet, all attempts at purification were of no avail.

Filled with a sense of security, the people scorned the warnings of the true prophets, saying,

The prophets will become wind;
The word is not in them. . . .
They are sure that the Lord . . . will do nothing,
No evil will come upon us,
Nor shall we see sword or famine.
Jeremiah 5:13; 5:12

Indeed,

They are all stubbornly rebellious,
Going about with slanders;
They are bronze and iron,
All of them act corruptly.
The bellows blow fiercely,
The lead is consumed by the fire;
In vain the refining goes on,
For the wicked are not removed.
Refuse silver they are called,
For the Lord has rejected them.
Jeremiah 6:28-30

Jeremiah's was a soul in pain, stern with gloom. To his wistful eye the city's walls seemed to reel. The days that were to come would be dreadful. He called, he urged his people to repent—and he failed. He screamed, wept, moaned—and was left with a terror in his soul.

THE AGE OF WRATH

Utterances denoting the wrath of God, the intent and threat of destruction, are found more frequently and expressed more strongly in Jeremiah than in any other prophet. For this reason, Jeremiah has often been called a prophet of wrath.

However, it would be more significant to say that Jeremiah lived in an age of wrath. His contemporaries had no understanding of the portent of their times, of the way in which God was present at the time. They did not care for time. But a prophet has a responsibility for the moment, an openness to what the moment reveals. He is a person who knows what time it is. To Jeremiah his time was an emergency, one instant away from a cataclysmic event.

> *Cut off your hair and cast it away;*
> *Raise a lamentation on the bare heights,*
> *For the Lord has rejected and forsaken*
> *The generation of His wrath.*
> *Jeremiah 7:29*

Jeremiah hurled a dreadful word at his people, accusing them of provoking or exciting God's anger, an expression not used by earlier prophets (cf. 7:18-19; 11:17-18; 25:6; 44:3-8) : "The sons of Israel and the sons of Judah . . . have done nothing but provoke Me to anger by the work of their hands, says the Lord. This city has aroused My anger and wrath, . . ." (32:30-32) . The words he proclaimed are merciless: "Thus says the Lord God: Behold, My anger and My wrath will be poured out on this place, upon man and beast, upon the trees of the field and the fruit of the ground; it will burn and not be quenched" (7:20) .

> *Behold, the storm of the Lord!*
> *Wrath has gone forth,*
> *A whirling tempest;*
> *It will burst upon the head of the wicked.*
> *The anger of the Lord will not turn back*
> *Until He has executed and accomplished*
> *The intents of His mind.*
> *In the latter days you will understand it clearly. . . .*
> *A lion has gone up from his thicket,*
> *A destroyer of nations has set out;*
> *He has gone forth from his place*
> *To make your land a waste;*
> *Your cities will be ruins*
> *Without inhabitant.*
> *Jeremiah 23:19-20, cf. 30:23-24; 4:7, 5:6*

The days would come when

the dead bodies of this people will be food for the birds of the air, and for the beasts of the earth; and none will frighten them away. And I will make to cease from the cities of Judah and from the streets of Jerusalem the voice of mirth and the voice of gladness, the voice of the bridegroom and the voice of the bride; for the land shall become a waste. . . . [Jerusalem will be] a heap of ruins, a lair of jackals [and] the cities of Judah a desolation, without inhabitant.

Jeremiah 7:33-34; 9:11

GOD'S LOVE OF ISRAEL

God's love of Israel is one of Israel's sacred certainties which Jeremiah, like Hosea and Isaiah before him, tried to instill in the minds of the people.

> *Thus says the Lord;*
> *The people who survived the sword*
> *Found grace in the wilderness; . . .*
> *With everlasting love have I loved you,*
> *Therefore I have continued My faithfulness to you.*
> *Jeremiah 31:2-3*

It was in love that God and Israel met.

The word of God came to me, saying: Go and proclaim in the hearing of Jerusalem, Thus says the Lord:

> *I remember the devotion of your youth,*
> *Your love as a bride,*
> *How you followed Me in the wilderness,*
> *In a land not sown.*
> *Israel was holy to the Lord,*
> *The first fruits of His harvest.*
> *All who would destroy him would be held guilty;*
> *Punishment would come to them,*
> *Says the Lord.*
> *Jeremiah 2:1-3*

"Father!—To God Himself we cannot give a holier name," said Wordsworth. Child—God Himself does not use a more tender word. In spite of Israel's failure, the voice of God avers:

> *For I am a father to Israel,*
> *And Ephraim—he is My first-born.*
> *Jeremiah 31:9*

Ephraim is "a precious son," "a darling child." Such was God's anticipation:

I thought
How I would set you among My sons,
And give you a pleasant land,
The most glorious inheritance among the nations.
And I thought you would call me, "My Father,"
And would not turn from following Me.

Jeremiah 3:19; cf. 3:4

Following the prophet Hosea, Jeremiah employed the analogy of married love to express the relationship of God and Israel. "I was their husband, says the Lord" (31:32).

Surely, as a faithless wife leaves her husband,
So have you been faithless to Me, O house of Israel,
Says the Lord. . . .
If a man divorces his wife,
And she goes from him
And becomes another man's wife,
Will he return to her?
Would not that land be greatly polluted?
You have played the harlot with many lovers;
And would you return to Me?
Says the Lord.
Lift up your eyes to the bare heights and see!
Where have you not been lain with?
By the wayside you have sat awaiting lovers,
Like an Arab in the wilderness,
You have polluted the land
With your vile harlotry.

Jeremiah 3:20; 3:1-2

THE INNER TENSION

Jeremiah depicted the dramatic tension in the inner life of God. As in Abraham's debate with God over the threatened destruction of Sodom, there was an implied desire not to let the judgment fall upon Judah.

Go to and fro in the streets of Jerusalem,
See, I entreat you, and know!
And look in its broad open places
To see whether you can find one
Who does justly,
Who practices faithfulness,
Says the Lord.

Jeremiah 5:1

On account of their sins, the land would be subjected to devastation. Yet the judgment seemed to be painful to the Supreme Judge, and Jeremiah tried to convey that God sought to justify His judgment. The words of God betray an inner oscillation:

> *How can I pardon you?*
> *Your children have forsaken Me,*
> *Have sworn by those who are no gods.*
> *When I fed them to the full,*
> *They committed adultery*
> *And trooped to the houses of harlots.*
> *They were well-fed lusty stallions,*
> *Each neighing for his neighbor's wife.*
> *Shall I not punish them for these things?*
> *Says the Lord.*
> *Shall I not avenge Myself*
> *On a nation such as this? ...*
> *They judge not with justice*
> *The cause of the fatherless, ...*
> *They do not defend the rights of the needy.*
> *Shall I not punish them for these things?*
> *Says the Lord.*
> *Shall I not avenge Myself*
> *On a nation such as this? ...*
> *Their tongue is a deadly arrow;*
> *It speaks deceitfully.*
> *With his mouth each speaks peaceably to his neighbor,*
> *But in his heart he plans an ambush for him.*
> *Shall I not punish them for these things?*
> *Says the Lord.*
> *Shall I not avenge Myself*
> *On a nation such as this?*
>
> Jeremiah 5:7-9, 28-29; 9:8-9 [H. 9:7-8]

"The Lord wrests the decision to judge from Himself: He would at once forgive, He has attempted to do so by means of disciplinary training, now He can no more forgive, He must avenge himself, ... He has been deceived, offended, betrayed: it is His own possession, with which He must part."[2]

THE SORROW AND ANGUISH OF THE LORD

A great hope was Israel; "the first fruits" were a foretaste of a harvest of blessing.[3] But as time passed, God's hope was dashed. The people deserted their Redeemer and worshiped instead "the works of their own hands" (1:16). God's pain and disappointment ring throughout the book of Jere-

---

[2] P. Volz, *Der Prophet Jeremia* (Leipzig, 1922), p. 60. See E. A. Leslie, *Jeremiah* (New York, 1954), p. 60, whose translation is the one quoted above.
[3] "The Lord once called you a green olive tree, fair with goodly fruit" (11:16; cf. 2:21).

miah. What a sublime paradox for the Creator of heaven and earth to
implore the people so humbly:

> *Thus says the Lord:*
> *What wrong did your fathers find in Me,*
> *That they went far away from Me,*
> *And pursued what is worthless,*
> *And became worthless?*
>
> *Jeremiah 2:5*

The heart of melancholy beats in God's words: "My people have forgotten
Me" (18:15); "they have forsaken Me" (2:13; cf. 1:16; 2:17, 19; 3:21; 5:7;
13:25; 16:11; 17:13; 19:4).

How much quiet tenderness, how much unsaid devotion is contained in
the way in which the Lord of heaven and earth spoke of Israel: "My
people," "My dear people" (*bath 'ami*).

> *For My people are foolish,*
> *They know Me not;*
> *They are stupid children,*
> *They have no understanding.*
>
> *Jeremiah 4:22*

"My people have been lost sheep" (50:6). "The shepherds who care for My
people . . . have scattered My flock and have driven them away" (23:2).
The false prophets "have healed the wound of My people lightly" (6:14).
They did not proclaim "My words to My people" (23:22). They "make My
people forget My name" (23:27), and "lead My people astray by their
lies" (23:32).

There were moments of compassion and moments of anger. But God's
attachment to Israel is eternal. It was "My people" when the blessing was
proclaimed (12:1, 16; 30:3); it was "My people Israel" when their wickedness was condemned (7:12) or punishment announced. In regard to the
external enemies of Israel, God said: "They have despised My people"
(33:24).

As great as God's wrath is His anguish. Together with proclaiming the
forthcoming disaster—"The people . . . shall be cast out in the streets of
Jerusalem, victims of famine and sword, with none to bury them" (14:16)
—the prophet was told by God:

> *You shall say to them this word:*
> *Let my eyes run down with tears night and day,*
> *And let them not cease,*
> *For My dearly beloved people* (bath 'ami)
> *is smitten with a great wound,*
> *With a very grievous blow.*
>
> *Jeremiah 14:17*

Again and again the prophet brought God's word to His beloved people: mourn, grieve, sorrow, lament. A sense of delicacy prevented the prophet from spelling out the meaning of the word: Mourn My people for Me as well. . . . [4]

> Thus says the Lord: . . .
> O My dear people (bath 'ami), gird on sackcloth,
> And roll in ashes;
> Make mourning as for an only son,
> Most bitter lamentation,
> For suddenly the destroyer will come upon us.
> > Jeremiah 6:22, 26

These words are aglow with a divine pathos that can be reflected, but not pronounced: God is mourning Himself. "Thus says the Lord. Behold, what I have built I am breaking down, and what I have planted I am plucking up . . ." (45:4). God's sorrow rises again and again to unconcealed heights of expression.

> I have forsaken My house,
> I have abandoned My heritage;
> I have given the beloved of My soul
> Into the hands of her enemies.
> My heritage has become to Me
> Like a lion in the forest,
> She has lifted up her voice against Me;
> Therefore I hate her.
> Is My heritage to Me like a speckled bird of prey?
> Are the birds of prey against her round about?
> Go, assemble all the wild beasts;
> Bring them to devour.
> Many shepherds have destroyed My vineyard,
> They have trampled down My portion,
> They have made My pleasant portion
> A desolate wilderness.
> They have made it a desolation;
> Desolate, it mourns to Me.
> The whole land is made desolate,
> But no man lays it to heart.
> Upon all the bare heights in the desert
> Destroyers have come;
> For the sword of the Lord devours
> From one end of the land to the other;
> No flesh has peace.
> They have sown wheat and have reaped thorns,

---

[4] This was sensed by the rabbis of the second and third centuries. Cf. their interpretations of pertinent passages in Jeremiah, particularly in the Midrash on Lamentations.

> *They have tired themselves out but profit nothing.*
> *They shall be ashamed of their harvests*
> *Because of the fierce anger of the Lord. . . .*
> *Thus says the Lord;*
> *A voice is heard in Ramah,*
> *Lamentation and bitter weeping.*
> *Rachel is weeping for her children;*
> *She refuses to be comforted for her children,*
> *Because they are not.*
> *Thus says the Lord;*
> *Keep your voice from weeping*
> *And your eyes from tears;*
> *For your work shall be rewarded, says the Lord,*
> *And they shall come back from the land of the enemy.*
> *There is hope for your future, says the Lord,*
> *And your children shall come back to their own country.*
> Jeremiah 12:7-13; 31:15-17

Israel's distress was more than a human tragedy. With Israel's distress came the affliction of God, His displacement, His homelessness in the land, in the world. And the prophet's prayer, "O save us," involved not only the fate of a people. It involved the fate of God in relation to the people. For Israel's desertion was not merely an injury to man; it was an insult to God. This was the voice of God Who felt shunned, pained, and offended:

> *Have I been a wilderness to Israel,*
> *Or a land of thick darkness?*
> *Why then do My people say,*
> *We are free,*
> *We will come no more to Thee?*
> *Can a maiden forget her ornaments,*
> *Or a bride her attire?*
> *Yet My people have forgotten Me*
> *Days without number*
> Jeremiah 2:31-32

The Lord Who had dwelt in the midst of Israel was abandoning His dwelling place. But should Israel cease to be His home, then God, we might say, would be without a home in the world. He would not have left His people altogether, but He would be among them like a stranger, like a wayfarer, withholding His power to save. It is as if there were an inner wrestling in God.

> *O Thou hope of Israel,*
> *Its savior in time of trouble!*
> *Why shouldst Thou be like a stranger in the land,*
> *Like a wayfarer who turns aside to tarry for a night?*
> *Why shouldst Thou be like a man astounded?*

Like a mighty man who cannot save?
Yet Thou, O Lord, art in the midst of us,
And we are called by Thy name,
Leave us not.

Jeremiah 14:8-9

When the calamity came, and death was "cutting off the children from the streets and the young men from the squares" (9:21 [H. 9:20]), He called upon the people to take up "weeping and wailing" (9:10 [H. 9:9]).

Thus says the Lord of hosts:
Consider, and call for the mourning women to come;
Let them make haste and raise a wailing over us,
That our eyes may run down with tears,
And our eyelids gush with water.

Jeremiah 9:17-18 [H. 9:16-17]

"Thus says the Lord of hosts: . . . raise a wailing *over us*, . . ." Does not the word of God mean: Cry for Israel and Me? The voice of God calling upon the people to weep, lament, and mourn, for the calamities are about to descend upon them, is itself a voice of grief, a voice of weeping.

O Lord, Thou hast deceived me,
And I was deceived;
Thou art stronger than I,
And Thou hast prevailed.

Jeremiah 20:7

This standard rendition misses completely the meaning of the text and ascribes to Jeremiah a pitiful platitude ("Thou art stronger than I"). The proper rendition of Jeremiah's exclamation would be:

O Lord, Thou hast seduced me,
And I am seduced;
Thou hast raped me
And I am overcome.

The meaning of this extraordinary confession becomes clear when we consider what commentators have failed to notice, namely, the specific meaning of the individual words. The striking feature of the verse is the use of two verbs *patah* and *ḥazak*. The first term is used in the Bible and in the special sense of wrongfully inducing a woman to consent to prenuptial intercourse (Exod. 22:16 [H. 22:15]; cf. Hos. 2:14 [H. 2:16]; Job 31:9). The second term denotes the violent forcing of a woman to submit to extranuptial intercourse, which is thus performed against her will (Deut. 22:15; cf. Judg. 19:25; II Sam. 13:11). The first denotes seduction or enticement; the second, rape. Seduction is distinguished from rape in that it does not involve violence. The woman seduced has consented, although her consent may

have been gained by allurements. The words used by Jeremiah to describe
the impact of God upon his life are identical with the terms for seduction
and rape in the legal terminology of the Bible.[5]

These terms used in immediate juxtaposition forcefully convey the complexity of the divine-human relationship: sweetness of enticement as well as
violence of rape. Jeremiah, who like Hosea thought of the relationship
between God and Israel in the image of love, interpreted his own involvement in the same image. This interpretation betrays an ambivalence in the
prophet's understanding of his own experience.

The call to be a prophet is more than an invitation. It is first of all a
feeling of being enticed, of acquiescence or willing surrender. But this win-
some feeling is only one aspect of the experience. The other aspect is a
sense of being ravished or carried away by violence, of yielding to overpowering force against one's own will. The prophet feels both the attraction
and the coercion of God, the appeal and the pressure, the charm and the
stress. He is conscious of both voluntary identification and forced capitu-
lation.

This dialectic of what takes place in the prophetic consciousness points to
the approach we have adopted in our analysis. Objectively considered, it is,
on the one hand, the divine pathos which stirs and entices the prophet, and,
on the other hand, unconditioned power which exercises sheer compulsion
over the prophet. Subjectively, it is in consequence the willing response of
sympathy to persuasion and also the sense of being utterly delivered up to
the overwhelming power of God. A man whose message is doom for the
people he loves not only forfeits his own capacity for joy, but also provokes
the hostility and outrage of his contemporaries. The sights of woe, the anticipation of disaster, nearly crush his soul.

And yet, the life of Jeremiah was not all misery, tension or pressure. He
also knew the bliss of being engaged to God, "the joy and delight" of being,
as it were, a bride.

> Thy words were found, and I ate them,
> Thy words became to me a joy,
> The delight of my heart,
> For I am called by Thy name,
> O Lord, God of hosts.
>
> Jeremiah 15:16

---

[5] The expression *patah* is often found in this meaning in the language of the Mishnah;
hazak has gained a precise significance in the Talmud: the idea and the term have become
of central importance for the notion of the right to property. As a consequence of its
specification in this sense, the expression in the sense of sexual violation was supplanted
by the term *'anas;* cf. *Ketuboth* 3, 4, where both terms occur. See also W. Rudolph,
Jeremia (Tübingen, 1947), p. 113.

The words "joy" and "delight" occur four other times in the book of Jeremiah, and always in connection with nuptial festivities (7:34; 16:9; 25:10; 33:11). The bearing of a name was a sign of betrothal. "Let us be called by your name," the unmarried women called to a man (Isa. 4:1). The prophet's situation was one of betrothal to the Lord, to the God of hosts.

SYMPATHY FOR GOD

1. "I am full of the wrath (ḥemah) of God" (6:11), exclaims Jeremiah. He was filled with a blazing passion, and it was this emotional intensity which drove him to discharge God's woeful errands. The ultimate purpose of a prophet is not to be inspired, but to inspire the people; not to be filled with a passion, but to impassion the people with understanding for God. Yet the ears of this people were closed: "The word of the Lord is to them an object of scorn" (6:10). Jeremiah was filled to overflowing with the wrath of God, which he could neither suppress nor contain, and which poured itself out therefore upon innocent "children in the street and upon the gatherings of young men" (6:11). The wrath of God was not the threat of judgment being poured forth, but the upsurge of wrath in Jeremiah himself. The compulsion to pour it forth must not be regarded as an ecstatic compulsion, for up to this point Jeremiah had been able to contain his anger.[6]

From this confession on the part of the prophet, it is clear with what agitation and passionate concern he was accustomed to fulfill his vocation. Again and again Jeremiah proclaimed the pathos of wrath. His being filled with divine wrath was his sympathy with it. Jeremiah not only experienced such sympathy; he was fully conscious of his experience.

2. The prophet of wrath did not merely proclaim it; he lived it, and was conscious of it.

> *I did not sit in the company of merrymakers,*
> *Nor did I rejoice;*
> *I sat alone, because Thy hand was upon me,*
> *For Thou hadst filled me with indignation* [za'am].
>
> *Jeremiah 15:17*

The question may be asked whether, to the mind of Jeremiah, his sympathy proceeded from an internal impulse or whether it was forced upon him from without. The phrase, "Thou hadst filled me with indignation," might justify the supposition that he experienced his agitation not as a personal response, but as an innoculated emotion, a state of being possessed. However, as we shall see, such a supposition is improbable.

---

[6] See D. P. Volz, *op. cit.*, p. 74.

According to Jer. 25:15-29, the prophet was told by the Lord: "Take from My hand this cup of wine of wrath (*hemah*), and make all the nations to whom I send you drink it. . . . Then you shall say to them, Thus says the Lord of hosts, the God of Israel: Drink, be drunk and vomit, fall and rise no more, because of the word I am sending among you." To drink of the divine wrath meant the same as to be doomed or to drink poison.[7] It would, therefore, be absurd to assume that Jeremiah drank or was filled with divine anger. It was the pathos that evoked in him an anger of sympathy.

3. Jeremiah's activity seemed both futile and distasteful. He tried to abstain from conveying his message to the people.

> *If I say, I will not mention Him;*
> *Or speak any more in His name,*
> *There is in my heart as it were a burning fire,*
> *Shut up in my bones,*
> *And I am weary with holding it in,*
> *And I cannot.*
>
> Jeremiah 20:9

The key to the understanding of this passage may be found in the phrase, "I am weary of holding it in," which is almost identical with the phrase in 6:11, quoted above, referring to the prophet's inability to suppress the divine wrath in him. In all likelihood the passage refers to the same theme, namely, the fire of wrath that glowed within him.

In the language of Jeremiah, fire is used in a twofold sense: as a symbol of destruction (21:14; 43:12; 48:45; 49:27; 50:32), and as a symbol of anger (4:4; 17:4; 21:12; cf. Deut. 32:22; Ezek. 21:31 [H. 21:36]; 22:31; 36:5; 38:19; Nah. 1:6; Ps. 39:3 [H. 39:4]; 79:5; 89:46 [H. 89:47]; Lam. 1:13; 2:4; Isa. 66:15). The identification of the divine word and fire has a double implication: the pathos, anger and its effect; and the threatened annihilation. The divine word moved in Jeremiah as fire because he lived through the experience of divine wrath. Just as the pathetic wrath of God could become a physical fire of destruction, so the wrathful word of the prophet could work itself out as a destructive fiery element.

The prophet was filled with a passion which demanded release; if he tried to contain it, its flame burned within him like a fever.[8] Jeremiah could not have felt it as a passion breathed into him by God. Biblical thought, as we have seen, regards every outburst of fire which comes from God over a

---

[7] To the Semitic mind, poison and wrath are integrally connected; see H. Gressmann, *Der Ursprung der Israelitisch-Juedischen Eschatologie* (Göttingen, 1905), pp. 130 f.

[8] The idea of "the burning fire in the heart and the bones" is reminiscent of the hot fever which is described as a "fire in the bones"; cf. the expressions *qadachath* (Lev. 26:16; Deut. 28:22) and *'esh shel 'aṣamoth* in the Babylonian Talmud, *Gittin* 70a.

people, a land or an individual, as a destructive force. Jeremiah felt the divine wrath as springing up from within.

There are, then, two separate themes in this confession. The fire of anger as the condition of the prophet's soul, and the sense of compulsion to bring it to expression. His inner condition is one of sympathy with the divine anger, the emotional and passionate character of which is indicated by the fact that Jeremiah localized his passion in the heart, which, according to ancient Hebrew conceptions, is the seat of emotion and passion.

A further implication of this confession is that the prophetic sympathy was stronger than the will, the inner passion more powerful than the personal disposition.

4. The prophet not only must learn to see how man behaves, but also must learn to sense God's feeling: His eternal love for Israel.

Thus said the Lord to me, Go and buy a linen waistcloth, and put it on your loins, and do not dip it in water. So I bought a waistcloth according to the word of the Lord, and put it on my loins. And the word of the Lord came to me a second time, Take the waistcloth which you have bought, which is upon your loins, and arise, go to the Euphrates, and hide it there in a cleft of the rock. So I went, and hid it by the Euphrates, as the Lord commanded me. And after many days the Lord said to me, Arise, go to the Euphrates, and take from there the waistcloth which I commanded you to hide there. Then I went to the Euphrates, and dug, and I took the waistcloth from the place where I had hidden it. And behold, the waistcloth was spoiled; it was good for nothing.

Then the word of the Lord come to me: Thus says the Lord: Even so will I spoil the pride of Judah and the great pride of Jerusalem. This evil people, who refuse to hear My words, who stubbornly follow their own heart and have gone after other gods to serve them and worship them, shall be like this waistcloth, which is good for nothing. For as the waistcloth clings to the loins of a man, so I made the whole house of Israel and the whole house of Judah cling to Me, says the Lord, that they might be for Me a people, a name, a praise, and a glory, but they would not listen.

Jeremiah 13:1-11

If the purpose of the story of the waistcloth were only to let the prophet see in a symbolic way the punishment of the people, he would not have been told to put it on his loins. But it is precisely this part of the story that seems to hold the central meaning of the act. The prophet must learn to feel for himself God's intimate attachment to Israel; he must not only know about it, but experience it from within. "For as the waistcloth clings to the loins of a man, so I made the whole house of Israel and the whole house of Judah cling to Me, . . . that they might be for Me a people, a name, a praise, and a glory, but they would not listen." Like Hosea in his marriage experience,

Jeremiah must learn the grief of God in having to spoil what is intimately precious to Him.

Thus there are two aspects to the story. The first aspect is didactic: to convey to the prophet symbolically the decision to punish the people (the buying of the waistcloth and its rotting). The second aspect is sympathetic: to let the prophet feel what that decision means to the life and pathos of God. Indeed, the command to the prophet to wear the waistcloth before placing it in the cleft of a rock would be devoid of meaning if the purpose of the story were only to demonstrate to the prophet the punishment to come.

5. Of his inner condition Jeremiah said:

> *My heart is broken within me,*
> *All my bones are out of joint;*
> *I am like a drunken man,*
> *Like a man overcome by wine,*
> *Because of the Lord,*
> *And because of His holy words.*
>   *Jeremiah 23:9*

What was the source of this dreadful condition? What emotion or what awareness brought this condition about? The prophet stated it briefly: "Because of the Lord, and because of His holy words." Had it been the sense of forthcoming disaster, or the awareness of the people's sins, he would have said, "Because of the people, and because of their fate or sins." What convulsed the prophet's whole being was God. His condition was a state of suffering in sympathy with the divine pathos.

The idea of drunkenness as a punishment occurs frequently in the book of Isaiah (25:15 ff.; 51:7, 39, 57; cf. Lam. 4:21; Isa. 63:6). Babel was the cup which contained the wine of destruction for the people. But the prophet was as far from describing himself as the bearer of annihilation as from describing himself as the object of punishment. Comparison with the speech about the wine of wrath (25:15) strongly suggests that in this confession, too, the prophet was thinking of an intoxication by the wrath of God.[9]

This supposition is confirmed by the following consideration. The prophecies of Jeremiah that we have examined are variations of one and the same theme. The striking recurrence of the "motif" leads one to suppose that a fundamental experience was in question, about the meaning of which the prophet was often concerned. Verses 23:9; 20:9; 6:9; and 15:17 constitute a series of formulae in which we can detect the increasing clarity of the idea.

---

[9] As regards the verb *῾abar,* cf. its meaning "to be angry" in the *hithpael;* Deut. 3:26; Ps. 78:21, 59, etc.; cf. also Num. 5:14.

6. Jeremiah hated his prophetic mission. To a soul full of love, it was horrible to be a prophet of castigation and wrath. What rewards did he receive for carrying the appalling burden?

> *I have become a laughingstock all the days;*
> *Every one mocks me.*
> *For as often as I speak I have to cry out,*
> *Have to complain of violence and abuse,*
> *For the word of the Lord has become for me*
> *A reproach and derision all day long.*
>
> *Jeremiah 20:7-8*

In spite of public rejection, in spite of inner misery, he felt unable to discard the divine burden, unable to disengage himself from the divine pathos. He knew why he had to yield; he knew how to explain his inability to resist the terrible errand.

SYMPATHY FOR ISRAEL

The modes of prophetic sympathy are determined by the modes of the divine pathos. The pathos of love and the pathos of anger awake corresponding tones in the heart of the prophet. In his confessions Jeremiah allows us to obtain a glimpse of the fervor of love as well as of the raging of anger against the people. Through insight into the nexus between prophetic emotion and divine pathos, it is possible to gain a clue to the meaning behind the conflicting and confusing emotions of Jeremiah's mind. His inconsolable grief over the destiny of the people is an expression of fellowship and love; the people's anguish is his anguish. However, his emotions are not simply an expression of instinctive attachment to his people or a feeling of personal involvement in their fate. At times Jeremiah even wished to abandon his people (19:1; cf. I Kings 19:3 ff.).

Ardent as was his love for the people, he was primarily driven by what God felt for Israel. Accord with divine pathos determined his attractions and aversions. Love involves an appreciation of what is precious in the beloved person. Israel was precious because it was the consort and the beloved of the Lord.

The prophet was fully conscious of his emotional nexus with God. It was the bidding of God that his compassion and lament were uttered.

> *Declare in Judah, and proclaim in Jerusalem, and say, . . .*
> *For this gird you with sackcloth,*
> *Lament and wail;*
> *For the fierce anger of the Lord*
> *Has not turned back from us.*
>
> *Jeremiah 4:5, 8; cf. 14:17*

Jeremiah loved his people. But he also trembled, knowing that God is just.

> *My anguish, my anguish! I writhe in pain!*
> *Oh, the walls of my heart!*
> *My heart is beating wildly;*
> *I cannot keep silent;*
> *For I hear the sound of the trumpet,*
> *The alarm of war,*
> *Disaster follows hard on disaster,*
> *The whole land is laid waste.*
> *Suddenly my tents are destroyed,*
> *My curtains in a moment.*
> *How long must I see the standard,*
> *And hear the sound of the trumpet?*
>
> *Jeremiah 4:19-21*

The prophet not only was a man concerned with right and wrong. He also had a soul of extreme sensitivity to human suffering. In the midst of hurling the harshest words of impending doom, he was suddenly gripped by what was in store for his people:

> *For I heard a cry as of a woman in travail,*
> *Anguish as of one bringing forth her first child,*
> *The cry of the daughter of Zion gasping for breath,*
> *Stretching out her hands,*
> *Woe is me! I am fainting before murderers.*
>
> *Jeremiah 4:31*

Impassioned with a sense of the divine disturbance, Jeremiah could condemn with a vehemence that was at times terrifying and devoid of charity. But his own heart was rich in tenderness and sensitivity to other people's suffering. He terrified in order to save. The disaster he threatened would be a disaster to him, sorrow and excruciating anguish. He had implored and warned them, He knew that if the people should remain dead to his words, he would drown in his own tears.

> *Hear and give ear; be not proud,*
> *For the Lord has spoken.*
> *Give glory to the Lord your God*
> *Before He brings darkness,*
> *Before your feet stumble*
> *On the twilight mountains,*
> *And while you look for light*
> *He turns it into gloom*
> *And makes it deep darkness.*
> *But if you will not listen,*

My soul will weep in secret for your pride;
My eyes will weep bitterly and run down with tears,
Because the Lord's flock has been taken captive.
                                        Jeremiah 13:15-17

This, indeed, was at the root of his anguish. Those whom he loved he was called upon to condemn. When the catastrophe came, and the enemy mercilessly killed men, women, and children, the prophet must have discovered that the agony was greater than the heart could feel, that his grief was more than his soul could weep for.

My grief is beyond healing
My heart is sick within me. . . .
For the wound of my beloved people is my heart wounded,
I mourn, and dismay has taken hold on me.
Is there nò balm in Gilead?
Is there no physician there?
Why then has the health of my beloved people
Not been restored?
O that my head were waters,
And my eyes a fountain of tears,
That I might weep day and night
For the slain of my beloved people! . . .
Who will have pity on you, O Jerusalem,
Or who will bemoan you?
Who will turn aside
To ask about your welfare?
                    Jeremiah 8:18—9:1 [H. 8:18-23]; 15:5

Instead of searching their own lives for the failures that brought down God's wrath on them, the people resented Jeremiah's prediction of doom, accusing him of ill-will, as if he were to blame for the disaster he predicted. Was Jeremiah an enemy of his people (15:10-11)?

Deeply hurt by the accusations, Jeremiah protested before God his innocence and his love of his people. The word of doom was not born in his heart (17:6).

Remember how I stood before Thee, . . .
To turn away Thy wrath from them.
                                        Jeremiah 18:20

Indeed, this was a part of the complexity of the prophet's inner existence. He was a person overwhelmed by sympathy for God and sympathy for man. Standing before the people he pleaded for God; standing before God he pleaded for his people. The prediction of doom was contrary to his own feelings. When the false prophet Hananiah predicted that within two years' time the captives of Judah, together with the vessels of the Temple which had been taken to Babylonia after the first Babylonian invasion, would be brought back to Jerusalem, Jeremiah exclaimed: "Amen! May the Lord do so; may the Lord make the words which you have prophesied come true" (28:6). In a moment of distress, while Babylon was waging war against Jerusalem, King Zedekiah turned to the prophet, saying: "Pray for us to the Lord our God" (37:3; cf. 7:16; 11:14; 14:11, 20-22; 18:20; 21:2).

Jeremiah prayed and pleaded for His people:

> *We acknowledge our wickedness, O Lord,*
> *And the iniquity of our fathers,*
> *For we have sinned against Thee.*
> *Do not spurn us, for Thy name's sake;*
> *Do not dishonor Thy glorious throne.*
> *Remember and do not break Thy covenant with us.*
>
> *Jeremiah 14:20-21*

God had a stake in the life of Israel. In spurning His people, He would dishonor the throne of His glory. Here, then, was a task of the prophet: to remind God of His own concern.

In pleading for his people, the prophet acknowledged their sins, recalled the covenant. Yet, the answer to his prayer was tinged with sadness: "Though Moses and Samuel stood before Me, My soul would not turn to this people. Send them out of My sight, and let them go!" (15:1.)

Awful as God's punishment would be, to be abandoned by Him would be incomparably worse. The prophet was haunted by the fear of ultimate calamity: God's rejection or loathing of the people. The plight of man was shrouded in what God felt about man. In his brooding about the situation of the people, Jeremiah's thought turned to God's soul and pathos.

> *Hast Thou utterly rejected Judah?*
> *Does Thy soul loathe Zion?*
> *Why hast Thou smitten us*
> *So that there is no healing for us?*
> *Jeremiah 14:19*

THE POLARITY WITHIN

> *See, I have set you this day over nations and over kingdoms,*
> *To pluck up and to break down,*
> *To destroy and to overthrow,*
> *To build and to plant.*
>
> *Jeremiah 1:10*

Jeremiah was called to an office both sublime and appalling. First he had to castigate, foretell doom and destruction; only after that could he comfort, offer hope, build and plant. Because of the ordeals he would have to face and the strength he would need, he was told: "Gird up your loins; arise and say to them everything that I command you. Do not be dismayed by them, lest I dismay you before them" (1:17). In order to be able to rise above dismay, to be able to persevere in the spirit of defiance, he was suddenly transformed into the stark opposite of his usual self. "Behold, I make you this day a fortified city, an iron pillar, and bronze walls, against the whole land, against the kings of Judah, its princes, its priests, and the people of the land" (1:18). He succeeded, indeed, in offending, chafing, even alarming his contemporaries. Dashing the people's sense of security, he added insult to gloom by chiding them for what they revered. Having been enabled to withstand like a fortress all the attacks that came from without, Jeremiah's inner life never turned to bronze or iron.

The role of the prophet was ambiguous in the eyes of some of his contemporaries. The indignation that flowed from him, the anger he displayed, even when extrinsic to his mind, became so intimate a part of his soul that those exposed to it could easily mistake it as his own antipathy rather than as sympathy with divine anger, and could assume that he had his own ax to grind, that he was giving vent to personal hostility. It seems that Jeremiah was accused of feeling delight in anticipating the disaster which he had announced in the name of the Lord. He who loved his people, whose life was dedicated to saving his people, was regarded as an enemy. Over and above the agony of sensing the imminent disaster, his soul was bruised by calumny. What protection was there against such backbiting? No one could look into his heart, but everybody was hurt by his words. Only the Lord knew the truth.

> *Heal me, O Lord, and I shall be healed;*
> *Save me, and I shall be saved;*
> *For Thou art my praise. . . .*
> *I have not pressed Thee to send evil,*
> *Nor have I desired the day of disaster,*
> *Thou knowest;*
> *That which came out of my lips*
> *Was before Thy face.*
>
> *Jeremiah 17:14, 16*

Jeremiah was gentle and compassionate by nature, and the mission he had to carry out was, to him, distasteful in the extreme. It made him contentious, petulant, irascible. People he had prayed for turned out to be his enemies. "Woe is me, my mother, that you bore me, a man of strife and contention to the whole land! I have not lent, nor have I borrowed, yet all of them curse me. So let it be, O Lord, if I have not entreated Thee for their good, if I have not pleaded with Thee on behalf of the enemy in the time of trouble and in the time of distress!" (15:10-11.) It seemed impossible to break through the wall of suspicion: "Can one break iron, iron from the north, and bronze?" (15:12.)

There were people who considered him a traitor. "You are telling a lie. The Lord our God did not send you . . . but Baruch . . . has set you against us, to deliver us into the hand of the Chaldeans [Babylonians], that they may kill us or take us into exile in Babylon" (42:2-3). The priests and the prophets pronounced him worthy of death (26:11). Even the men of his own village, Anathoth, those closest to him, were in full cry after him, seeking to take his life (11:21; 12:6). The shock of discovering how those who spoke "fair words" to him were seeking his life came as a bolt of lightning to a soul riven with pain, tortured by visions of imminent disaster.

> I was like a gentle lamb
> Led to the slaughter.
> I did not know it was against me
> They devised schemes, saying:
> Let us destroy the tree with its fruit,
> Let us cut him off from the land of the living,
> That his name be remembered no more.
> O Lord of hosts, Who judgest righteously,
> Who triest the heart and the mind,
> Let me see Thy vengeance upon them,
> For to Thee I have committed my cause.
>   Jeremiah 11:19-20

He was called upon to deny the charge of forsaking his country and of going to the enemy camp. "It is false; I am not deserting to the Chaldeans!" (37:14.) When Jeremiah became aware of a conspiracy to slay him (18:23), it was more than he could bear. There had been the promise at the time of his call to be a prophet: "They will fight against you; but they shall not prevail against you, for I am with you, says the Lord, to deliver you" (1:19).

At the crucial moment of history, Jeremiah was the hope, the anchor, and the promise. The slaying of Jeremiah would have meant the death blow to Israel as well, a collapse of God's mission.

It was not his vested interests, honor, or prestige that the prophet was fighting for. He was fighting for the physical survival of his people. Those members of the people who sought to destroy him must have been regarded by him as traitors, as a deadly menace to his prophetic mission. Since all attempts at persuasion had proved futile, and even the Lord's call was of no avail, what else was left for the prophet to do except to pray that his enemies be destroyed so that the whole people could be saved? (11:20; 12:3; 15:15; 17:18; 18:21.)

Polarity of emotion is a striking fact in the life of Jeremiah. We encounter him in the pit of utter agony and at the height of extreme joy, carried away by divine wrath and aching with supreme compassion. There are words of railing accusation and denunciation; the lips that pleaded for mercy utter petitions for retribution, for the destruction of those who stand in the way of the people's accepting his prophetic word. Indeed, the commission he received at the time of his call endowed him with the power to carry out two opposite roles:

> *To pluck up and to break down,*
> *To destroy and to overthrow,*
> *To build and to plant.*
>   *Jeremiah 1:10*

Aside from the moral problem involved in the harsh petitions, there is the personal problem. Do not such contrasts or opposing attitudes indicate a lack of integrity? Is not his pleading for the destruction of his opponents a collapse of his power of mercy? A way of comprehending these contradictions as being parts of a unified personality is to remember that the prophet's inner life was not wholly his own. His emotional situation reflected the divine relation to Israel: compassion as well as anger. What he felt was not always original with him. "Filled with the wrath of God," it was beyond his ability to weigh, measure or control the outburst of anger. The actual occasion of such an outburst may at times have been a personal one; its possibility and intensity derived from sympathy. The tension of being caught, heart and soul, in two opposing currents of violent emotion, was more than a human being could bear.

> *Cursed be the day*
> *On which I was born!*
> *The day when my mother bore me,*
> *Let it not be blessed!*
> *Cursed be the man*
> *Who brought the news to my father,*
> *A son is born to you,*
> *Making him very glad...*
> *Because He did not kill me in the womb.*
> *So my mother would have been my grave,*
> *And her womb for ever great.*

Why did I come forth from the womb
To see toil and sorrow,
And spend my days in shame? . . .
O that I had in the desert
A wayfarers' lodging place,
That I might leave my people
And go away from them!
                              Jeremiah 20:14-15, 17-18;
                                        9:2 [H. 9:1]

THE HYPERTROPHY OF SYMPATHY

Jeremiah seems to have suffered at times from a hypertrophy of sympathy for God. Inherent in sympathetic emotion is a tendency to become divorced from the occasion or the subject by which it was called forth. What starts out, for example, as a feeling of sadness in sympathy for a bereaved person, may become a condition of sadness as such, no longer associated with the particular person. It may also surpass in intensity the feeling of the person for whom one has sympathy. Sympathy may continue even when the bereaved person has found comfort and overcome his grief.

Jeremiah's sympathy seems at times to have become an independent pathos, even deviating from the divine pathos. Such deviation led to a conflict between the pathos of the Lord and the pathos of the prophet. Therefore, the Lord had to correct and enlighten him about the nonfinality of pathos. The anger had become the prophet's own, rather than remaining a true reflection of the divine pathos. Such excess of sympathy with the divine wrath shows the danger of a sympathy grown absolute. "Avenge me on my persecutors" (15:15), the prophet prayed. Adversaries endangered the preaching of God's word; the prophet lost patience. He exhorted God to depart from merciful longsuffering. Thus it developed that the prophet's indignation was stronger than God's anger, that the prophet's sympathy for the divine pathos went beyond the divine pathos. Divine forbearance and human indignation conflicted, and the prophet had to be told that God was concerned about the disciplining, not the destruction, of His adversaries; it was not the business of the prophet to recommend that the Lord punish, but that He test and purify (5:1, 4 f.; 6:9 f., 27 f.; 8:6).

In answer to Jeremiah's prayer, "Avenge me on my persecutors" (15:15), the Lord said to him:

If you return, I will restore you,
And you shall stand before Me.
If you utter what is precious, and not what is base,
You shall be as My mouth.

                              Jeremiah 15:19

Instead of a modicum of satisfaction or a hint of understanding for the dreadful burden he faithfully bore, instead of a new promise of protection, aid or solace, Jeremiah received a rebuke. The words he had dared to speak before the Lord were worthless; the state of mind he had exhibited was gently and implicitly condemned as apostasy. How often had he condemned the people and called upon them to repent and to return. Now he himself, the prophet, the servant, the watchman, was told by God to repent, to return.

The ambitendency of Jeremiah's invectives and maledictions characterized the prophet's mission from the start. His appointment, as we have seen, was

> *To pluck up and to break down,*
> *To destroy and to overthrow,*
> *To build and to plant.*
>
> *Jeremiah 1:10*

He offered both grief and rebirth, both doom and redemption.

> *If you return, O Israel, says the Lord,*
> *To Me you should return.*
> *If you remove your abominations from My presence,*
> *And do not waver;*
> *If you swear, As the Lord lives,*
> *In truth, in justice, and in uprightness,*
> *Then nations shall bless themselves in Him,*
> *And in Him shall they glory.*
>
> *Jeremiah 4:1-2*

Beyond all indignation and imprecations lay the certainty that Israel as God's creation would abide, Israel would exist.

> *Thus says the Lord,*
> *Who gives the sun for light by day*
> *And the fixed order of the moon*
> *And the stars for light by night,*
> *Who stirs up the sea so that its waves roar—*
> *The Lord of hosts in His name.*
> *If this fixed order departs*
> *From before Me, says the Lord,*
> *Then shall the descendants of Israel cease*
> *From being a nation before Me for ever....*
> *Thus says the Lord:*
> *Behold I will restore the fortunes of the tents of Jacob,*
> *And have compassion on his dwellings;*
> *The city shall be rebuilt upon its mound,*
> *And the palace shall stand where it used to be.*
>
> *Jeremiah 31:35-36; 30:18*

PROPHECY NOT THE ONLY INSTRUMENT

There was no sense of guilt, no feeling of shame. Judah said, "I am innocent." But the Lord proclaimed: "Behold, I will bring you to judgment for saying, I have not sinned" (2:35). "Were they ashamed when they committed abominations? No, they were not at all ashamed; they did not know how to blush" (6:15; 8:12). The Lord implored His people: "Only acknowledge your guilt, that you rebelled against the Lord your God" (3:13). And the prophet enjoined the people: "Let us lie down in our shame, and let our dishonor cover us, for we have sinned against the Lord our God, we and our fathers . . ." (3:25).

> I, the Lord, search the mind
> And try the heart,
> To give every man according to his ways,
> According to the fruit of his doings.
> Jeremiah 17:10; cf. 11:20; 20:12

Jeremiah knew that the malady was not primarily in the wickedness of the deeds, but in "the stubbornness of their evil hearts" (3:17; 7:24; 9:14 [H. 9:13]; 11:8; 13:10; 14:14; 16:12; 18:12; 23:17); in their "evil thoughts" (4:14), not only in their evil manners. "This people has a stubborn and rebellious heart" (6:23). They are circumcised in body but "uncircumcised in heart" (9:26). "Remove the foreskin of your hearts" (4:4). "Wash your heart from wickedness" (4:14). "Where is the word of the Lord? Let it come" (17:15), they said. "The word of God is to them an object of scorn. . . . To whom shall I speak and give warning, that they may hear?" (6:10.) In such despondency the prophet began to question the possibility of succeeding in his mission.

> Can the Ethiopian change his skin
> Or the leopard his spots?
> Then also you can do good
> Who are accustomed to do evil. . . .
> The heart is deceitful above all things.
> And desperately corrupt;
> Who can understand it?
> Jeremiah 13:23; 17:9

Man is unable to redeem himself, to cure the sickness of the heart. What hurts the soul, the soul adores. Can man be remade? A prophet can give man a new word, but not a new heart. It is God who must give man a heart to know that He is God (24:7).

Prophecy is not God's only instrument. What prophecy fails to bring about, the new covenant will accomplish: the complete transformation of every individual.

Behold, the days are coming, says the Lord, when I will make a new covenant with the house of Israel and the house of Judah, not like the covenant which I made with their fathers when I took them by the hand to bring them out of the land of Egypt, My covenant which they broke, though I was their husband, says the Lord. But this is the covenant which I will make with the house of Israel after those days, says the Lord: I will put My law within them, and I will write it upon their hearts; and I will be their God, and they shall be My people. And no longer shall each man teach his neighbor and each his brother, saying, Know the Lord, for they shall all know Me, from the least of them to the greatest, says the Lord; for I will forgive their iniquity, and I will remember their sin no more.

Jeremiah 31:31-34 [H. 31:30-33];
cf. Ezekiel 11:19 ff.; 36:26 f.

For many years Jeremiah had predicted pestilence, slaughter, famine, and captivity (15:2). However, when calamity arrived, in the hour of panic and terror, when every face was turned pale with dark despair, the prophet came to instill hope, to comfort, to console.[10]

It is a time of distress for Jacob;
Yet he shall be saved out of it. . . .
Then fear not, O Jacob My servant, says the Lord,
Nor be dismayed, O Israel;
For lo, I will save you from afar,
And your offspring from the land of captivity.
Jacob shall return and have quiet and ease,
And none shall make him afraid.
For I am with you to save you, says the Lord.

Jeremiah 30:7, 10-11

The rule of Babylon shall pass, but God's covenant with Israel shall last forever. The day will come when "the people of Israel and the people of Judah shall come together, weeping as they come, and they shall seek the Lord their God. They shall ask the way to Zion, with faces turned toward it, saying, Come, let us join ourselves to the Lord in an everlasting covenant which will never be forgotten" (50:4-5). Jerusalem will dwell secure under the watchword, "The Lord is our vindication" (33:16).

The climax of Jeremiah's prophecy is the promise of a covenant which will mean not only complete forgiveness of sin (33:8; 50:20), but also a complete

---

[10] I do not share the view advanced by Rudolph, *Jeremia*, p. 159, that chs. 30 and 31 date from the reign of King Josiah, and that the references to Judah (30:3-4, 8-9; 31:1, 23-30, 38-40) are insertions by a later editor.

transformation of Israel. In time to come God will give Israel "one heart and one way" and make with them "an everlasting covenant" (32:39-40), which will never be violated (50:40).

THE COLLAPSE OF ASSYRIA

During his last years Hezekiah had been completely under the influence of Isaiah. His death in 687/6 brought the twelve-year-old Manasseh to the beginning of his long reign (687/6-642 B.C.E.), during which the reforms that had been introduced by Hezekiah were abolished. All the high altars and shrines were restored. Manasseh remained a docile vassal of Nineveh, and even assisted Assyria's campaign against Egypt, which was conquered by the Assyrian army under Esarhaddon (681-669 B.C.E.) and Ashurbanipal (ca. 669-633 B.C.E.).

King Josiah (640-609 B.C.E.), who ascended the throne following the assassination of his father Amon (642-640 B.C.E.), made a total break with the policy of Manasseh. The rapid decline of Assyrian power and influence made it easier for those who abhorred Manasseh's idolatry. Young King Josiah inaugurated a reformation which marks an epoch in the religious history of Israel. He undertook, first of all, a consistent purge of foreign cults and practices. Various solar and astral cults, mostly of Mesopotamian origin and imported into Judah in the wake of Assyrian dominion, as well as native cults—some introduced by Manasseh (II Kings 21:1-9), some of very long standing—were removed and destroyed (II Kings 23:4 ff.). Josiah further took advantage of Assyria's weakness to free his people from political dependence upon her.

The year in which Jeremiah received his call to be a prophet was a turning point in history. Ashurbanipal died in 633(?), leaving the Assyrian empire in a state of weakness, ripe for dissolution. During his reign Nineveh had lost her grip on the provinces; Egypt, Judah, and other states in Palestine and Syria regained their independence. Ashurbanipal's brutality and punitive raids into the territory of his neighbors had increased the hatred for Assyria to a passion.[11] For ages, Assyria had plundered all the peoples within her range. Wherever her name was known it was execrated. Now her end was approaching. Nineveh, the exultant city that said to herself, "I am, and there is no one else," was about to become a desolation, a dry waste like the desert. "Everyone who passes by her hisses and shakes his fist" (Zeph. 2:15).

---

[11] *ANET*, pp. 291, 294.

Woe to the bloody city,
All full of lies and booty—
No end to the plunder! ...
Behold I am against you,
Says the Lord of hosts,
And will lift up your skirts over your face;
I will let nations look on your nakedness,
And kingdoms on your shame. ...
There is no assuaging your hurt,
Your wound is grievous.
All who hear the news of you
Clap their hands over you.
For upon whom has not come
Your unceasing evil?

Nahum 3:1, 5, 19;
cf. Ezekiel 31:3 ff.; 32:22 ff.

On the other hand, God's compassion for "Nineveh, that great city, in which there are more than a hundred and twenty thousand persons who do not know their right hand from their left, and also much cattle," is the theme of the book of Jonah (4:11).

The death of Ashurbanipal, who like his predecessors was also ruler of Babylon, was the signal for a new revolt by the Babylonians, long held in subjugation by Assyria, and anxious to regain the power and prestige they once possessed and to restore to their city the glory of former times. At once we find Nabopolassar (626-605 B.C.E.) king of Babylon. With the change of rulers from Ashurbanipal to Nabopolassar, the hegemony of Assyria came to an end, and the leadership among the Semitic peoples of Asia passed to the Chaldeans, or Babylonians.

With Babylonia firmly in his possession, Nabopolassar joined the Median tribes and their king Cyaxares (*ca.* 625-585 B.C.E.) in the final assault upon Assyria. In the year 612, Nineveh fell before the onslaught. Briefly and almost contemptuously Nabopolassar wrote the epitaph of the overthrown empire: "I slaughtered the land of Subarum, I turned the hostile land into heaps and ruins." "The Assyrian, who since distant days has ruled over the peoples and with his heavy yoke had brought injury to the people of the Land, their feet from Akkad I turned back, their yoke I threw off."[12] The Assyrian kingdom disappeared from history, and there was no longer an Assyrian people. The dreaded empire collapsed with surprising speed, only

---

[12] A. T. Olmstead, *History of Assyria* (New York, 1923), p. 640.

a short time after it had reached the zenith of her power. Her strength suddenly flagged, and she fell prey to her enemies.

The Babylonians had emerged as a major power, and Josiah seems to have supported them in their plans to destroy the might of Assyria. Egypt, on the other hand, which two generations earlier had been the last great target of Assyrian aggression, was Assyria's sole ally in her death agony. Apprehensive of the growing might of new Babylonia, Egypt had been intermittently supporting Assyria against the Babylonians and their allies. At the same time, she began to nurture the hope of regaining possession of Palestine and Syria, which had once belonged to Egypt. So, at the outset of his reign, the Pharaoh Neco II (609-593 B.C.E.) marched into Palestine. While other local kings now almost independent were too dispirited to offer battle, Josiah, who by this time was practically independent and had no desire to come under the control of Assyria, tried to stop the Egyptians. The clash occurred in the year 609, near Megiddo, and ended in tragedy for Judah. Josiah was slain, and his army returned to Jerusalem, where his son Jehoahaz was proclaimed king. Neco, who now considered himself overlord of Judah, deposed the new king and deported him to Egypt. Jehoahaz' brother Johoiakim was placed on the throne as an Egyptian vassal, and the land was laid under heavy tribute. Judah's independence was ended. Neco was master of the erstwhile Assyrian provinces as far as the Euphrates.

As said above, the call to be a prophet came to Jeremiah during the reign of Josiah, in the year 625, but we do not know with any degree of certainty of public activity on the part of Jeremiah during Josiah's reign. He clashed with public authorities during the reign of Johoiakim (609-598 B.C.E.) when he delivered his message first in Topheth and then in the Temple court in Jerusalem. Pashur, the Temple officer struck him publicly and put him in prison (19:14—20:3). Another such prophecy spoken in the Temple court announcing the destruction of the Temple as well as of the city of Jerusalem, enraged the priests, the false prophets, and the people. Jeremiah was put on trial and threatened with the penalty of death, but was saved by some officers.

The rise of Nebuchadnezzar (605/4-562 B.C.E.) brought the activity of Jeremiah to a climax. He was charged to write down in the form of a scroll all his prophecies since the days of Josiah (36:1 f.), the gist of which was the message: "The king of Babylon will certainly come and destroy this land" (36:29). Copied by his secretary, Baruch, these prophecies were read to the people by Baruch in the court of the Temple. The people were deeply moved by the prophet's message, and when the story of this episode reached the court, king and princes asked to hear it.

King Jehoiakim was a petty tyrant who shed much blood in Jerusalem (II Kings 24:4). Knowing the terrible temper of the king, who had already put one prophet to death (Jer. 26:23), the princes advised both Jeremiah and Baruch to hide. The king, to whom the prophecies were read, did not hesitate to cast into the fire Jeremiah's scroll, section by section. He ordered Jeremiah imprisoned, but the prophet could not be found (ch. 36). However, after some time he came out of hiding and resumed his public activity.

There could hardly be a greater incompatibility than that between Jeremiah and King Jehoiakim, whose chief interest was to enlarge his palace, apparently using forced labor to do so.

> Woe to him who builds his house by unrighteousness,
> And his upper rooms by injustice;
> Who makes his neighbor serve him for nothing,
> And does not give him his wages;
> Who says, I will build myself a great house
> With spacious upper rooms,
> And cuts out windows for it,
> Paneling it with cedar,
> And painting it with vermilion.
> Do you think you are a king
> Because you compete in cedar?
> Did not your father eat and drink
> And do justice and righteousness?
> Then it was well with him.
> He judged the cause of the poor and needy;
> Then it was well.
> Is not this to know Me?
> Says the Lord.
> But you have eyes and heart
> Only for your dishonest gain,
> For shedding innocent blood,
> And for practicing oppression and violence.
> Therefore thus says the Lord
> Concerning Jehoiakim the son of Josiah, king of Judah:
> They shall not lament for him, saying,
> Ah, my brother! or, Ah sister!
> They shall not lament for him, saying,
> Ah, lord! or, Ah his majesty!
> With the burial of an ass he shall be buried,
> Dragged and cast forth beyond the gates of Jerusalem.
>
> Jeremiah 22:13-19

THE EMERGENCE OF THE BABYLONIAN EMPIRE

In 605, a change in the balance of power placed Judah in a new danger. The Egyptian Neco, determined to extend his dominion beyond the Euphrates into the northern part of Mesopotamia, put in the field an immense army and reached Carchemish, on the Euphrates, without opposition. Nebuchadnezzar, the son of Nabopolassar, gave battle, and won a crushing victory. Neco was undone and his army fled in confusion, pursued by Nebuchadnezzar; the latter might have overrun Egypt had he not been apprised of his father's sudden death, which compelled him to return to Babylon. A new Babylonian empire came into being, and for many years it was to dominate the Near East.

Judah was thrown into consternation by this turn of events (Jer. 46). Jehoiakim transferred his allegiance to Nebuchadnezzar and became his vassal (II Kings 24:1).

Quietly, however, Jehoiakim seems to have been convinced that the security of Judah was tied to the destiny of Egypt. He was therefore determined to throw off the Babylonian yoke. Many leading citizens apparently supported his policy. The only clear voice raised against such a fatal venture was that of Jeremiah who, like Isaiah in a similar crisis, warned the nation against such suicidal folly. Nebuchadnezzar, he proclaimed, had been designated by the Lord to carry out His will; Judah as well as many other lands would be in his hand (25:15 f.; 27:6). It was futile to resist him, and those who relied on Egypt would be put to shame as were those who had once relied on Assyria (2:36 f.).

> Thus says the Lord of hosts:
> Behold, evil is going forth
> From nation to nation,
> And a great tempest is stirring
> From the farthest parts of the earth! ...
> Wail, you shepherds, and cry,
> And roll in ashes, you lords of the flock,
> For the days of your slaughter and dispersion have come,
> And you shall fall like choice rams.
> No refuge will remain for the shepherds,
> Nor escape for the lords of the flock.
> Hark, the cry of the shepherds,
> And the wail of the lords of the flock!
> For the Lord is despoiling their pasture,
> And the peaceful folds are devastated,
> Because of the fierce anger of the Lord.
> Like a lion He has left His covert,

For their land has become a waste
Because of the sword of the Lord,
And because of His fierce anger.
Jeremiah 25:32, 34-38

At last the king omitted the payment of the tribute, and the issue was joined. Nebuchadnezzar, though occupied elsewhere, had no intention of tolerating such an act. Pending the time when he could act in person, he encouraged marauding nomadic hordes, friendly to the Babylonians, to ravage the land of Judah (II Kings 24:2; Jer. 35:11). Subsequently, in 597, he arrived in person at the head of an army to besiege Jerusalem. Before the Babylonian army laid seige to the capital, King Jehoiakim died, and his son, the new king Jehoiachin, a lad of eighteen years, realizing the hopelessness of the situation, decided to surrender before an assault should be undertaken. With his mother and the entire court he was carried into captivity, followed by seven thousand men capable of carrying arms and one thousand workers in iron, together with their families, and an enormous booty. A boy of twenty-one named Zedekiah was made king of Judah.

The eleven years (597-587 B.C.E.) of Zedekiah's reign were notable for a steady decline in Judah's power and for the desperate efforts of Jeremiah to avert the coming disaster. A ruler of good intentions, not entirely unresponsive to warnings of the prophet, whom he consulted on occasion on matters of state (37:3-10, 16-21; 38:14-28), Zedekiah felt himself helpless among his headstrong officials, and he was under their domination (38:5).

Meanwhile, the cherished holy vessels, the king Jehoiachin, and the upper class of Judean leaders were being kept in Babylonian exile. The king was a servant of Nebuchadnezzar. Patriots in Judah as well as in the neighboring kingdoms subject to Babylonian domination were clamoring for revolt, encouraged by diviners, soothsayers, and false prophets who announced that exile and the rule of Babylon would soon end. Egypt, to the south, continued to stir up revolt among the small states against the yoke of the Babylonians, and high officials in Jerusalem were ready to play the dangerous game, as had Hezekiah a century earlier. Emissaries from five kingdoms in the area came to Jerusalem to organize the rebellion. At that moment, Jeremiah, at the command of God, resorted to a strange and bold act. He harnessed a wooden yoke to his neck with thongs and bars, just as would be done to an ox when plowing or threshing, and thus the prophet appeared before the foreign statesmen proclaiming the word of God:

Thus says the Lord of hosts, the God of Israel: This is what you shall say
to your masters: It is I Who by My great power and My outstretched arm
have made the earth, with the men and animals that are on the earth, and I

*give it to whomever it seems right to Me. Now I have given all these lands
into the hand of Nebuchadnezzar, the king of Babylon, my servant, and I
have given him also the beasts of the field to serve him. All the nations shall
serve him and his son and his grandson, until the time of his own land
comes; then many nations and great kings shall make him their slave.*

*But if any nation or kingdom will not serve this Nebuchadnezzar king of
Babylon, and put its neck under the yoke of the king of Babylon, I will punish that nation with the sword, with famine, and with pestilence, says the
Lord, until I have consumed it by his hand. So do not listen to your prophets, your diviners, your dreamers, your soothsayers, or your sorcerers, who are
saying to you, You shall not serve the king of Babylon. For it is a lie which
they are prophesying to you, with the result that you will be removed far
from your land, and I will drive you out, and you will perish. But any nation
which will bring its neck under the yoke of the king of Babylon and serve
him, I will leave on its own land, to till it and dwell there, says the Lord.*

Jeremiah 27:4-11

Jeremiah repeated the same stern warning to King Zedekiah as well as to
the priests who were influenced by the prediction of the false prophets:
"Bring your necks under the yoke of the king of Babylon, serve him and
his people, and you will live" (27:12). The acceptance of Babylonian overlordship, unlike the submission to Assyria which Isaiah had called upon the
people to reject, did not involve the danger of complete expulsion and
national extinction.

THE FALL OF JERUSALEM

In spite of historical experience, forced upon the people for close to one
hundred and fifty years, many voices were raised in favor of rebellion against
Babylon (28:1 ff.). In vain did Jeremiah plead for obedience to Nebuchadnezzar as the one into whose hands the Lord had transferred world rule
(37:11 ff.).

Disregarding Jeremiah's warnings, Zedekiah yielded at the end to his
leading officials and to the clamor of the people to take the insane step of
renouncing his allegiance to Nebuchadnezzar, and sent ambassadors to
Egypt seeking military protection against the Babylonians. Nebuchadnezzar
had made a treaty (*berith*) with Zedekiah, which Zedekiah confirmed with
an imprecatory oath; now, Zedekiah broke the treaty and his oath (Ezek.
17:13-21; II Chron. 36:13). Nebuchadnezzar's reaction was swift. Early in
588 (or 589) his army arrived, placing Jerusalem under blockade and
occupying the rest of the country.

While the Babylonian army was fighting Jerusalem, Jeremiah confronted
the king, and declaring it to be the will of God that Jerusalem should fall to
the Babylonians, demanded surrender to Babylonia (34:1-5; 21:3-7). Such a

demand must have outraged both the devout and the zealots of Jerusalem. To surrender the holy city to a pagan conqueror! Jeremiah's advice was resented. Courageously the people continued to hold out, believing that just as God had delivered Jerusalem from Sennacherib, He would deliver it from Nebuchadnezzar.

Jeremiah's demand to surrender to Nebuchadnezzar was not primarily a plea to accept the foreign yoke as punishment for sins, but rather a call for understanding God's design to turn over the dominion of the entire area to the Babylonian empire, which was to last seventy years (24:7 ff.; 29:10 ff.) . Even during his confinement in the court of the guard, while Jerusalem was besieged and doomed to be captured, Jeremiah proclaimed,

Thus says the Lord: In this place of which you say, it is a waste without man or beast, in the cities of Judah and the streets of Jerusalem that are desolate, without man or inhabitant or beast, there shall be heard again the voice of mirth and the voice of gladness, the voice of the bridegroom and the voice of the bride, the voices of those who sing, as they bring thank offerings to the house of the Lord;

> *Give thanks to the Lord of hosts,*
> *For the Lord is good,*
> *For his steadfast love endures for ever!*

For I will restore the fortunes of the land as at first, says the Lord.

Jeremiah 33:10-11[13]

Meanwhile an Egyptian army arrived from the southwest which forced the Babylonians to suspend the siege of Jerusalem for a time (37:5; 34:21) . But Jeremiah persisted in predicting defeat, publicly discouraging the people from fighting, disparaging the effectiveness of Egyptian help, even advocating that the people and the army desert to the Babylonians.

Taking advantage of the temporary lifting of the siege, Jeremiah desired to go to his native town on a personal matter; he was arrested at the gate of Jerusalem and, accused of deserting to the Babylonians, was thrown into a dungeon cell (37:11-16) . It was at the intervention of the king that he was transferred to the court of the guard and supplied with ample rations (37:17-21) . There the prophet continued to express his seditious opinions: resistance to the Babylonians was futile, and dying was wrong. In the name of the Lord he appealed to individuals to leave the city and to surrender (21:8-10) . The king's officers threw him into an empty cistern. It was an Ethiopian eunuch, Ebed-melech, who, with the king's permission, saved him from death by starvation (chs. 37—38) . Jeremiah remained in the lighter

---

[13] Compare Y. Kaufmann, *The Religion of Israel* (Eng.; Chicago, 1960) , pp. 422 f.

captivity of the court prison until he was liberated at the capture of Jerusalem by the Babylonians.

Meanwhile the Egyptian relief force was defeated and the siege of Jerusalem resumed. Zedekiah, whose only hope now was for a miracle from God, sent a delegation to Jeremiah, saying: "Pray for us. Perhaps the Lord will make the Babylonian king withdraw from us." But the prophet's answer was stern: Your resistance will get weaker. God Himself will fight against you "with outstretched hand and strong arm, in anger, in fury, and in great wrath." The city will be captured; some of the people shall die of pestilence, the rest will be carried away in captivity (see 21:44).

Jerusalem held out for one and one-half years, until famine decided the issue. In 587 the city fell. The holy city was plundered and burned by the conquerors: the Temple of Solomon went up in flames. The prophet who had served as a voice castigating the people was now, in sorrow, the voice of the people.

> *Woe is me because of my hurt!*
> *My wound is grievous.*
> *But I said: Truly this is an affliction,*
> *And I must bear it.*
> *My tent is destroyed,*
> *All my cords are broken;*
> *My children have gone from me,*
> *They are not;*
> *There is no one to spread my tent again,*
> *To set up my curtains.*
> *Jeremiah 10:19-20*

To us today, Zedekiah's rebellion against Nebuchadnezzar appears as a gross miscalculation of the political circumstances. Judah's defiance against a power that crushed Assyria was as foolhardy as her reliance on Egypt was self-deceptive. The new empire did not threaten Judah's existence and seems to have been satisfied with acknowledgment of its overlordship and the payment of tribute. Judah could have survived under Babylonian overlordship even more easily than it did under Assyrian or Egyptian tutelage.

Yet, it is not political sagacity that explains Jeremiah's opposition to the stand taken by the rulers of the kingdom, implying a reversal of the position taken by Isaiah when he had insisted that Judah should not capitulate to Assyria. The prophet does not see the world from the point of view of a political theory; he is a person who sees the world from the point of view of God; he sees the world through the eyes of God. To Jeremiah, the relationship to Nebuchadnezzar was much less important than the relationship to God.

Jeremiah was constantly exposed to the situation of God, and tirelessly attentive to the mood of the people, offering boldly the call, the challenge, and the warning, attempting to unravel the knots in the relationship between God and Israel.

He has seen like no other prophet "affliction under the rod of His wrath," but he was also imbued with the certainty of God's attachment, which surpasses His wrath. ". . . as I have watched over them to pluck up and break down, to overthrow, destroy, and bring evil, so I will watch over them to build and to plant, says the Lord" (31:28; see 1:10). "Behold, the days are coming, says the Lord, when I will raise up for David a righteous branch, and he shall reign as king and deal wisely, and shall execute justice and righteousness in the land. In his days Judah will be saved, and Israel will dwell securely. And this is the name by which He will be called: 'The Lord is our righteousness' " (23:5-6).

> *Their children shall be as they were of old,*
> *Their congregation shall be established before Me;*
> *I will punish all who oppress them.*
>
> > *Jeremiah 30:20*

> *They shall come and sing aloud on the height of Zion,*
> *They shall be radiant over the goodness of the Lord . . .*
>
> > *Jeremiah 31:12*

Nebuchadnezzar's soldiers burned the temple, the king's palace, the larger houses of Jerusalem. The walls were razed, most of the inhabitants were deported.

The Jerusalem man is busy destroying, God is erecting.

7. HABAKKUK

The life of Habakkuk is unknown to us. Presumably the prophet was a native of Judah who prophesied during the reign of Jehoiakim (609-598 B.C.E.), at the time of the triumphs of Nebuchadnezzar.

The world of Habakkuk is known to us through the little book that bears his name. What is that world like? It is a place in which "justice never goes forth" (1:4) except in perverted form.

> O Lord, how long shall I cry for help,
> And Thou wilt not hear?
> Or cry to Thee, Violence!
> And Thou wilt not save?
> Why dost Thou make me see wrongs
> And look upon trouble?
> Destruction and violence are before me;
> Strife and contention arise.
> So the law is slacked
> And justice never goes forth.
> For the wicked surround the righteous,
> So justice goes forth perverted.
>
> *Habakkuk 1:2-4*

A startled, tormented man is Habakkuk. He is distressed at the fact that violence prevails and agonized by the thought that God tolerates evil. He prays, "How long?" He cries, "Why?"

His prayer and his cry do not remain unanswered. However, the response given to him is not the comfort of an explanation. The Voice that comes to him says,

> Look . . . see,
> Wonder and be astounded.
> For I am doing a work in your days

SELECTED BIBLIOGRAPHY: Stonehouse, *The Book of Habakkuk* (London, 1911); G. A. Smith, *The Book of the Twelve Prophets* (New York, 1929), pp. 117-160.

> *That you would not believe if told.*
> *For lo, I am rousing the Chaldeans,*
> *That bitter and hasty nation,*
> *Who march through the breadth of the earth,*
> *To seize habitations not their own.*
> *Dread and terrible are they;*
> *Their justice and dignity proceed from themselves.*
> *Their horses are swifter than leopards,*
> *More fierce than the evening wolves;*
> *Their horsemen press proudly on,*
> *Yea, their horsemen come from afar;*
> *They fly like an eagle swift to devour.*
> *They all come for violence;*
> *Terror of them goes before them.*
> *They gather captives like sand.*
> *At kings they scoff,*
> *And of rulers they make sport.*
> *They laugh at every fortress,*
> *For they heap up earth and take it.*
> *Then they sweep by like the wind and go on,*
> *Guilty men, whose own might is their god!*
> *Habakkuk 1:5-11 [H. 1:6-11]*

The Voice does not explain why God should rouse the terrible Chaldeans to march through the breadth of the earth. On the contrary, the message represents another assault upon Habakkuk's understanding, adding mystery to amazement. While God's design is veiled in an enigma, it is the prophet who volunteers an explanation. The nations are guilty; punishment must follow the guilt. The Chaldeans are the instrument of God's justice.

> *O Lord, Thou hast ordained them as a judgment;*
> *And Thou, O Rock, hast established them for chastisement.*
> *Habakkuk 1:12*

Comforting as the thought is that crime does not go unpunished, it is a thought that gives rise to grave and bitter questions. Is this the way to let justice prevail? Should "guilty men, whose own might is their god" be the instrument to carry out the will of God? Is this the way of justice: that innocent men should perish so that the wicked may be punished?

> *Thou who art of purer eyes than to behold evil*
> *And canst not look on wrong,*
> *Why dost Thou look on faithless men,*
> *And art silent when the wicked swallows up*
> *The man more righteous than he?*
> *Habakkuk 1:13*

Justice is meaningless to the great powers of the world. Merciless are they, and absolutely worthless is man in their eyes. God, Who so loves man that He does not tire of uttering through the prophets His outrage at the wrongs done unto man, is now accused by Habakkuk of being responsible for the vitiation of man.

> For Thou makest men like the fish of the sea,
> Like crawling things that have no ruler.
> Habakkuk 1:14

The ruthless king

> . . . brings all of them up with a book; . . .
> He gathers them in his seine;
> So he rejoices and exults.
> Habakkuk 1:15

Net and seine are his gods; to them he sacrifices and brings incense, "for by them he lives in luxury, and his food is rich."

> His greed is as wide as Sheol;
> Like death he has never enough.
> He gathers for himself all nations,
> And collects as his own all peoples. . . .
> Is he then to keep on emptying his net,
> And mercilessly slaying nations for ever?
> Habakkuk 2:5; 1:17

There is darkness in the world and anguish in the heart. Should one abandon God and burn incense to net and seine? Should one abandon mercy?

In his anguish Habakkuk decides to wait for another encounter with God.

> I will take my stand to watch
> And station myself on the tower,
> And look forth to see what He will say to me,
> And what I will answer concerning my complaint.
> Habakkuk 2:1

Two things he wishes to know: God's word and his own answer, for the first is meaningless without the second. This is the insight Habakkuk receives:

> Write the vision;
> Make it plain upon tablets,
> So he may run who reads it.
> For still the vision awaits its time;
> It hastens to the end—it will not lie.
> If it seem slow, wait for it.
> It will surely come, it will not delay.

Behold, he whose soul is puffed up in him shall fail,
But the righteous shall live by his faith.

Habakkuk 2:2-4

Habakkuk's vision remains unknown to us. Its content is not put into words. It clearly was a vision of redemption at the end of days. There is an answer to Habakkuk's question. It is an answer, not in terms of thought, but in terms of events. God's answer will happen, but it cannot be spelled out in words. The answer will surely come; "if it seem slow, wait for it." True, the interim is hard to bear; the righteous one is horrified by what he sees. To this the great answer is given: "The righteous shall live by his faith." It is an answer, again not in terms of thought, but in terms of existence. Prophetic faith is trust in Him, in Whose presence stillness is a form of understanding.

The Lord is in His holy temple;
Let all the earth keep silence before Him!

Habakkuk 2:20

The book of Habakkuk concludes with a vision and a prayer. The prophet sees the future in the perfect tense and employs figures of nature as symbols of history. The great theophany has come: the Lord is arriving upon a chariot of victory. His glory covers the heavens, and the earth is full of His praise. But His appearance is dreadful. Before Him goes pestilence, and close behind follows plague. He bestrides the earth in indignation, trampling the nations in anger. He comes forth for the salvation of His people, of His anointed, to crush "the head from the house of the wicked" who rejoice in devouring the poor in secret. Dismay clutches at the prophet:

I hear, and my body trembles,
My lips quiver at the sound;
Rottenness enters into my bones,
I tremble where I stand.
I will quietly wait for the day of trouble
To come upon people who invade us.

Habakkuk 3:16

Habakkuk realizes and accepts the mystery of divine anger. He knows it is an instrument necessary for redemption. Humbly he prays: "In anger remember mercy" (3:2).

The prophet trembles, but he also has the power to wait on the Lord. However, the depth of his experience lies deeper than trust and faith. What the prophet faces is not his own faith. He faces God. To sense the living God is to sense infinite goodness, infinite wisdom, infinite beauty. Such a sensation is a sensation of joy. The world may be dismal; the wrath may turn the gardens into a desert; yet the prophet "will rejoice in the Lord." This, it seems, is Habakkuk's personal answer to the vision:

> *Though the fig tree do not blossom,*
> *Nor fruit be on the vines,*
> *The produce of the olive fail*
> *And the fields yield no food,*
> *The flock be cut off from the fold*
> *And there be no herd in the stalls,*
> *Yet I will rejoice in the Lord*
> *I will joy in the God of my salvation.*
>
> *Habakkuk 3:17-18*

8. SECOND ISAIAH

ON THE EVE OF REDEMPTION

The Neo-Babylonian empire did not last long. It declined rapidly after the death of Nebuchadnezzar in the year 562 B.C.E. Cyrus, the Persian king of the little principality of Elam, succeeded in overpowering the two powers that had divided the Near Eastern world at the fall of Assyria. He defeated the king of the Median empire in 550 and the king of Babylonia in 539. Cyrus was now the head of the great Persian empire, and his power extended as far as the western coast of Asia Minor.

It was in this exciting period that a prophet arose who lifted the meaning of these events from the level of political history to the level of understanding world history as a drama of redemption. He proclaimed that the Lord was about to redeem His people, that Babylon would fall, and that Cyrus, who had been called and empowered by the Lord to carry out His will in history (41:5-7; 44:28; 45:1 f.), was destined to play an important part in the return of Israel to Zion and in the restoration of Jerusalem. The majestic words of this prophet, whose name is unknown, are found in the later chapters of the book of Isaiah (chs. 40—66). The message of Second Isaiah, as he is conventionally called, is of no age. It is prophecy tempered with human tears, mixed with a joy that heals all scars, clearing a way for understanding the future in spite of the present. No words have ever gone further in offering comfort when the sick world cries.

MY RIGHT IS DISREGARDED BY GOD

The Lord had carried out His threat and punished without pity (Lam. 2:17). But what had His punishment accomplished? Devastation, famine,

SELECTED BIBLIOGRAPHY: J. Muilenburg, "Introduction and Exegesis to Isaiah, chs. 40-66," in G. A. Buttrick, ed., *The Interpreter's Bible*, V (Nashville, 1956), 381-773; M. Buber, *The Prophetic Faith* (New York, 1949); Y. Kaufmann, *The Religion of Israel*, IV (Heb.; Jerusalem, 1956), 51-156; C. C. Torrey, *The Second Isaiah* (New York, 1928); E. J. Kissane, *The Book of Isaiah*, vol. II (Dublin, 1943).

death, and distress; Jerusalem was destroyed, Israel in exile, and her sons
were "like an antelope in a net" (51:20). The tormentors had said to Israel:
"Bow down, that we may pass over," and she made her "back like the ground
and like the street for them to pass over" (51:23). The exiles lived in con-
tinual fear "because of the fury of the oppressor when he sets himself to
destroy" (51:13). Yet, even in distress, with the Temple destroyed, Jerusalem in ruins, and liberty lost, Israel remained faithful to her God. "The
Lord is in the right, for I have rebelled against His word" (Lam. 1:18).
"Is it not from the mouth of the Most High that good and evil come?"
(Lam. 3:38). Why should a man complain about the punishment of his
sins?

The suffering servant "opened not his mouth, like a lamb that is led to the
slaughter" (53:7). Yet, Second Isaiah does not passively accept Zion's lot.
Far from being silent, he challenges the Lord, putting the Lord in
remembrance.

> For Zion's sake I will not keep silent,
> And for Jerusalem's sake I will not rest,
> Until her triumph goes forth as brightness,
> And her rescue as a burning torch. . . .
> Upon your walls, O Jerusalem,
> I have set watchmen;
> All the day and all the night
> They shall never be silent.
> You who put the Lord in remembrance,
> Take no rest. . . .
> Awake, awake, put on strength,
> O arm of the Lord.
>
>   Isaiah 62:1, 6-7; 51:9

The prophet voices his bewilderment at the silence of the Almighty.

> O Lord, Thou art our Father;
> We are the clay, and Thou art our potter;
> We are all the work of Thy hand.
> Be not exceedingly angry, O Lord,
> And remember not iniquity for ever.
> Behold, consider, we are all Thy people.
> Thy holy cities have become a wilderness,
> Zion has become a wilderness,
> Jerusalem a desolation.
> Our holy and beautiful house,
> Where our fathers praised Thee,
> Has been burned by fire,
> All our pleasant places have become ruins.

Wilt Thou restrain Thyself at these things, O Lord?
Wilt Thou keep silent, and afflict us to the utmost? . . .
Look down from heaven and see,
From Thy holy and glorious habitation.
Where are Thy zeal and Thy might?
The yearning of Thy heart and Thy compassion
Are withheld from me.

> *Isaiah 64:8-12 [H. 64:7-11]; 63:15*

More excruciating than the experience of suffering is the agony of sensing no meaning in suffering, the inability to say, "Thy rod and Thy staff, they comfort me." Can He Who "has destroyed without mercy all the habitations of Jacob," Who "has become like an enemy" (Lam. 2:2, 5), still be trusted as the God Who is our Father?

Zion said: The Lord has forsaken me,
My Lord has forgotten me. . . .
I have labored in vain,
I have spent my strength for nothing and vanity. . . .
My way is hid from the Lord,
My right is disregarded by my God.

> *Isaiah 49:14, 4; 40:27*

Israel's misery seemed out of all proportion to her guilt, and its justice belied by other facts of history.

Was this to be hailed as justice: agony for Israel and glory for Babylon? The beloved of God bruised and despised while the "mistress of kingdoms" (47:5) "felt secure in . . . wickedness" (47:10) ? Was it not obvious that God did not care? Or was it beyond His power to save those for whom He cared? (See 59:1.)

To comfort is to throw a glimmer of meaning into a cave of wretchedness. Jerusalem—"she has none to comfort her" (Lam. 1:2, 9, 16, 17, 21) . Who will condole with you? How may I comfort you? (51:19) Why was Israel driven into exile? Why did Israel continue to be in exile?

WHO TAUGHT HIM THE PATH OF JUSTICE?

In an atmosphere of bewilderment, confusion, and despondency, and speaking to

A people robbed and plundered, . . .
All of them trapped in holes
And hidden in prisons . .

> *Isaiah 42:22*

the prophet first accepts the burden of the mystery of divine wisdom before
attempting to illumine His ways.

> For My thoughts are not your thoughts,
> Neither are your ways My ways, says the Lord.
> For as the heaven is higher than the earth,
> So are My ways higher than your ways
> And My thoughts than your thoughts.
>
> Isaiah 55:8-9

Living in the certainty of a divine wisdom which defies human understanding, those who question Him expect the Lord to adjust His thought to
their thoughts, His design to their conceptions. The prophet maintains that
those who question Him try to enlighten Him; that those who contend with
Him presume to instruct Him in "the path of justice," "the way of understanding." The overwhelming grandeur of His wisdom as manifested in the
realm of nature should inspire humility when reflecting about His ways in
the realm of history.

> Who has measured the waters in the hollow of his hand,
> Marked off the heavens with a span,
> Enclosed the dust of the earth in a measure,
> Weighed the mountains in scales
> And the hills in a balance?
> Who has directed the Spirit of the Lord,
> Or as His counselor has instructed Him?
> Whom did He consult for His enlightenment,
> Who taught Him the path of justice,
> Who taught Him knowledge,
> Who showed Him the way of understanding? . . .
> Woe to him who strives with his Maker,
> An earthen vessel with the potters!
> Does the clay say to him who fashions it, What are you making?
> Or, Your work has no handles?
> Woe to him who says to a father, What are you begetting?
> Or, to a woman, With what are you in travail? . . .
> Will you command Me concerning the work of My hands?
>
> Isaiah 40:12-14; 45:9-11[1]

THE SUFFERING SERVANT

God's thoughts are higher than human thoughts. Yet just as God may
share the sufferings of man, so man may share the thoughts of God.

Amos had proclaimed:

---

[1] According to Rashi, in his *Commentary*, this passage contains an answer to the problem
of why the Lord lets the wicked prosper and Israel suffer.

> *You only have I known*
> *Of all the families of the earth;*
> *Therefore I will punish you*
> *For all your iniquities.*
>
> > *Amos 3:2*

Second Isaiah would phrase the last words to read: "For all their iniquities."
What Israel endured was not simply chastisement for her sins; her agony far
exceeded her guilt. Indeed,

> *She has received from the Lord's hand*
> *Double for all her sins.*
>
> > *Isaiah 40:2*

She is the suffering servant of the Lord.[2]

As a rule we reflect on the problem of suffering in relation to him who
suffers. The prophet's message insists that suffering is not to be understood
exclusively in terms of the sufferer's own situation. In Israel's agony, all
nations are involved. Israel's suffering is not a penalty, but a privilege, a
sacrifice; its endurance is a ritual, its meaning is to be disclosed to all men
in the hour of Israel's redemption.

Deliverance, redemption, is what the Lord has in store for Israel, and
through Israel for all men. Her suffering and agony are the birth-pangs of
salvation which, the prophet proclaims, is about to unfold. In answer to the
prophet's fervent invocation (51:9), the Lord is about to bare His arm or
His might before the eyes of all the nations. (Cf. 52:10 with 53:1.)

> *How beautiful upon the mountains*
> *Are the feet of him who brings good tidings,*
> *Who publishes peace, who brings good tidings of good,*
> *Who publishes salvation,*
> *Who says to Zion, Your God reigns.*
> *Hark, your watchmen lift up their voice,*

---

[2] The outstanding songs of the servant of the Lord are 42:1-4; 49:1-6; 50:4-9; 52:13–53:12.
Perhaps no other problem in the Hebrew Bible has occupied the minds of scholars more
than the identification and interpretation of the servant. For a survey of the vast literature,
see C. R. North, *The Suffering Servant in Deutero-Isaiah* (Oxford, 1956). In the main, four
theories have been proposed. The servant is (1) an anonymous contemporary of Second
Isaiah; (2) Second Isaiah himself; (3) Israel; (4) a purely ideal or imaginary figure. To
quote J. Muilenburg, in *The Interpreter's Bible*, V, 408, 411, "The servant is certainly
Israel. . . . Israel, and Israel alone, is able to bear all that is said about the servant of the
Lord. For the fundamental fact outweighing all others is the repeated equation of the two
in the poems." See 41:8 ff.; 43:8-13; 44:1-2, 21; 45:4; 49:3. According to H. H. Rowley, *The
Faith of Israel* (London, 1956), p. 122, "The servant is at once Israel and an individual, who
both represents the whole community and carries to its supreme point the mission of the
nation, while calling the whole people to enter into that mission, so that it shall be its mission and not merely his. . . . The servant is Israel today and tomorrow; but Israel may be
all or a few or one of its members."

Together they sing for joy;
For eye to eye they see
The return of the Lord to Zion.
Break forth together into singing,
You waste places of Jerusalem;
For the Lord has comforted His people,
He has redeemed Jerusalem. . . .
Behold, My servant shall prosper,
He shall be exalted and lifted up,
And shall be very high.
As many were astonished at him—
His appearance was so marred, beyond human semblance,
And his form beyond that of the sons of men—
So shall he startle many nations;
Kings shall shut their mouths because of him;
For that which has not been told them they shall see,
And that which they have not heard they shall understand.
Who has believed what we have heard?
And to whom has the arm of the Lord been revealed?
For he grew up before Him like a young plant,
And like a root out of dry ground;
He had no form or comeliness that we should look at him,
And no beauty that we should desire him.
He was despised and rejected by men;
A man of sorrows, and acquainted with grief;
And as one from whom men hide their faces
He was despised, and we esteemed him not.
Surely he has borne our griefs
And carried our sorrows;
Yet we esteemed him stricken,
Smitten by God, and afflicted.
But he was wounded for our transgressions,
He was bruised for our iniquities;
Upon him was the chastisement that made us whole,
And with his stripes we are healed. . . .
And like a sheep that before its shearers is dumb,
So he opened not his mouth. . . .
By his knowledge shall the righteous one, My servant,
Make many to be accounted righteous;
And he shall bear their iniquities.
Therefore I will divide him a portion with the great,
And he shall divide the spoil with the strong;
Because he poured out his soul to death,
And was numbered with the transgressors;
Yet he bore the sin of many,
And made intercession for the transgressors.

Isaiah 52:7-9, 13—53:5, 7, 11-12

Suffering as chastisement is man's own responsibility; suffering as redemption is God's responsibility. It was He Who had chosen Israel as His servant; it was He Who had placed upon Israel the task of suffering for others. The meaning of her agony was shifted from the sphere of man to the sphere of God, from the moment to eternity.

IN ALL THEIR AFFLICTION, HE WAS AFFLICTED

Israel's suffering is God's grief. In reflecting on what this people has endured, His words sound like pangs of remorse.

> *I was angry with My people,*
> *I profaned My heritage.*
> > *Isaiah 47:6*

Not all the evils that befell Israel go back to the will of God. The Babylonians, who in His providence became the leading power in the world and into whose hand He handed over His people, "showed them no mercy"; on the aged they made their yoke "exceedingly heavy." While Israel suffered, the Lord restrained Himself. But the time of His restraint and silence is over. He can wait no longer for the display of His might and mercy.

> *For a long time I have kept silent,*
> *I have kept still and restrained Myself;*
> *Now I will cry out like a woman in travail,*
> *I will gasp and pant.*
> > *Isaiah 42:14*

The allusion to the Lord as "a woman in travail," the boldest figure used by any prophet, conveys not only the sense of supreme urgency of His action, but also a sense of the deep intensity of His suffering. Of the person who cleaves to Him in love, the Lord says:

> *When he calls to Me, I will answer him;*
> *I will be with him in affliction.*
> > *Psalm 91:15*

Of God's involvement in human suffering the prophet declares courageously:

> *In all their affliction He was afflicted . . .*
> *In His love and in His pity He redeemed them,*
> *He lifted them up and carried them all the days of old.*
> > *Isaiah 63:9*

It is God's involvement in the suffering of man (see pp. 109 ff.) that explains this particular concern for the downtrodden and contrite. (Cf. 57:15.)

To extricate the people from despondency, to attach meaning to their past and present misery, was the task that the prophet and God had in common. "Comfort ye, comfort ye My people, says your God" (40:1). And also, "I, I am He that comforts you" (51:12). "As one whom his mother comforts, so I will comfort you" (66:13). His comfort comes from compassion (49:13), and will bring about joy (51:3), deliverance from captivity and the restoration of Zion and Jerusalem.

> *For soon My salvation will come,*
> *And My deliverance be revealed. . . .*
> *Israel is saved by the Lord*
> *With everlasting salvation. . . .*
> *Behold, the Lord has proclaimed*
> *To the end of the earth:*
> *Say to dear Zion,*
> *Behold, your salvation comes,*
> *Behold, His reward is with Him,*
> *His recompense before Him.*
> *They shall be called the holy people,*
> *The redeemed of the Lord;*
> *You shall be called Sought out,*
> *A city not forsaken.*
>   *Isaiah 56:1; 45:17; 62:11-12*

BECAUSE I LOVE YOU

Earlier prophets, absorbed in guilt and punishment, addressed Israel as "sinful nation, a people laden with iniquity" (Isa. 1:4); Second Isaiah, radiant with triumph and joy, addresses Israel as "you who pursue righteousness, you who seek the Lord" (51:1).

What Jeremiah proclaimed as the Lord's promise for the future, "I will put My teaching within them, and I will write it upon their hearts" (Jer. 31:33 [H. 31:32]), Second Isaiah seems to regard as fulfilled:

> *Hearken to me, you who know righteousness,*
> *The people in whose heart is My teaching.*
>   *Isaiah 51:7*

"Deeply despised, abhorred by the nations, servant of rulers" (49:7), Israel is given the spirit to say to the world,

> *The Lord has called me from the womb, . . .*
> *And said to me, You are My servant,*
> *Israel, in whom I am glorified.*
>   *Isaiah 49:1, 3*

Earlier, God was challenging Israel; now, Israel is questioning God. The task of the early prophets was to threaten and to shock; Second Isaiah's task is to give "power to the faint" and "strength to him who has no might" (40:29). They called upon Israel to mourn; he calls upon her to sing and to rejoice.

Israel's transgressions are trivial and insignificant when compared with God's love. Iniquities pass, even their memory may vanish in forgiveness, but God's love for Israel will never pass, will never vanish.

> *I, I am He*
> *Who blots out your transgressions for My own sake,*
> *And I will not remember your sins....*
> *I have swept away your transgressions like a cloud,*
> *And your sins like mist;*
> *Return to Me, for I have redeemed you.*
>   *Isaiah 43:25; 44:22*

There was no rejection on His part, He did not divorce His people (50:1). There was no detachment or personal alienation, but rather a spurious separation.

> *Your iniquities have made a separation*
> *Between you and your God,*
> *And your sins have hid His face from you*
> *So that He does not hear*
>   *Isaiah 59:2*

Sins affect His attitude temporarily; they cannot alter His relationship radically. God's love of Israel is eternal. Is it conceivable that sin, the work of man, should destroy what is intimately divine and eternal? For the reason of His eternal attachment is

> *Because you are precious in My eyes,*
> *And honored, and I love you....*
> *For a brief moment I forsook you,*
> *But with great compassion I will gather you.*
> *In overflowing wrath for a moment*
> *I hid My face from you,*
> *But with everlasting love I will have compassion on you,*
> *Says the Lord, your Redeemer.*
> *Can a woman forget her suckling child,*
> *That she should have no compassion on the son of her womb?*
> *Even these may forget*
> *Yet I will not forget you*
> *For the mountains may depart*
> *And the hills be removed*
> *But My steadfast love shall not depart from you,*

And My covenant of peace shall not be removed,
Says the Lord, Who has compassion on you.
                    Isaiah 43:4; 54:7-8; 49:15; 54:10

THE LORD'S OATH

"For I am God, and there is no other" (45:22). The Father of all men is committed to all men. Second Isaiah not only conveys the Lord's invitation and commitment to every man on earth; he proclaims that God has sworn that all men will worship Him. Here is a divine oath, not merely a hope. Here is a statement transcending all doubts.

> *By Myself I have sworn,*
> *From My mouth has gone forth in righteousness*
> *A word that shall not return:*
> *To Me every knee shall bow,*
> *Every tongue shall swear.*
>
>   *Isaiah 45:23*

While the coming salvation is the redemption of His people and the restoration of Jerusalem and Zion, the end of His design is that

> *The glory of the Lord shall be revealed,*
> *And all flesh shall see it together.*
>   *Isaiah 40:5*

It is the paradox of the human situation that those who do not even know God are chosen by Him to be the instruments in enabling men to know God. Cyrus, who did not know Him (45:4-5), is consecrated, called, and equipped for his great mission, so

> *. . . that men may know, from the rising of the sun*
> *And from the west, that there is none besides Me;*
> *I am the Lord, and there is no other.*
>
>   *Isaiah 45:6*

Even as Cyrus may not know Him and is yet chosen to carry out God's mission, the nations of the world who may not know Him are waiting for God, for His teaching and redemption (42:4; 51:4-5). Idolatry will disappear (42:16-17; 45:16-17). To all nations the call goes forth:

> *Turn to Me and be saved,*
> *All the ends of the earth!*
>   *Isaiah 45:22*

The Lord is coming "to gather all nations and tongues, and they shall come and shall see My glory" (66:18), and they will all be His servants.

The foreigners who join themselves to the Lord,
To minister to Him, to love the name of the Lord,
And to be His servants,
Every one who keeps the Sabbath, and does not profane it,
And holds fast My covenant—
These I will bring to My holy mountain,
And make them joyful in My house of prayer;
Their burnt offerings and their sacrifices
Will be accepted on My altar;
For My house shall be a house of prayer
For all peoples.

                                                    Isaiah 56:6-7

A LIGHT TO THE NATIONS

In contrast to the books of earlier prophets where the word of God speaks of Israel in the third person, now the Voice speaks to Israel directly in the second person. It is not a prophet speaking in His name; it is predominantly God addressing Himself to the people; it is I, not He. Prophetic receptivity is shared by all. Meaning is manifest, insight is common. It is as if in fulfillment of Moses' prayer, "Would that all the Lord's people were prophets, that the Lord would put His spirit upon them!" (Num. 11:29), Israel is declared to be God's spokesman, or prophet (49:2). Just as the Lord said to Jeremiah, "I appointed you a prophet to the nations" (Jer. 1:5), He said to Israel, "I appointed you a light to the nations" (49:6). The term "servant of the Lord," used to designate the prophets (I Kings 14:18; 15:29; II Kings 9:7, 36; 14:25; 17:13, 23; 21:10; 24:2; Amos 3:7; Isa. 20:3; Jer. 7:25; 25:4; 26:5), is now applied to Israel.

"As for Me, this is My covenant with them, says the Lord: My spirit which is upon you, and My words which I have put in your mouth, shall not depart out of your mouth, or out of the mouth of your children, or out of the mouth of your children's children, says the Lord, from this time forth and for evermore" (59:21). "All your sons shall be taught by the Lord" (54:13).

I will pour My spirit upon your descendants,
And My blessing on your offspring.
I have put My words in your mouth,
And hid you in the shadow of My hand,
To plant heaven,
To establish earth,
Saying to Zion, You are My people.
     Isaiah 44:3; 51:16; cf. Joel 2:28 [H. 3:1]

Just as prior to the exile individual prophets addressed themselves to Israel, Israel now addresses herself to the nations. Like Jeremiah, Israel was called to her task from the earliest moment of her existence (Jer. 1:5).

> Listen to me, O coastlands,
> Hearken, you peoples from afar.
> The Lord called me from the womb,
> From the body of my mother He named my name.
> He made my mouth like a sharp sword,
> In the shadow of His hand He hid me;
> He made me a polished arrow,
> In His quiver He hid me away.
> He said to me, You are My servant,
> Israel, in whom I will be glorified.
>
> *Isaiah 49:1-3*

Israel is more than an instrument in God's design. Israel is made to be "a witness to the peoples" (55:4). "You are My witnesses!" (44:8). Israel is called to be

> A light to the nations,
> To open the eyes that are blind,
> To bring out the prisoners from the dungeon,
> From the prison those who sit in darkness.
>
> *Isaiah 42:6-7*

For the accomplishment of His grand design, the Lord waits for the help of man (cf. 63:5). This is the meaning of being His servant: to be a light to the nations so that His salvation "may reach to the end of the earth" (49:6).

> Behold My servant, whom I uphold,
> My chosen, in whom My soul delights;
> I have put My spirit upon him,
> He will bring forth justice to the nations.
> He will not cry or lift up his voice,
> Or make it heard in the street;
> A bruised reed he will not break,
> And a dimly burning wick he will not quench;
> He will faithfully bring forth justice.
> He will not fail or be discouraged
> Till he has established justice in the earth,
> And the coastlands wait for his teaching.
>
> *Isaiah 42:1-4*

THE WORD OF OUR GOD WILL STAND FOREVER

The grandeur and presence of God are strikingly apparent, heaven and earth are radiant with His glory. It is enough to lift up the eyes on high and see Who created these (40:26). Yet men are blind; spiritually, they live in a dungeon. Israel's destiny is, as we have seen, "to open the eyes that are blind." Yet the tragedy is that the servant himself fails to understand the meaning of his mission.

> Who is blind but My servant,
> Or deaf as My messenger whom I send?
> Who is blind as My dedicated one,
> Or blind as the servant of the Lord?
> He sees many things, but does not observe them;
> His ears are open, but he does not hear.
>
> Isaiah 42:19-20

There were those who though walking in the darkness trusted in the name of the Lord and relied on Him (50:10), while others, "stubborn of heart," did not respond to the message of redemption proclaimed by the prophet (46:12), or even forsook the Lord and forgot Zion (65:11). An extremely bitter, crushing cry bursts out of the prophet:

> We have all become like one who is unclean;
> All our righteous deeds are like a polluted garment.
> We all fade like a leaf,
> Our iniquities, like the wind, take us away.
>
> Isaiah 64:6[3]

The prophet continues to stress the sharp contrast between the Creator and His creation, the eternal and the evanescent, the thoughts of God and the thoughts of man, the sublimity of the Lord and the triviality of man (40:17, 22), heaven and earth (55:8-9), the reality of God and the nothingness of idols, the everlastingness of His Word and the impermanence of human kindness.

> All flesh is grass,
> And all its kindness is like the flower in the field.
> The grass withers, the flower fades, . . .
> But the word of our God will stand for ever.
>
> Isaiah 40:6-8

He stresses the contrast between the wisdom of God's works and the limited worth of human deeds, the eternity of God's love and the temporariness of His wrath (54:7-8), the marvel of God's presence and the enigma of His silence.

> Who are you that you are afraid of man who dies,
> Of the son of man who is made like grass, . . .

---

[3] See A. J. Heschel, *God in Search of Man* (New York, 1955), pp. 393 f.

> *And fear continually all the day*
> *Because of the fury of the oppressor,*
> *When he sets himself to destroy? . . .*
> *Truly, Thou art a God who hidest Thyself,*
> *O God of Israel, the Savior.*
>
>   *Isaiah 51:12-13; 45:15*

Heaven, the most permanent and sublime part of God's creation, as well as the earth, mankind's dearest shelter, which according to Ecclesiastes (1:4) endures forever, are considered evanescent when compared with God's salvation.

> *Lift up your eyes to the heaven,*
> *And look at the earth beneath;*
> *For the heaven will vanish like smoke,*
> *The earth will wear out like a garment,*
> *And they who dwell in it will die like gnats;*
> *But My salvation will be for ever,*
> *And My deliverance will never be ended.*
>
>   *Isaiah 51:6*

The deliverance of Israel and the return to Zion are depicted as an event of both universal and cosmic significance. From distant lands, nations will come to Zion and declare: "God is with you only, and there is no other" (45:14), and will sing to the Lord a new song (42:10-12).

Heaven and the depths of the earth, mountains and every tree in the forest will break forth into singing, "for the Lord has redeemed Jacob" (44:23).

"For behold, I create a new heaven and a new earth" (65:17; cf. 66:22). Salvation will come; "in its time I will hasten it" (60:22). "Those who wait for Me shall not be put to shame" (49:23).

9. HISTORY

THE IDOLATRY OF MIGHT

Why were so few voices raised in the ancient world in protest against the ruthlessness of man? Why are human beings so obsequious, ready to kill and ready to die at the call of kings and chieftains? Perhaps it is because they worship might, venerate those who command might, and are convinced that it is by force that man prevails. The splendor and the pride of kings blind the people. The Mesopotamian, for example, felt convinced that authorities were always right: "The command of the palace, like the command of Anu, cannot be altered. The king's word is right; his utterance, like that of a god, cannot be changed!"[1] The prophets repudiated the work as well as the power of man as an object of supreme adoration. They denounced "arrogant boasting" and "haughty pride" (Isa. 10:12), the kings who ruled the nations in anger, the oppressors (Isa. 14:4-6), the destroyers of nations, who went forth to inflict waste, ruin, and death (Jer. 4:7), the "guilty men, whose own might is their god" (Hab. 1:11).

> Their course is evil,
> Their might is not right.
> Jeremiah 23:10

The end of public authority is to realize the moral law, a task for which both knowledge and understanding as well as the possession of power are indispensable means. Yet inherent in power is the tendency to breed conceit. ". . . one of the most striking and one of the most pervasive features of the prophetic polemic [is] the denunciation and distrust of power in all its forms and guises. The hunger of the powerful knows no satiety; the appetite grows on what it feeds. Power exalts itself and is incapable of yielding to any

---

[1] T. Jacobsen, in H. Frankfort, et al., eds., The Intellectual Adventure of Ancient Man (Chicago, 1946), p. 203.

transcendent judgment; it 'listens to no voice' (Zeph. 3:2) ."[2] It is the bitter irony of history that the common people, who are devoid of power and are the prospective victims of its abuse, are the first to become the ally of him who accumulates power. Power is spectacular, while its end, the moral law, is inconspicuous.

"Material force is the *ultima ratio* of political society everywhere. Arms alone can keep the peace."[3] This was and still remains the axiom with men everywhere. The sword is not only the source of security; it is also the symbol of honor and glory; it is bliss and song.

When the prophets appeared, they proclaimed that might is not supreme, that the sword is an abomination, that violence is obscene. The sword, they said, shall be destroyed.

> *They shall beat their swords into plowshares,*
> *And their spears into pruning hooks;*
> *Nation shall not lift up sword against nation,*
> *Neither shall they learn war any more.*
>   Isaiah 2:4

The prophets, questioning man's infatuation with might, insisted not only on the immorality but also on the futility and absurdity of war. In a later era Napoleon, we are told, solemnly declared to his Minister of Education: "Do you know, Fontanes, what astonishes me most in this world? The inability of force to create anything. In the long run the sword is always beaten by the spirit."[4] Yet, the most astonishing thing in the world is the perennial disregard of the impotence of force. What is the ultimate profit of all the arms, alliances, and victories? Destruction, agony, death.

> *Peoples labor only for fire,*
> *Nations weary themselves for naught.*
>   Habakkuk 2:13

Egypt and Mesopotamia were involved recurrently in a struggle for supremacy. At the same time, Mesopotamia was beset by internal conflicts between the rival peoples of Babylonia and Assyria. Those two countries carried on frequent wars against sedentary and migratory peoples in the Near East who were considered threats to the empires or who were simply tempting prey for the insatiable kings and warlords. They fell upon the quiet people in the villages, "all of them dwelling without walls, and having no bars or gates; to seize spoil and carry off plunder; . . . to carry away silver and gold, to take away cattle and goods" (Ezek. 38:11-13) .

---

[2] J. Muilenburg, *The Way of Israel* (New York, 1961) , p. 89.
[3] John Henry Cardinal Newman, *Discussions and Arguments* (London, 1872) ; p. 203.
[4] J. C. Herold, *The Mind of Napoleon* (New York, 1955) , p. 76.

As it was in the age of the prophets, so it is in nearly every age: we all go mad, not only individually, but also nationally. We check manslaughter and isolated murders; we wage wars and slaughter whole peoples. Ferocity appears natural; generosity, superimposed. Since the natural often seems sacred, we seldom dare suppress or try to remake what has been called "all that fine belligerence within us." We measure manhood by the sword and are convinced that history is ultimately determined on the fields of battle. "There is no peace, says my God, for the wicked" (Isa. 57:21; cf. 48:22). "Perpetual peace is a dream—and not even a beautiful dream—and war is an integral part of God's ordering of the Universe. In war, Man's noblest virtues come into play: courage and renunciation, fidelity to duty and a readiness for sacrifice that does not stop short of offering up Life itself. Without war the world would become swamped in materialism."[5]

David at one time assembled at Jerusalem all officials of Israel—the officers, the commanders, the mighty men, and all the seasoned warriors. Then he rose to his feet and said: "Hear me, my brethren and my people. I had it in my heart to build a house of rest for the Ark of the covenant of the Lord, . . . and I made preparations for building. But God said to me: You may not build a house for My name, for you are a warrior and have shed blood. . . . It is Solomon your son who shall build My house . . ." (I Chron. 28:1-3, 6).[6]

The Chronicler did not regard the wars of David as wrong. Far from it; God was with David wherever he went, and his victories over the enemies assured security to Israel, so that "violent men shall waste them no more, as formerly," and established his throne forever (I Chron. 17:8-14). David's wars were regarded as a necessary evil, but the fierce doings David was involved in made him unfit to build the house for the Lord.

The prophets did not isolate the evil of war, and they seem to have regarded it as the extension of a condition that prevails even in time of peace.

Noise, fury, tumult are usually associated with battles of war, when nation seeks to destroy nation. The cheating, the cunning, the humiliations by which individuals seek to destroy each other are pursued discreetly, with no one feeling hurt, consciously, except the victim. The walls within which secret crimes are committed remain quiet. But to the ear of the prophet,

[5] H. von Moltke, as quoted by A. Toynbee, *War and Civilization* (New York, 1950), p. 16.
[6] The word of the Lord came to David through the prophet Nathan, commanding him not to build a Temple (II Sam. 7; I Chron. 17); but here a different reason is given. The statement in I Kings 5:3 that David had been too busy fighting to have time to erect the Temple is often characterized by modern interpreters as "abysmally lower" than the reason given in I Chron. These interpreters fail to observe that the reason mentioned in I Kings is contained in a communication sent by Solomon to Hiram, the king of Tyre.

> *The stone will cry out from the wall,...*
> *Woe to him who builds a town with blood,*
> *And founds a city on iniquity!*
>
> Habakkuk 2:11-12

Righteousness and peace are interdependent (cf. Ps. 85:10). "The effect of righteousness will be peace, And the result of righteousness quietness and trust for ever" (Isa. 32:17).

> *Woe to those who devise wickedness*
> *And work evil upon their beds!*
> *When the morning dawns, they perform it,*
> *Because it is in the power of their hand.*
> *They covet fields, and seize them;*
> *And houses, and take them away;*
> *They oppress a man and his house,*
> *A man and his inheritance.*
>
> Micah 2:1-2

Amos castigated the individuals "who store up violence and robbery in their strongholds" (3:10). "Your rich men are full of violence!" Micah exclaimed (6:12). The condemnation of violence (*hamas, shod, 'oshek*) is a major theme in the prophets' speeches.

On the other hand, the denunciation of violence committed by private individuals applied a millionfold to the brutal wars of aggression waged by insatiable and arrogant empires. Although Assyria, for example, was used as a tool for the merited chastisement of other peoples, the prophets insisted that the guilt was the aggressor's. Amos cried out against the cruelties inflicted by the various nations upon each other—nations which, casting off all pity, pursued one another with the sword, ripping up women with child, slaughtering people, driving them into captivity, selling them into slavery. (Amos 1:3, 13). On the day of battle, Hosea reminds us, cities were devastated by the conqueror, and mothers were dashed to pieces with their children (Hos. 10:14).

Isaiah was filled with disgust for the military boots, for every mantle rolled in blood (Isa. 9:5 [H. 9:4]), for the scepter and the pomp of the wicked rulers (Isa. 14:5, 11), for the arrogance, pride, and insolence of the rulers. Above all, Isaiah entertained extreme disgust for the Assyrians. The prophet's vehement denunciation of the individuals oppressing the poor and crushing the needy, and his sense of outrage at those who were accumulating dishonest gain applied even more to the brutalities suffered by entire communities at the hand of hostile armies and their leaders.

Assyria has often been called the most ruthless nation of antiquity. For ages she plundered all peoples within her reach, like a lion which "filled his caves with prey and his dens with torn flesh" (Nah. 2:12 [H. 2:13]) . Her warfare abounded in atrocities; cutting off the heads of conquered peoples was a common procedure. The kings of Assyria boasted of towns destroyed, dismantled or burned, leveled as if by a hurricane or reduced to a heap of rubble. The victors took away everything they could carry. Upon capturing a city,

> the king's throne would be set up before the gates of the city and the prisoners would be paraded before him, led by the monarch of the captured town, who would undergo the most agonizing torture, such as having his eyes put out or confinement in a cage, until the king of Assyria set a term to his long-drawn agony. Sargon had the defeated king of Damascus burned alive before his eyes. The wives and daughters of the captured king were destined for the Assyrian harems and those who were not of noble blood were condemned to slavery. Meanwhile the soldiery had been massacring the population, and brought the heads of their victims into the king's presence, where they were counted up by the scribes. Not all the male prisoners were put to death, for the boys and craftsmen were led into captivity, where they would be assigned to the hardest tasks on the royal building projects, where the swamps which cover so much of Mesopotamia must have caused an enormously high rate of mortality. The remainder of the population were uprooted and sent to the other end of the Empire.[7]

Isaiah spoke to Israel as well as to "all . . . inhabitants of the world" (Isa. 18:3) . What went on in Israel on a small scale went on in the world on a grand scale. The misdeeds of individuals who deprived their fellow men of their rightful possessions—"Woe to those who join house to house, who add field to field" (Isa. 5:8) —were trifling compared to the crimes of Assyria. "The oppressor" (Isa. 14:4) tried to turn the world into a desert, overthrowing cities and refusing to let his prisoners go home (Isa. 14:17) . What a passion for war, what a pleasure in destruction!

The great powers spread not only ruin and destruction, but also guilt and moral corruption. In the case of Assyria, she was condemned for her "countless harlotries," for betraying nations "with her harlotries, and peoples with her charms" (Nah. 3:4) . The small nations were first subdued and then forced to become allies, fellow travelers, supplying soldiers, joining Assyria in the slaughter of other nations.[8] Seeking glory, booty, and power, van-

---

[7] G. Contenau, *Everyday Life in Babylon and Assyria* (London, 1954) , p. 148. Assyrian art was "great only in portraying the dying agonies of men and of beasts. . . . Nothing comparable is to be found in ancient art to the 'stele of the vultures' feeding on the carrion of the vanquished." (R. H. Bainton, *Christian Attitudes toward War and Peace* [New York, 1960], p. 19.) See also A. T. Olmstead, *History of Assyria* (New York, 1923) , p. 295; D. D. Lucken-bill, *Ancient Records of Babylonia and Assyria*, I (Chicago, 1926) , 145; H. Schmokel, *Geschichte des alten Vorderasiens* ("Handbuch der Orientalistik," II, 3) , pp. 252 f.

[8] The army of Assyria was composed of many nations, see Isa. 10:8; 13:4; 17:12; 22:6; for Babylonia, see Jer. 34:1.

quished kings became commanders in Assyria's army, sharing her glories, partaking in the slaughter. It was about such enticement that Habakkuk exclaimed:

> Woe to him who makes his neighbors drink,
> Causing them to join him in his fury,
> Who makes them drunk,
> To gaze on their shame!
> You will be sated with contempt instead of glory, . . .
> Shame will come upon your glory! . . .
> For the blood of men and violence to the earth,
> To cities and all who dwell therein.
>
> *Habakkuk 2:15-17*

A few decades later, after the downfall of Assyria, it was Babylonia whose might and splendor held many nations in her spell. A state of intoxication, a voluntary madness, overcame the world, eager to join and to aid the destroyer, accessories to aggression.

> Babylon was a golden cup in the hand of the Lord,
> Making the whole earth drunk;
> The nations drank of her wine,
> Therefore the nations went mad.
>
> *Jeremiah 51:7*

THERE IS NO REGARD FOR MAN

How ugly and weird the world is: drunk with lust for power, infatuated with war, merciless and sad.

> The envoys of peace weep bitterly,
> The highways lie waste, . . .
> Covenants are broken,
> Witnesses are despised,
> There is no regard for man.
>
> *Isaiah 33:7-8*[9]

Of course, there is religion in the world. There are even men who worship the Righteous One:

> From the ends of the earth we hear songs of praise,
> Of glory to the Righteous One.
> But I say, I pine away,
> I pine away. Woe is me!

---

[9] Both Driver and Kissane ascribe the poem to Isaiah; see E. J. Kissane, *The Book of Isaiah* (Dublin, 1941), p. 369.

For the treacherous deal treacherously,
The treacherous deal very treacherously.[10]
Isaiah 24:16

Before the fall of Assyria, nations lived in dread of that country, whose design was "to destroy and to cut off nations not a few" (Isa. 10:7). The tyrant says in his heart:

I will ascend to heaven;
Above the stars of God I will set my throne on high. . . .
I will ascend above the heights of the clouds,
I will be like the Most High.

Isaiah 14:13-14

The root of all evil is, according to Isaiah, man's false sense of sovereignty and, stemming from it, man's pride, arrogance, and presumption. Assyria said:

By the strength of my hand I have done it,
And by my wisdom, for I have understanding;
I have removed the boundaries of peoples,
And have plundered their treasures;
Like a bull I have brought down those who sat on thrones.
My hand has found like a nest
The wealth of the peoples;
And as men gather eggs that have been forsaken
So I have gathered all the earth;
And there was none that moved a wing,
Or opened the mouth, or chirped.

Isaiah 10:13-14

Even little Moab, a tiny kingdom west of the Dead Sea, was full of arrogance, pride, insolence, and false boasts (Isa. 15:6).

There is no limit to cruelty when man begins to think that he is the master. Such a claim is as dangerous as it is absurd.

Shall the ax boast over him who hews with it,
Or the saw magnify itself against him who wields it?
As if the rod should swing him who lifts it,
Or as if the staff should lift him who is not wood!

Isaiah 10:15

Such presumption will not last forever. The design of the Lord is "to humble the pride of all glory, to dishonor all the honored of the earth" (Isa. 23:9).

---

[10] The meaning of the verse is uncertain. Most critics assign it to a time after the destruction of Jerusalem in 587. According to Kissane, *op. cit.*, p. 270, "the poem is just as applicable to the period of Isaiah as to any other period."

Enter into the rock,
And hide in the dust
Before the terror of the Lord,
Before the glory of his majesty.
The naughtiness of man shall be brought low,
And the pride of men shall be humbled;
And the Lord alone shall be exalted
In that day.
For the Lord of hosts has a day
Against all that is proud and haughty,
Against all that is exalted and high;
Against all the cedars of Lebanon,
The high and exalted;
And against all the oaks of Bashan;
Against all the high mountains,
And against all the lofty hills;
Against every high tower,
And against every fortified wall;
Against all the ships of Tarshish,
And against all the beautiful galleys;
And the haughtiness of man shall be humbled,
And the pride of men shall be brought low;
And the Lord alone will be exalted in that day.
                              Isaiah 2:10-17

FOR NOT BY FORCE SHALL MAN PREVAIL

The prophets were the first men in history to regard a nation's reliance upon force as evil. Hosea condemned militarism as idolatrous.

Israel has forgotten his Maker
And built palaces;
Judah has multiplied fortified cities....
You have trusted in your chariots
And in the multitude of your warriors, ...
[Israel has] gone up to Assyria,
A wild ass wandering alone; ...
They hire allies among the nations....
When Ephraim saw his sickness,
And Judah his wound,
Then Ephraim went to Assyria,
And sent to the great [?] king.[11]
But he is not able to cure you
Or heal your wound.
             Hosea 8:14; 10:13; 8:9-10; 5:13

---

[11] According to Rashi, the reference is to Hoshea and Ahaz; according to Kimhi, the reference is to Menahem and Ahaz.

Having anticipated Isaiah's vision of enduring peace, Hosea proclaimed in the name of the Lord: "I will not deliver them by bow, nor by sword, nor by war, nor by horses, nor by horsemen. . . . I will make for you a covenant on that day with the beasts of the field, the birds of the air, and the creeping things of the ground; I will abolish the bow, the sword, and war from the land, and I will make you lie down in safety" (Hos. 1:7; 2:18).

"The gods are on the side of the stronger," according to Tacitus. The prophets proclaimed that the heart of God is on the side of the weaker. God's special concern is not for the mighty and the successful, but for the lowly and the downtrodden, for the stranger and the poor, for the widow and the orphan.

The heart of God goes out to the humble, to the vanquished, to those not cared for.

> *I will restore health to you,*
> *And your wounds I will heal, says the Lord,*
> *Because they have called you an outcast:*
> *It is Zion, for whom no one cares.*
> *Jeremiah 30:17*

> *The Lord has founded Zion,*
> *And in her the afflicted of His people find refuge. . . .*
> *The meek shall obtain fresh joy in the Lord,*
> *And the poor among men shall exult in the Holy One of Israel.*
> *Isaiah 14:32; 29:19*

"For not by force shall man prevail" (I Sam. 2:9). "The nations shall see and be ashamed of all their might" (Mic. 7:16). "Not by might, . . . says the Lord of hosts" (Zech. 4:6).

> *Some boast of chariots, and some of horses;*
> *But we boast of the name of the Lord our God. . . .*
> *His delight is not in the strength of the horse,*
> *Nor is His pleasure in the legs of a man.*
> *But the Lord takes pleasure in those who fear Him,*
> *In those who hope in His steadfast love.*
> *Psalms 20:7; 147:10-11*

> *This is the man to whom I will look,*
> *He that is humble and contrite in spirit,*
> *And trembles at My word. . . .*
> *For thus says the high and the lofty One*
> *Who inhabits eternity, Whose name is Holy:*
> *I dwell in the high and holy place,*
> *And also with him who is a contrite and humble spirit,*
> *To revive the spirit of the humble,*
> *To revive the heart of the contrite. . .*

Zion shall be redeemed by justice,
And those in her who repent, by righteousness.
                              Isaiah 66:2; 57:15; 1:27

THE PANTHEISM OF HISTORY

One must not confound biblical theology with the mystical view that God is all, and all is God. The prophets never taught that God and history are one, or that whatever happens below reflects the will of God above. Their vision is of man defying God, and God seeking man to reconcile with Him.

History is where God is defied, where justice suffers defeats. God's purpose is neither clearly apparent nor translatable into rational categories of order and design. There are only moments in which it is revealed.

God's power in history does not endure as a process; it occurs at extraordinary events.[12] There is a divine involvement and concern, involvement in what is done, for that which is. Even where His power is absent, His concern is present.

There was a moment when God looked at the universe made by Him and said: "It is good." But there was no moment in which God could have looked at history made by man and said: "It is good."[13]

To the ancient Greeks, a man's home is in nature, and the urgent problem is knowledge of nature, of cosmos. Because cosmos is the most comprehensive concept, all ideas, all problems can be understood once the laws of the cosmos are discovered. Historic events are part of the species of natural events, just as man is but part of the animal species. The gods being themselves a part of nature have no power over history. The only thing that Herodotus would say about the divine power that ordains the course of history is that it rejoices in upsetting and disturbing things. "He was only repeating what every Greek knew: that the power of Zeus is manifested in the thunderbolt, that of Poseidon in the earthquake, that of Apollo in pestilence, and that of Aphrodite in the passion that destroyed at once the pride of Phaedra and the chastity of Hippolytus."[14]

To the prophets, man's home is in history, and their central concern is what is happening in history. Both nature and history are subject to God's

---

[12] On the distinction between process and event, see p. 431.

[13] On the significance of the prophetic understanding of history see M. Eliade, *Cosmos and History*: The Myth of the Eternal Return, (New York, 1954); R. Niebuhr, *Faith and History* (New York, 1949), pp. 126 f.; *idem, The Self and the Dramas of History* (New York, 1955), pp. 75 ff.; J. P. Hyatt, *Prophetic Religion* (New York, 1947), pp. 76 ff.; E. Jacob, *Theology of the Old Testament* (New York, 1958); J. Muilenburg, *op. cit.* pp. 74 ff. See also A. J. Heschel, *The Sabbath* (New York, 1951); J. Muilenburg, "The Biblical View of Time," *Harvard Theological Review*, LIV (1961), 225-252.

[14] R. G. Collingwood, *The Idea of History* (Oxford, 1946), p. 22; cf. Herodotus, *History*, I, 32.

dominion. Just as the word is the vessel for His revelation, history is the vessel for His action and the material for man's achievement.

THE UNITY OF HISTORY

The prophet may be regarded as the first universal man in history; he is concerned with, and addresses himself to, all men. It was not an emperor, but a prophet, who first conceived of the unity of all men.

"The prophets who preceded you and me from ancient times," said Jeremiah to Hananiah, "prophesied . . . against many countries and great kingdoms" (Jer. 28:8).

Amos spoke in the name of Him who decides the destiny of all nations (Amos 9:7), and proclaimed His judgment over Damascus, Gaza, Tyre, Edom, the Ammonites, and Moab as well as over Israel and Judah (Amos 1:3—2:6). Isaiah proclaimed God's purpose and design "concerning the whole earth" (14:26), and actually addressed himself to "all you inhabitants of the world, you who dwell on the earth" (Isa. 18:3; cf. 33:13; 34:1), delivering special prophecies concerning Babylon, Moab, Damascus, Egypt, Tyre, and others (chs. 13—23). It is the God of Israel Who summons the mighty men to execute His designs (Isa. 13:3, 5), Who calls the nations of the world into judgment, and it is He Whom one day all nations shall worship in Zion (Isa. 2:2 ff.; 11:10; 18:7).

> The Lord of hosts has sworn:
> As I have resolved
> So shall it be,
> As I have planned
> So shall it stand:
> I will break Assyria in My land,
> And trample him upon My mountains;
> His yoke shall depart from them,
> And his burden from their shoulder.
> This is the plan that is planned
> Concerning the whole earth,
> This is the hand that is stretched out
> Over all nations.
> For the Lord of hosts has planned,
> And who will annul it?
> His hand is stretched out,
> And who will turn it back? . . .
> Behold, the Lord, the Lord of hosts
> Will lop the boughs with terrifying power;
> The great in height will be hewn down,
> The lofty will be brought low.
>
> Isaiah 14:24-27; 10:33

Jeremiah was appointed "a prophet to the nations" (Jer. 1:5), not merely

to Israel, and like Isaiah he proclaimed prophecies concerning many nations.[15] He was told to give a charge to the envoys of the kings of Edom,
Moab, Ammon, Tyre, and Sidon who had come to Jerusalem (Jer. 27:2 ff.) :
All nations are accountable to One God; they are declared to be full of guilt
against the Holy One of Israel. "Every man is stupid and without knowledge" (Jer. 51:17). "The Lord has an indictment against the nations; He
is entering into judgment with all flesh" (Jer. 25:31). All nations are made
to drink the cup of wrath (Jer. 25:17 ff.; cf. 1:14). The nations cannot endure His indignation (Jer. 10:10). Jeremiah proclaimed: "At that time
Jerusalem shall be called the throne of the Lord, and all nations shall
gather to it, to the presence of the Lord in Jerusalem, and they shall no
more stubbornly follow their own evil heart" (Jer. 3:17; cf. 4:2; 10:7).

In the words of a later prophet: "Have we not all one father? Has not one
God created us? Why then are we faithless to one another, profaning the
covenant of our fathers?" (Mal. 2:10.)

> *What then shall I do when God rises up?*
> *When He remembers, what shall I answer Him?*
> *Did not He Who made me in the womb make him?*
> *Did not One fashion us in the womb?*
>
> *Job 31:14-15*

Thus was born the idea of one history. The particular event or situation
is related to Him Who rules over all nations. Just as the knowledge of
nature was born with the discovery of principles determining all happenings
in nature, so is consciousness of history the result of an awareness of One
God judging all events in history.

THE HUMAN EVENT AS A DIVINE EXPERIENCE

History is first of all what man does with power. To the prophets, power
is a divine assignment; emperors are mere tools in the hand of God, and the
word of the prophet is, according to Jeremiah, mightier than the power of
kings.

> *See, I have set you this day over nations and over kingdoms,*
> *To pluck up and to break down,*
> *To destroy and to overthrow,*
> *To build and to plant.*
>
> *Jeremiah 1:10*

The Lord chooses agents from the ends of the earth (Isa. 5:20) through
whom His will is carried out. He says of Cyrus, the king of Persia: "He is
My shepherd, and he shall fulfill all My purpose" (Isa. 44:28), and of

---

[15] See H. Bardtke, *"Jeremia der Fremdvölkerprophet," ZAW,* LIII (1935), 20 ff.

Assyria: "the rod of My anger, the staff of My fury" (Isa. 10:5), "the weapons of His indignation" (13:5). As an agent of God, Nebuchadnezzar is called God's servant (Jer. 25:9; 27:6; 43:10; cf. Ezek. 26:7). Egypt and Assyria are like tiny insects, comparable to a fly and a bee in the eyes of God. The Assyrian king may boast of his might, his army may invade the land of Judah, but the word of God proclaims:

> I will put My hook in your nose,
> And My bridle in your mouth,
> And I will turn you back
> On the way by which you came.
> The Assyrian shall fall by a sword, not of man,
> And a sword, not of man, shall devour him.
>
> Isaiah 31:8

To all men, both near and far, Isaiah addresses the word of God: "Acknowledge My might" (33:13). Assyria's masters are planning to conquer the whole earth (Isa. 5:25-29). Her greed is reckless, her weapons devastating, her armies formidable, crushing all resistance, sweeping to victories. No one seems to question her invincibility except Isaiah, who foresees the doom of the oppressor, the collapse of the monster.

> The people who walked in darkness
> Have seen a great light;
> Those who dwelt in gloom,
> Upon them a light shines, . . .
> For the yoke they endured,
> The staff on their shoulders,
> The rod of their oppressors,
> Thou hast broken as on the day of Midian.
> For every boot that tramped in tumult,
> And every mantle rolled in blood
> Will be burned as fuel for the fire.
>
> Isaiah 9:2, 4-5 [H. 9:1, 3-4]

It is generally assumed that politics, warfare, and economic activities are the substance and the subject matter of history. To the prophets, God's judgment of man's conduct is the main issue; all else is marginal.

Others have considered history from the point of view of power, judging its course in terms of victory and defeat, of wealth and success; the prophets look at history from the point of view of justice, judging its course in terms of righteousness and corruption, of compassion and violence.[16]

---

[16] A modern historian, e.g., relates that the Assyrian king Sennacherib, a ruler notable for his ruthlessness in war, "was followed by a sentimental son, who undid his father's work. . . . Had Assyria been more mercilessly consistent, the fall of the Assyrian empire might have been indefinitely postponed." (A. T. Olmstead, *History of Assyria* [New York, 1923], p. 296; cf. pp. 294 f.)

To the modern historian, history is not the understanding of events, but rather the understanding of man's experience of events. What concerns the prophet is the human event as a divine experience. History to us is the record of human experience; to the prophet it is a record of God's experience.

There is nothing we forget as eagerly, as quickly, as the wickedness of man. The earth holds such a terrifying secret. Ruins are removed, the dead are buried, and the crimes forgotten. Bland complacency, splendid mansions, fortresses of cruel oblivion, top the graves. The dead have no voice, but God will disclose the secret of the earth.

> *For behold, the Lord will go forth from His place,*
> *To punish the iniquity of the inhabitants of the earth,*
> *And the earth shall disclose the blood shed upon her,*
> *And shall no longer cover up her slain.*
>
> Isaiah 26:21

Human power is not the stuff of which history is made. For history is not what is displayed at the moment, but what is concealed in the mind of the Lord.

THE CONTINGENCY OF CIVILIZATION

Of one thing men are sure: The earth is a steadfast thing, and the world will go on forever. One may doubt everything except that civilization will continue. But the prophet had no such certainty.

The prophet depicts the Lord when about to visit iniquities upon mankind.

> *Behold the Lord will lay waste the earth and make it desolate,*
> *He will twist its surface and scatter its inhabitants. . . .*
> *The world languishes and withers,*
> *The heavens languish together with the earth. . . .*
> *The earth lies polluted under its inhabitants,*
> *For they have transgressed the laws,*
> *Violated the statutes, broken the everlasting covenant.*
> *Therefore a curse devours the earth,*
> *Its inhabitants suffer for their guilt;*
> *Therefore the inhabitants of the earth are scorched,*
> *Few men are left.*
>
> Isaiah 24:1, 4-6

Dislike for the world or disparagement of civilization is alien to the prophet. His attachment to God calls upon him to be involved with humanity. Yet in the face of idle and false impositions, he announces the contingency and insecurity of civilization, the sickness and liability of man. Israel is under judgment; the covenant with God must not be taken as immunity from judgment.

> O Lord, Thou art my God,
> I will exalt Thee, I will praise Thy name,
> For Thou hast done marvelous things,
> Plans formed of old, faithful and sure.
> For Thou hast made the city a heap,
> The fortified city a ruin;
> The castle of the aliens is a city no more,
> It shall never be rebuilt.
> Therefore, strong peoples will glorify Thee,
> Cities of ruthless nations will fear Thee.
> Because Thou hast been a refuge to the poor,
> A refuge to the needy in his distress,
> A shelter from the storm, a shade from the heat.
> Though the fury of the ruthless be like a storm,
> Though the noise of the aliens be like heat in a dry land,
> Thou allayest heat by the shade of a cloud,
> The song of the mighty shall be subdued.
>
> Isaiah 25:1-5

High over the scandals and illusions of triumphant tyrants rises the mighty voice:

> I will punish the world for its evil,
> And the wicked for their iniquity;
> I will put an end to the pride of the arrogant,
> And humble the haughtiness of the tyrants. . . .
> For the ruthless shall come to nought,
> The scoffer shall vanish,
> And all who watch to do evil shall be cut off.
>
> Isaiah 13:11; 29:20

THE POLARITY OF HISTORY

Awareness of a problem means awareness of a conflict or a tension between two ideas, forces or situations. In this sense the prophets discovered the problem of history as a tension between what happens now and what may happen next. The future is no simple continuation of the present. Just as the present, in their eyes, represented a violation of what was established in the past (Israel's commitment to God), so may the future overturn the seeming solidity of what is being done in the present.

Moreover, the situation here and now is but a stage in the drama of history. Whatever happens now affects the past; it either shapes or distorts events that are going on. By history we do not mean the "gone" or the dead past, but the present in which past and future are interlocked. Sin is repudiation of history. Sacred events, sacred moments are commitments. The conscience stands still, but commitments go on.

Jeremiah was told to go to a potter's house where he would receive a revelation. "So I went down to the potter's house, and there he was working at his wheel. Whenever the vessel he was making went wrong, as clay is apt to do in a potter's hand, he would remake it in a different shape, such as he thought suitable. Thereupon the word of the Lord came to me: Am I not able to act toward you, O Israel, like this potter? You are in my hands as clay is in the hands of the potter" (Jer. 18:3-4).

Life is not as fate designs, nor is history a realm to be tyrannized by man. Events are not like rocks on the shore shaped by wind and water. Choice, design, is what determines the shape of events. God is at work on man, intent to fashion history in accord with Himself.

The tragic sense in man interprets a catastrophe as that which has to be, that which is fated to be. The relentless power of fate cannot be resisted. The greatest Greek drama rests on the interplay between fate and character, "between what man cannot change and what remains within his power."[17]

In contrast, Jeremiah was told: "If at any time I declare concerning a nation or a kingdom, that I will pluck up and break down and destroy it, and if that nation, concerning which I have spoken, turns from its evil, I will repent of the evil that I intended to do to it. And if at any time I declare concerning a nation or a kingdom that I will build and plant it, and if it does evil in My sight, not listening to My voice, then I will repent of the good which I had intended to do to it . . ." (Jer. 18:7-8).

Sin is not a *cul de sac,* nor is guilt a final trap. Sin may be washed away by repentance and return, and beyond guilt is the dawn of forgiveness. The door is never locked, the threat of doom is not the last word.

Ultimately there is only one will by which history is shaped: the will of God; and there is only one factor upon which the shape of history depends: the moral conduct of the nations. The history of mankind moves between these two poles.[18]

STRANGE IS HIS DEED, ALIEN IS HIS WORK

Strongly as Isaiah is convinced that history is not an arena where willful nations carry out their evil designs, but rather an area where God's will comes to expression, he also knows that not all history is a performance of

---

[17] W. C. Greene, *Moira* (Cambridge, 1944), p. 92.
[18] See P. Volz, *Der Prophet Jeremia* (Leipzig, 1922), p. 191.

God; that He often detaches Himself from the affairs of man; that His judgments are not always "wrought in the earth." The presence of God in history, the manifestation of His will in the affairs of the world, is the object of the prophet's longing. It is not mystical experience he yearns for in the night, but historical justice. Mystical experience is the illumination of an individual; historical justice is the illumination of all men, enabling the inhabitants of the world to learn righteousness.

> *In the way of Thy judgments,*
> *O Lord, we wait for Thee;*
> *Thy name and the thought of Thee is the delight of our soul.*
> *My soul yearns for Thee in the night,*
> *My spirit within me earnestly seeks Thee.*
> *For as Thy judgments are wrought in the earth,*
> *The inhabitants of the world learn righteousness.*
>
> *Isaiah 26:8-9*

To Isaiah, God is strength, song, salvation (Isa. 12:2), "a rock of refuge" (17:10); but He can also become "a stone of offence, a rock of stumbling, . . . a trap and a snare" (Isa. 8:14).

For the Lord is often passive, seemingly indifferent to Israel's fate. He does not act at once; He does not always intervene, but he is watching the course of events. Thus the Lord said to Isaiah:

> *I will quietly look for My abode,*
> *Like clear heat in sunshine,*
> *Like a cloud of dew in the heat of harvest.*
>
> *Isaiah 18:4*

The summer heat and the dew promote the maturing of the grape. Destroyers and oppressors are allowed to continue until just before the fruit matures, when the branches together with the fruit will be ruthlessly cut off (Isa. 18:5-6).[19] "The Lord waits to be gracious to you" (Isa. 30:18). When the moment is ripe and His purpose complete,

> *Now I will arise, says the Lord,*
> *Now I will lift Myself up,*
> *Now I will be exalted.*
>
> *Isaiah 33:10*

God's ways are just, right, wise, but neither transparent nor immune to misunderstanding. There is an unfolding and a shrouding, a concealing within a disclosing, consoling as well as confusing.

It is hard to see how history and justice are always one. "The Lord will

---

[19] See E. J. Kissane, *op. cit.,* p. 207.

rise up . . . to do His deed—strange is His deed; to work His work—alien
is His work" (Isa. 28:21). It is a dawn of meaning to some, and darkness to
others. God is "wonderful in counsel, excellent in wisdom" (Isa. 28:29). Yet
His work often stuns man's power of comprehension. He does

> . . . marvelous things with this people,
> Wonderful and marvelous;
> The wisdom of their wise men shall fail,
> And the prudence of their prudent men shall be hid.
>
> *Isaiah 29:14*

What is unequivocal in God's wisdom becomes ambiguous to man's intelligence.

> Whoever is wise, let him understand these things;
> Whoever is discerning, let him know them;
> For the ways of the Lord are right,
> The upright walk in them,
> But transgressors stumble in them.
>
> *Hosea 14:9 [H. 14:10]*

Exceedingly intricate are His ways. Any attempt to formulate a theory, to
stamp a dogma, to define God's itinerary through history, is a sham, fraught
with pretension. In the realm of theology, shallowness is treason.

The psalmist is overwhelmed by the sublime grandeur of God's righteousness and the unfathomable depth of His judgments. They are like mighty
mountains beyond the reach of man, like the abyss too deep to fathom. Only
His love and faithfulness are everywhere.

> Thy love, O Lord, extends to the heavens,
> Thy faithfulness to the clouds.
> Thy righteousness is like the mighty mountains,
> Thy judgments are like the great abyss.
>
> *Psalm 36:5-6*[20]

Jeremiah is a person who stands "in the council of the Lord," but at the
same time is exasperated by the mysterious remoteness of the Lord. God is
his strength, stronghold, and refuge (Jer. 16:19), but at times God appears
"like a man confused, like a mighty man who cannot save" (Jer. 14:9). At
times Jeremiah sings of the joy and delight in being "called by Thy name"
(Jer. 15:16), and at times he cries out, "Be not a terror to me!" (Jer. 17:17.)
At times he maintains, "The Lord is with me a dread warrior, therefore my
persecutors will stumble; they will not overcome me" (Jer. 20:11), and at

---

[20] See Ibn Ezra, *Commentary, ad loc.*

times he exclaims, "Wilt Thou be to me like a deceitful brook? Like waters that fail?" (Jer. 15:18.)

It is one of the essential paradoxes of prophetic thinking that, although the prophet speaks continually of the people's guilt and of dreadful punishment in store for them, once the disaster comes he is stunned, puzzled, unable to justify completely the full measure of suffering.

> *Is Israel a slave? Is he a homeborn servant?*
> *Why then has he become a prey?*
> *The lions have roared against him,*
> *They have roared loudly.*
> *They have made his land a waste;*
> *His cities are in ruins, without inhabitant. . . .*
> *O Thou hope of Israel,*
> *Its savior in time of trouble,*
> *Why shouldst Thou be like a stranger in the land,*
> *Like a wayfarer who turns aside to tarry for a night?*
> *Jeremiah 2:14-15; 14:8*

In an imaginary dialogue with Israel, the Lord apologizes, as it were, for abandoning His people. The wrath is not of His own choice. It is the people who are responsible for it. The prophet hears "the cry of my dear people from the length and breadth of the Land": "Is the Lord not in Zion? Is her King not in her?" And to this God responds: "Why have they provoked Me to anger with their graven images and with their foreign idols?" (Jer. 8:19.)

For all the inner identification with God, the prophet is not always ready to accept divine judgment as final (Amos 7:2, 5). He does not hesitate to complain about God's way. Isaiah asks: "How long, O Lord?" (Isa. 6:11); and Habakkuk: "O Lord, how long shall I cry for help, and Thou wilt not hear?" (Hab. 1:2). Yet, once God acts and the scourge takes its bitter toll, the prophets are neither crushed nor resentful. Ill follows ill, woe succeeds woe, and no grumbling (cf. Lam. 2:20). "The Lord is in the right, for I have rebelled against His word" (Lam. 1:18).

"I have dealt you the blow of an enemy, the punishment of a merciless foe, because your guilt is great, because your sins are flagrant" (Jer. 30:14). Oppressed and afflicted, Israel does not question God's judgment. Affliction only demonstrates God's power and justice.

"It is not so much the suffering as the senselessness of it that is unendurable," declared Nietzsche. Pain was the price the people had to pay for having been chosen and then having sinned. "The Lord has done what He purposed, has carried out His threat; as He ordained long ago . . ." (Lam. 2:17). Pain had a purpose: to purify the people; and the people did not despise the Lord's discipline, nor become weary of His reproof, "for the

Lord reproves him whom He loves, as a father the son in whom he delights"
(Prov. 3:11-12). "Know then in your heart that, as a man castigates his
son, so the Lord your God castigates you" (Deut. 8:5). "Blessed is the man
whom Thou dost chasten, O Lord . . ." (Ps. 93:12). Out of anguish comes
the people's prayer:

> Thou hast chastened me, and I was chastened,
> Like an untrained calf;
> Bring me back that I may be restored,
> For Thou art the Lord my God.
> For after I turned away I repented;
> After I was instructed, I smote upon my thigh;
> I was ashamed, I was confounded,
> Because I bore the disgrace of my youth.
> > Jeremiah 31:18-19

And yet, God is not absent even though His work may be silent. His
presence in history does not continually come to expression in cataclysmic
events. The ways in which He acts are perceptible at rare moments, but
usually they are indiscernible—just as the work of him who tills the soil is
only occasionally spectacular. He does not always plow or harrow; there are
many small, inconspicuous labors to be carried out in order to achieve the
main goal. In fact, the undramatic art of tilling the soil reflects God's
counsel and wisdom.

> Give ear, and hear my voice;
> Hearken, and hear my speech.
> Is the ploughman continually plowing?
> Does he continually break up and harrow his ground?
> Does he not, when he has leveled its surface,
> Scatter dill, sow cummin,
> Plant wheat, corn and barley,
> And spelt as the border?
> For he is instructed aright;
> His God teaches him.
> Dill is not threshed with a sledge,
> Nor is a cart wheel rolled over cummin;
> But dill is beaten out with a stick,
> And cummin with a rod.
> Does one crush bread grain?
> No, he does not thresh it for ever;
> When he drives his cart wheel over it
> With his horses, he does not crush it.
> This also comes from the Lord of hosts;
> He is wonderful in counsel,
> And excellent in wisdom.
> > Isaiah 28:23-29

The prophet is prepared for pain. One of the effects of his presence is to intensify the people's capacity for suffering, to rend the veil that lies between life and pain. And yet Jeremiah knew how shattering the outpouring of God's anger could be. "Chastise, O Lord, but in just measure; not in Thy anger, lest Thou bring me to nothing" (Jer. 10:24). In a moment of anguish he cried out:

> Why is my pain unceasing,
> My wound incurable,
> Refusing to be healed,
> Wilt Thou be to me like a deceitful brook?
> Like waters that fail?
>
> Jeremiah 15:18

Man is ready to accept a God Who is close at hand, Whose power is present, Whose judgment can be understood, Whose glory can be experienced. But the invisible God of Israel is hard on man, for His power is often absent, His judgment obscure, His glory concealed.

> Am I a God close at hand,
> And not a God far off?
> Says the Lord.
> Can anyone hide himself in secret places
> Where I shall not see him?
> Do I not fill heaven and earth?
> Says the Lord.
>
> Jeremiah 23:23-24[21]

Hopes are wrecked, faith is mocked. What must not happen, does. Is history, then, a distortion of what God wills, misrepresenting and defying His will? Or does God's itinerary in history lead through a maze of seeming contradictions? Is His design for justice woven of more threads than man comprehends? You shall be patient, for I the Lord your God am patient.

> The anger of the Lord will not turn back
> Until he has executed and accomplished
> The intents of His mind.
> In the latter days you will understand it clearly.
>
> Jeremiah 23:20; cf. 30:24

In the eyes of man, what comes about and what is still to come may be an age apart; in the eyes of God, they are one. The darkness of history, therefore, conceals a light. Beyond the mystery is meaning. And the meaning is destined to be disclosed.

---

[21] These verses do not belong in the context of ch. 23.

LIKE A STRANGER IN THE LAND

Perplexity is not alien to the prophets. Jeremiah continually proclaims that God's justice is revealed in the events of history, that the Lord is the Righteous Judge Who gives to every man according to his deeds (Jer. 17:10), that God's justice never rests until it reaches and defeats those who are wicked and defiant. This certainty is a stronghold in which his teaching is sheltered. However, experience and observation lead him to the haunting realization that the magnificent rock is not impregnable; what he is called upon to proclaim he finds difficult to sustain.

Significantly, the question he raises is not why the righteous suffer, but rather why the wicked prosper.

> *Righteous art Thou, O Lord, when I complain to Thee;*
> *Yet I would plead my case before Thee.*
> *Why does the way of the wicked prosper?*
> *Why do all who are treacherous thrive?*
> *Thou plantest them, and they take root;*
> *They grow and bring forth fruit.*
>
>   *Jeremiah 12:1-2*

The answer he is given is a rebuke; the issue that puzzles him is minor compared with issues he may still face.[22]

> *If you have raced with men on foot, and they have wearied you,*
> *How will you compete with horses?*
> *And if in a safe land you fall down,*
> *How will you do in the jungle of Jordan?*
>
>   *Jeremiah 12:5*[23]

Indeed, the greatest question of all regarding the problem of justice is yet to confront him. It is the question, "Why do the righteous suffer?" Is suffering an index of guilt? Is it not a fact that suffering is meted out beyond the measure of guilt? The land of Israel was destroyed, and the misery seemed out of proportion to the guilt.

> *How long will the land mourn,*
> *The grass of every field wither?*
>   *Jeremiah 12:4*

> *Behold, He snatches away; who can hinder Him?*
> *Who will say to Him: What doest Thou?*
>   *Job 9:12*

---

[22] Compare and contrast Jer. 2:18.
[23] Cf. Kimhi, *Commentary, ad loc.* It seems that vs. 5 follows directly vs. 2a. Vs. 6 follows 11:22. In the interpretation, I follow P. Volz, *op. cit.,* pp. 141 f.

A HISTORY OF WAITING FOR GOD

This is what the prophets discovered. *History is a nightmare.* There are more scandals, more acts of corruption, than are dreamed of in philosophy. It would be blasphemous to believe that what we witness is the end of God's creation. It is an act of evil to accept the state of evil as either inevitable or final. Others may be satisfied with improvement, the prophets insist upon redemption. The way man acts is a disgrace, and it must not go on forever. Together with condemnation, the prophets offer a promise. The heart of stone will be taken away, a heart of flesh will be given instead (Ezek. 11:19). Even the nature of the beasts will change to match the glory of the age. The end of days will be the end of fear, the end of war; idolatry will disappear, knowledge of God will prevail.

The inner history of Israel is a history of waiting for God, of waiting for His arrival. Just as Israel is certain of the reality of the Promised Land, so is she certain of the coming of "the promised day." She lives by a promise of "the day of the Lord," a day of judgment followed by salvation, when evil will be consumed and an age of glory will ensue.

In contrast to Amos, who stressed the aspect of judgment of the day, Isaiah unfolds the total vision of the darkness and the glory.

> *The earth staggers like a drunken man,*
> *It sways like a hut; . . .*
> *On that day the Lord will punish*
> *The host of heaven, in heaven,*
> *And the kings of the earth, on the earth.*
> *Isaiah 24:20-21*

Yet, following the judgment "it will be said on that day: Lo, this is our God; we have waited for Him, that He might save us. This is the Lord; we have waited for Him; let us be glad and rejoice in His salvation" (Isa. 25:9).

In words contained in the book of Isaiah we hear of the time when "the terror of defeat and captivity will be merely a memory."

> *Your eyes will see the king in his beauty;*
> *They will behold a land that stretches afar.*
> *Your mind will muse on the terror:*
> *Where is he who counted, where is he who weighed the tribute?*
> *Where is he who counted the towers? . . .*
> *Your eyes will see Jerusalem,*
> *A quiet habitation, an immovable tent,*
> *Whose stakes will never be plucked up,*
> *Nor will any of its cords be broken.*
>
> *Isaiah 33:17-20*

The day will come when God "will destroy the covering that is cast over all peoples, the veil that is spread over all nations. He will swallow up death for ever, the Lord God will wipe away tears from all faces, the reproach of His people He will take away from all the earth; for the Lord has spoken" (Isa. 25:7-8) . "Those who err in spirit will come to understanding, and those who murmur will accept instruction." (Isa. 29:24) .

In a world where images are holy, where idols are both feared and adored, where paganism rules triumphantly, Isaiah predicts:

> *The idols shall utterly pass away!*
> *And the holes of the ground,*
> *From before the terror of the Lord,*
> *And from the glory of His majesty,*
> *When He rises to terrify the earth.*
> *In that day men will cast forth*
> *Their idols of silver and their idols of gold,*
> *Which they made for themselves to worship,*
> *To the moles and to the bats,*
> *To enter the caverns of the rocks,*
> *And the clefts of the cliffs,*
> *From before the terror of the Lord,*
> *And from the glory of His majesty,*
> *When He rises to terrify the earth.*
>
> *Isaiah 2:18-21*

"In that day men will regard their Maker, and their eyes will look to the Holy One of Israel; they will not have regard for the altars, the work of their hands, and they will not look to what their own fingers have made, either the Asherim or the altars of incense" (Isa. 17:7-8) .

The people will be purified by suffering. "Though the Lord give you the bread of adversity and the water of affliction, yet your Teacher will not hide Himself any more, but your eyes shall see your Teacher, and your ears shall hear a word behind you saying: This is the way, walk in it, when you turn to the right or when you turn to the left" (Isa. 30:20-21) .[24]

The promise made to Abraham will be fulfilled. "In you shall all the families of the earth be blessed" (Gen. 12:3).[25] Israel will flourish, and all nations will come to understanding.

> *Thus says the Lord, Who redeemed Abraham,*
>   *concerning Jacob:*
> *Jacob shall no more be ashamed,*
> *No more shall his face grow pale.*
> *For when he sees his children,*

---

[24] Isaiah's authorship of this passage is maintained by Kissane, *op. cit.*, p. 337.
[25] Cf. Gen. 18:18; 22:18; 26:4; 28:14; see also C. R. North, *The Old Testament Interpretations of History* (London, 1946) , p. 26.

The work of My hands in his midst,
They will hallow My name;
They will hallow the Holy One of Jacob,
And will stand in awe of the God of Israel.
And those who err in spirit will come to understanding,
And those who murmur will accept instruction.

Isaiah 29:22-24

THEY SHALL NOT HURT OR DESTROY

The sword is the pride of man; arsenals, forts, and chariots lend supremacy to nations. War is the climax of human ingenuity, the object of supreme efforts: men slaughtering each other, cities battered into ruins. What is left behind is agony, death, and desolation. At the same time, men think very highly of themselves; "they are wise in their own hearts, shrewd in their own sight" (Isa. 5:21). Idols of silver and gold are what they worship. Nineveh, "the bloody city, all full of lies and booty," held the world in spell with her "countless harlotries," with her "graceful and deadly charms" (Nah. 3:1, 4).

Into a world fascinated with idolatry, drunk with power, bloated with arrogance, enters Isaiah's word that the swords will be beaten into plowshares, that nations will search, not for gold, power or harlotries, but for God's word.

The power and splendor of Nineveh were unrivaled in the world. For centuries it was the city to which the eyes of the civilized world were turned. The immense tribute that flowed from many lands into the capital of the empire not only helped to maintain a huge army, but also lust, luster, and luxury.

Jerusalem, in contrast, was "a quiet habitation," little known to the nations except as a target for invaders. But in the vision of Isaiah the nations will no more turn their eyes to Nineveh, the seat of human power, but to Jerusalem, the seat of divine learning, eager to learn God's ways, eager to learn how to walk in His paths.

In that day the root of Jesse shall stand as an ensign to the peoples; him shall the nations seek, and his dwellings shall be glorious (Isa. 11:10).

It shall come to pass at the end of days
That the mountain of the house of the Lord
Shall be established as the highest of the mountains,
And shall be raised above the hills,
And all the nations shall flow to it.
And many people shall come and say:
Come, let us go up to the mountain of the Lord,
To the house of the God of Jacob;

> *That He may teach us His ways*
> *And that we may walk in His paths.*
> *For out of Zion shall go forth teaching,*
> *And the word of the Lord from Jerusalem.*
> *He shall judge between the nations,*
> *And shall decide for many peoples;*
> *And they shall beat their swords into plowshares,*
> *And their spears into pruning hooks.*
> *Nation shall not lift up sword against nation,*
> *Neither shall they learn war any more.*
>
> *Isaiah 2:2-4*

What to us seems inconceivable, to Isaiah was a certainty: War will be abolished. They shall not learn war any more because they shall seek knowledge of the word of God. Passion for war will be subdued by a greater passion: the passion to discover God's ways.[26]

Had the prophets relied on human resources for justice and righteousness, on man's ability to fulfill all of God's demands, on man's power to achieve redemption, they would not have insisted upon the promise of messianic redemption, for messianism implies that any course of living, even the supreme efforts of man by himself, must fail in redeeming the world. In other words, human history is not sufficient unto itself. Man's conscience is timid, while the world is ablaze with agony. His perception of justice is shallow, often defective, and his judgment liable to deception.

> *There shall come forth a shoot from the stump of Jesse,*
> *And a branch shall grow out of his roots,*
> *And the Spirit of the Lord shall rest upon him,*
> *The spirit of wisdom and understanding,*
> *The spirit of counsel and might,*
> *The spirit of knowledge and the fear of the Lord.*
> *Through the fear of the Lord he will have supreme sensitivity.*
> *He shall not judge by what his eyes see,[27]*
> *Or decide by what his ears hear;*
> *But with righteousness shall he judge the helpless,*
> *And decide with equity for the meek of the earth;*
> *And he shall smite the earth with the rod of his mouth,*
> *And with the breath of his lips he shall slay the wicked.*
> *Righteousness shall be the girdle of his waist,*
> *And faithfulness the girdle of his loins.*
> *The wolf shall dwell with the lamb,*
> *And the leopard shall lie down with the kid,*

---

[26] The study by H. Gross, *Die Idee des ewigen und allgemeinen Weltfriedens* (Trier, 1946), reached the author after the completion of this manuscript.
[27] See I Sam. 16:7.

And the calf and the lion and the fatling together,
And a little child shall lead them.
The cow and the bear shall feed;
Their young shall lie down together;
And the lion shall eat straw like the ox.
The sucking child shall play over the hole of the asp,
And the weaned child shall put his hand on the adder's den.
They shall not hurt or destroy
In all My holy mountain;
For the earth shall be full of the knowledge of the Lord
As the waters cover the sea.

Isaiah 11:1-9

BLESSED BE MY PEOPLE EGYPT

What is history? Wars, victories, and wars. So many dead. So many tears. So little regret. So many fears. And who could sit in judgment over the victims of cruelty when their horror turns to hatred? Is it easy to keep the horror of wickedness from turning into a hatred of the wicked? The world is drenched in blood, and the guilt is endless. Should not all hope be abandoned?

What saved the prophets from despair was their messianic vision and the idea of man's capacity for repentance. That vision and that idea affected their understanding of history.

History is not a blind alley, and guilt is not an abyss. There is always a way that leads out of guilt: repentance, or turning to God. The prophet is a person who, living in dismay, has the power to transcend his dismay. Over all the darkness of experience hovers the vision of a different day. "In that day there shall be a highway from Egypt to Assyria; the Assyrian will come to Egypt, and the Egyptian into Assyria, and the Egyptians will worship with the Assyrians.[28] In that day Israel shall be a third with Egypt and Assyria, a blessing in the midst of the earth, which the Lord of hosts has blessed, saying, Blessed be My people Egypt, and Assyria, the work of My hands, and Israel, My inheritance" (Isa. 19:23-25).[29]

Egypt and Assyria are locked in deadly wars. Hating each other, they are both the enemies of Israel. Abominable are their idolatries, and frightful are their crimes. In the days of Abraham and Moses, as in the days of Isaiah,

---

[28] See A. B. Ehrlich, *Randglossen zur Hebräischen Bibel*, IV (Leipzig, 1912), 73.

[29] Duhm, followed by many critics, maintains that 19:16–25 is postexilic. Assyria is taken to stand for Seleucid Syria, and Egypt for Ptolemaic Egypt. Others maintain that the prophecy belongs to Isaiah; see Y. Kaufmann, *The Religion of Israel* (Heb.), p. 226, n. 80; (Eng.), p. 350, n. 2; Kissane, *op. cit.*, pp. 209 f. For our purpose it matters little whether Isaiah or another composed this chapter.

the repudiation of both Mesopotamia and Egypt was the very destiny of
Israel. How does Isaiah, the son of a people which cherishes the privilege
of being called by the Lord, "My people, the work of My hands," feel about
Egypt and Assyria? The God of Israel is also the God of her enemies, without their knowing Him and despite their defying Him. The enmity between
the nations will turn to friendship. They will live together when they
worship together.[30]

---

[30] A similar thought is found in Zech. 2:15: "Many nations shall join themselves to the
Lord in that day, and shall be My people." Cf. Isa. 56:1-7: "My house shall be called a
house of prayer for all peoples." See also I Kings 8:41-43; Isa. 45:20; 60:6-7; 66:18-19; Jer.
3:17; 4:2; 12:16; 16:19; Zeph. 3:9-10; Zech. 8:20-23; 14:16-21; Mal. 1:11; Ps. 22:28;
47:2; 65:3; 67:46; 68:3-33; 76:12; 96:7-8;102:23;117:1.

10. CHASTISEMENT

THE FUTILITY OF CHASTISEMENT

The threat of punishment is one of the most prominent themes of the prophetic orations. Yet the prophets themselves seem to have questioned the efficacy of punishment. Punishment has three aims: retributive, deterrent, and reformatory.[1]

The divine intention, according to the prophets, is not primarily retributive, to impose penalty in consequence of wrongdoing; but rather deterrent, to discourage transgression by fear of punishment; and reformatory, to repair, to refine, to make pure by affliction: God's purpose is not to destroy but to purify (cf. Isa. 27:7-8; 28:29), "to purge away your dross as with lye and remove all your alloy; . . . afterward you shall be called the city of righteousness, the faithful city" (Isa. 1:25-26; cf. 4:4). "Behold, I will refine them and test them, for what else can I do, because of My dear people?" (Jer. 9:7 [H. 9:6].) "I have tried you in the furnace of affliction," said a later prophet (Isa. 48:10). Through suffering lies the way to restoration and to the implanting of His will in the hearts of regenerated people (Isa. 1:26; Hos. 6; 10:12, 14; Jer. 24:7; 31:33 f.). In distress they may seek Him (Hos. 5:15).

---

[1] According to L. R. Farnell, *The Attributes of God* (Oxford, 1925), p. 174, the vindictive theory was first challenged by the humanitarian ethics and philosophy of the Greeks. He refers to Plato's theory of human punishment, the intention of which should be reformative and remedial only, and to Homer's suggestion, *Odyssey* 1, 31, that the gods send no evil to men, either in this life or in the next. However, according to Homer, the purpose of punishment is retributive and deterrent. For the Greeks, justice was the retribution that countered wrongdoing. Thus, "justice and revenge are not very different, indeed they coincide when vengeance is taken for wrongdoing. A product of this kind of justice is the *ius talionis* which was usual in early times and finds pregnant expression in the saying 'an eye for an eye, a tooth for a tooth.' This is to be traced among the Greeks also; for them, justice is retributive justice." (M. P. Nilsson, *Greek Piety* [Oxford, 1948], pp. 35 f.) The Greek word for punishment, *poine*, has a coercive element. "*Poine* overtakes the evildoer as a spirit of revenge, sometimes at the hand of others, sometimes through the dispensation of fate, generally through his own misdeeds." (*Encyclopaedia of Social Sciences*, XII, 712.) A combination of the retributive and the deterrent intentions of justice is found in Deut. 19:19 ff.; cf. K. F. Nägelsbach, *Die Homerische Theologie* (Nürnberg, 1861), p. 320.

The prophets, however, discovered that suffering does not necessarily bring about purification, nor is punishment effective as a deterrent. The futility of chastisement was a problem that occupied the minds of the prophets. Jeremiah, for example, knew that punishment is not the answer:

> O Lord, do not thy eyes look for truth?
> Thou hast smitten them,
> But they felt no anguish;
> Thou hast consumed them,
> But they refused to take correction.
> They have made their faces harder than rock;
> They have refused to repent. . . .
> In vain have I smitten your children,
> They took no correction.
>
> Jeremiah 5:3; 2:30

THE STRANGE DISPARITY

The two staggering facts in the life of a prophet are: God's turning to him, and man's turning away from him. This is often his lot: to be chosen by God and to be rejected by the people. The word of God, so clear to him, is unintelligible to them.

> To whom will he impart knowledge,
> And to whom will he convey a message?
> Those who are weaned from the milk,
> Those taken from the breast?
> For it is precept upon precept, precept upon precept,
> Line upon line, line upon line,
> Here a little, there a little.
> Nay, but by men of strange lips
> And with an alien tongue
> The Lord will speak to this people,
> To whom He has said:
> This is rest;
> Give rest to the weary
> And this is repose;
> Yet they refused to hear.
> Therefore the word of the Lord will be to them
> Precept upon precept, precept upon precept,
> Line upon line, line upon line,
> Here a little, there a little;
> That they may go, and fall backward,
> And be broken, snared, and caught.
>
> Isaiah 28:9-13

What baffles the prophet is the disparity between the power and impact of God and the immense indifference, unyieldingness, sluggishness, and inertia of the heart. God's thunderous voice is shaking heaven and earth, and man does not hear the faintest sound. The Lord roars like a lion (Amos 3:8). His word is like fire, like a hammer which breaks the rock in pieces (Jer. 23:29), and the people go about unmoved, undisturbed, unaware. What to the prophet is like the sun piercing the thickest cloud remains unnoticed by the people.

> *Woe to those who call evil good,*
> *And good evil,*
> *Who put darkness for light,*
> *And light for darkness,*
> *Who put bitter for sweet,*
> *And sweet for bitter.*
> *Isaiah 5:20*

The prophet is scorched by the word of God—"There is in my heart as it were a burning fire shut up in my bones" (Jer. 21:9)—but the hearts of the people are asbestos, fireproof.

> *I have become a laughingstock all the day,*
> *Everyone mocks me. . . .*
> *The word of God has become for me*
> *A reproach and derision all day long.*
> *They refuse to hear the instruction of the Lord.*
> *Jeremiah 20:7-8*

> *They say to the seers: See not!*
> *And to prophets: Prophesy not to us what is right!*
> *Speak to us smooth things,*
> *Prophesy illusions!*
> *Depart from the way, turn aside from the path,*
> *Let us hear no more of the Holy One of Israel!*
> *Isaiah 30:10-11*

The prophet Amos was forbidden to appear in Bethel and Jeremiah was imprisoned because their message shocked those in power.

It was a major enigma that confronted the prophet: How is it possible not to see the majesty of the Lord (Isa. 26:10), not to sense that the whole earth is full of His glory (Isa. 6:3), not to understand God's sign in the happenings of history? What we call the irrational nature of man, they called hardness of heart.

> *O Lord, Thy hand is exalted,*
> *But they see not.*
> *Isaiah 26:11*

It is a recurring complaint: "O foolish and senseless people, who have eyes, but see not, who have ears, but hear not" (Jer. 5:21; Ezek. 12:2; Isa.

43:8). "Sons who will not hear the instructions of the Lord" (Isa. 30:9). "Like a stubborn heifer, Israel is stubborn" (Hos. 4:16). "Ephraim is like a dove, silly and without sense, calling to Egypt, going to Assyria" (Hos. 7:11). "My people are destroyed for lack of knowledge!" (Hos. 4:6) "Their ears are closed, they cannot listen (Jer. 6:10). The Lord set watchmen over the people, saying: "Give heed to the sound of the trumpet!" But they said, "We will not give heed" (Jer. 6:17). How abysmal stubbornness can be. Man rears his own despots—idols, lies, perversions; he labors to prepare his own disaster. Is he insane?

THE FAILURE OF FREEDOM

The central message of the prophets is the insistence that *the human situation can be understood only in conjunction with the divine situation.* The absurdity of isolating the human situation and treating it in disregard of the divine involvement is exemplified by the self-defeating course of man-made history.

Modern interpretations see history as the arena in which man reigns supreme, with the forces of nature as his only possible adversaries. Man is alone, free, and growing stronger. God is either nonexistent or unconcerned. It is human initiative that makes history, and it is primarily by force that constellations change. Man can attain his own salvation.

This view of history, starting with man's consciousness of freedom and sense of sovereignty, arrives at the antinomy of freedom and fate: the frustration and collapse of freedom. Man is not the master of his own destiny. Forces he cannot completely control emerge imperceptibly to stifle him and to defy his intentions, his plans, and his visions.

Prophetic reflection begins, we might say, with the abuse and consequent failure of freedom, with the irrationality of human conduct, and it points to God Who stands above history. Man-made history is not history's only dimension. The pathos and judgment of God transcend the human dimension. Great conquerors are seen as mere tools of His mysterious will. Man has choice, but not sovereignty.

History is not a meaningless conglomeration of neutral facts, but a drama unfolding the relationship between God and man. The drama is staged in time and encompasses the wide arena of human affairs. A battle is raging: man in his presumption undertakes to fashion history in disregard and defiance of God. The prophets witness the misery that man endures as well as man's wickedness that God endures, and even tolerates. But God is wrestling with man. History is where God is defied, where His judgment is enacted, and where His kingship is to be established. For it is of the realm of space, not of the realm of history, that the seraphim proclaim: "It is full of His glory." Only a sprinkling of His glory is found in history.

THE SUSPENSION OF FREEDOM

The opposite of freedom is not determinism, but hardness of heart. Freedom presupposes openness of heart, of mind, of eye and ear.

According to Hegel, the history of the world is none other than the progress of the consciousness of freedom. With some qualification one might say in the spirit of the prophets that the history of the world with which they dealt was none other than the progress of the condition of hardness of heart.

Freedom is not a natural disposition, but God's precious gift to man. Those in whom viciousness becomes second nature, those in whom brutality is linked with haughtiness, forfeit their ability and therefore their right to receive that gift. Hardening of the heart is the suspension of freedom.[2] Sin becomes compulsory and self-destructive. Guilt and punishment become one.

In other words, the ability to understand, to see or to hear the divine significance of events, may be granted or withheld from man. One may see great wonders, but remain entirely insensitive. "You have seen all that the Lord did before your eyes in the land of Egypt . . . the great trials which *your eyes saw,* the signs, and those great wonders. But to this day the Lord *has not given you* a mind to understand, or *eyes to see,* or ears to hear" (Deut. 29:2-4 [H. 29:1-3]).

The normal soul is fit and pliable, open to truth, sensitive to God. But if the people "have eyes, but see not, have ears, but hear not," it is because of "a stubborn and rebellious heart" (Jer. 5:23). Sin has its cause in the hardness, stiffness, or the stubbornness of heart.[3] To be callous is to be blind to the presence of God in the world, blind to "the glory of His majesty" (Isa. 2:21). Such blindness results in pride, haughtiness, and arrogance.

Hardness of heart is a condition of which the person afflicted is unaware. Not knowing what ails him, he is unable to repent and to recover. However, when hardness is intensified from above, responsibility is assumed by God. He smites and He restores, bringing about a revival of sensitivity.

It seems that the only cure for willful hardness is to make it absolute.

---

[2] See Maimonides, *Eight Chapters,* ch. 8.

[3] In the Bible, callousness is the root of sin. There are many words to express it: "stubbornness of heart," "hardness of heart" (Deut. 29:18; Lam. 3:65); "brazen-faced and stiffhearted" (Ezek. 2:4); "stubborn of heart" (Isa. 46:12); "uncircumcised in the heart" (Jer. 9:25). "The heart [of the godless] is gross like fat," exclaims the psalmist (119:70). The prophets continually reproach Israel for lack of sensibility (Isa. 42:20; 48:8; cf. Ps. 106:7; Prov. 28:14; 29:1; cf. also E. La B. Cherbonnier, *Hardness of Heart* [New York, 1955]).

Half-callousness, paired with obstinate conceit, seeks no cure. When hardness is complete, it becomes despair, the end of conceit. Out of despair, out of total inability to believe, prayer bursts forth.

Prophets came and went; words had no effect, turbulent punishments, miseries, were of no avail. Man is of many minds. "The heart is deceitful above all things, and desperately corrupt; who can understand it?" (Jer. 17:9.) Where signs and words from without fail, despair within may succeed.

The dark fact of callousness, just like the luminous power of understanding, goes back to God who creates light as well as darkness in the heart of man. The weird miracle of callousness, resistance to God, may be due to an obstinacy imposed by God. Punishment and guilt become one.

While not denying that the people sin of their own free will, there is a subtle awareness of God's being involved in man's going astray, an involvement that adds bafflement to injury.

> O Lord, why dost Thou make us err from Thy ways
> And harden our heart, so that we fear Thee not?
> Return for the sake of Thy servants,
> The tribes of Thy heritage.
>
> Isaiah 63:17

One might ask: Do not these lines imply the thought that God shares in human responsibility and is involved in human guilt? It is a thought that may also be evoked by the words in God's speech to Job:

> [The ostrich] deals cruelly with her young as if they were not hers. . . .
> Because God has made her forget wisdom,
> And given her no share of understanding.
>
> Job 39:16-17

"Ah, Lord God, surely Thou hast utterly deceived this people and Jerusalem, saying: It shall be well with you; whereas the sword has reached their very life" (Jer. 4:10). In other words: Since Thou hast been patient with the false prophets who misled and persuaded the people that all is well, it is as if though Thou hast deceived them. The false prophets have led the people astray by insisting that there is no reason for anxiety; what the future holds in store is peace and prosperity. The leaders are responsible for the people. But who is responsible for the leaders? Witnessing the disaster that came upon Judah, Jeremiah exclaims: "For most of the people think that the Lord has spoken to those prophets, and they are confused as to whether to listen to me or to them, and the majority is inclined to follow them, because they are many."[4]

---

[4] Kimhi, Commentary, ad loc.

NO WORD IS GOD'S LAST WORD

Agony is the final test. When all hopes are dashed and all conceit is shattered, man begins to miss what he has long spurned. In darkness, God becomes near and clear. "He shall go through it suffering and hungry, and then when hungry he shall break out in anger and curse his king and his gods; He shall turn his face upwards, and look upon the earth, and behold distress and darkness, the gloom of darkness, and he will be thrust into thick darkness. But there will be no gloom for her that was in anguish. . . . The people that walked in darkness behold a great light; those who dwelt in a land of deep darkness, on them a light shines" (Isa. 8:21—9:2 [H. 8:21—9:1]).

When all pretensions are abandoned, one begins to feel the burden of guilt. It is easier to return from an extreme distance than from the complacency of a good conscience, from spurious proximity.

God smites and He restores, He hurts and He heals, He obstructs and He exposes hearts and eyes. Such exposing, the liquidation of Isaiah's first assignment (see above, p. 89) is perhaps alluded to in the words: "He has taken away the covering of Judah" (Isa. 22:8).

Isaiah's original charge must have early come to an end. Did he not insist that his mission was to "strengthen the weak hands and make firm the feeble knees" (Isa. 35:3)? And did he not appeal in words designed to bring about insight and understanding: "O house of Jacob, come let us walk in the light of the Lord" (Isa. 2:5)? "Wash yourselves, make yourselves clean, remove the evil of your doings from before My eyes" (1:16).

God is invisible, distant, dwelling in darkness (I Kings 8:12). His thoughts are not our thoughts; His ways in history are shrouded and perplexing. Prophecy is a moment of unshrouding, an opening of the eyes, a lifting of the curtain. Such moments are rare in history. "With their flocks and herds they shall go to seek the Lord, but they will not find Him; He has withdrawn from them" (Hos. 5:6). Moments did come when the prophets obtained no vision from the Lord (Lam. 2:9).

> *We do not see our signs;*
> *There is no longer any prophet.*
> Psalm 74:9

What Isaiah suggested in terms of human insensitivity was expressed by Amos in terms of divine inaccessibility. Generation after generation, it was as if God had opened a door: in the prophets His word was revealed. Prophecy had become a commonplace, and the word wearisome, obtrusive. Not forever, the prophet is told. The Lord will shut the door, and the word will obtrude no more.

> *Behold, the days are coming, says the Lord,*
> *When I will send a famine on the land;*
> *Not a famine of bread, nor a thirst for water,*
> *But of hearing the words of the Lord.*
> *They shall wander from sea to sea, and from north to east;*
> *They shall run to and fro, to seek the word of the Lord,*
> *But they shall not find it.*
>
> *Amos 8:11-12*

And yet, the word of God never comes to an end. For this reason, prophetic predictions are seldom final. No word is God's final word. Judgment, far from being absolute, is conditional. A change in man's conduct brings about a change in God's judgment. No word is God's final word.

> *Yea, O people in Zion who dwell in Jerusalem; you shall weep no more. He will surely be gracious to you at the sound of your cry; when he hears it, he will answer you. And though the Lord give you the bread of adversity and the water of affliction, yet your Teacher will not hide himself any more, and your eyes shall see your Teacher. And your ears shall hear a word behind you, saying: This is the way, walk in it. . . . In that day the deaf shall hear the words of a book, and out of their gloom and darkness the eyes of the blind shall see. . . . Then the eyes of the blind shall be opened, and the ears of the deaf unstopped; then shall the lame man leap like a hart, and the tongue of the dumb sing for joy.*
>
> *Isaiah 30:19-21; 29:18; 35:5-6*

God's anger must not obscure His redeeming love.

> *Behold, God is my salvation;*
> *I will trust, and will not be afraid;*
> *For the Lord God is my strength and my song,*
> *And He has become my salvation.*
>
> *Isaiah 12:2*

"We have waited for Him, that He might save us" (Isa. 25:9). And the day will surely come "when the Lord binds up the hurt of His people, and heals the wounds inflicted by His blow" (Isa. 30:26). He hurts, and He heals.

11. JUSTICE

SACRIFICE

Sacred fire is burning on the altars in many lands. Animals are being offered to the glory of the gods. Priests burn incense, songs of solemn assemblies fill the air. Pilgrims are on the roads, pageantries in the sacred places. The atmosphere is thick with sanctity. In Israel, too, sacrifice is an essential act of worship. It is the experience of giving oneself vicariously to God and of being received by Him. And yet, the pre-exilic prophets uttered violent attacks on sacrifices (Amos 5:21-27; Hos. 6:6; Isa. 1:11-17; Mic. 6:6-8; Jer. 6:20; 7:21-23; Isa. 61:1-2; Pss. 40:7; 50:12-13). Samuel insisted: "Has the Lord as great delight in burnt offerings and sacrifices, as in obeying the voice of the Lord? Behold, to obey is better than sacrifice, and to hearken than the fat of rams" (I Sam. 15:22).[1] However, while Samuel stressed the primacy of obedience over sacrifice, Amos and the prophets who followed him not only stressed the primacy of morality over sacrifice, but even proclaimed that the worth of worship, far from being absolute, is contingent upon moral living, and that when immorality prevails, worship is detestable. Questioning man's right to worship through offerings and songs, they maintained that the primary way of serving God is through love, justice, and righteousness.

This is a paradox to be sure, and like every paradox its opposite is a view that is orthodox. It contains both a negation and an affirmation, the negation being more intelligible than the affirmation. It is difficult for us today to appreciate the boldness and defiance contained in these pronouncements. The distinction between the holy and the profane, between the divine and

---

[1] A sentence expressing a similar view is found in the *Instruction for King Merikare* who ruled Egypt in the second half of the third millennium B.C.E. "More acceptable is the character of one upright of heart than the ox of the evildoer." (*ANET*, pp. 417 f.) For other statements in later literature which have a bearing upon the attitude of the prophets to animal sacrifice, see R. S. Cripps, *A Critical and Exegetical Commentary on the Book of Amos* (London, 1929), pp. 342 ff.; A. J. Heschel, *Theology of Ancient Judaism*, I (Heb.; London and New York, 1962), 33 ff.

the mundane, is the basis of religious thinking. A line is drawn between the interests of man and the demands of God. What is it that all gods demand? Sacrifice, incense, reverence for their power. Sacrifice, the strength and the measure of piety, acts wherein God and man meet—all this should be called obnoxious?

Of course, the prophets did not condemn the practice of sacrifice in itself; otherwise, we should have to conclude that Isaiah intended to discourage the practice of prayer (Isa. 1:14-15).[2] They did, however, claim that deeds of injustice vitiate both sacrifice and prayer. Men may not drown the cries of the oppressed with the noise of hymns, nor buy off the Lord with increased offerings. The prophets disparaged the cult when it became a substitute for righteousness. It is precisely the implied recognition of the value of the cult that lends force to their insistence that there is something far more precious than sacrifice.

These feasts and assemblies, offerings and rites, hallowed by the loyalty of many generations, had become the essence of piety. One cannot doubt the sacred authenticity of the cult. It had a place and a procedure of its own, a sacred nimbus, a mysterious glory. It differed from all other pursuits; exceptional, striking, set apart, it conferred unique blessings. In the sacrificial acts something happened, something sacred was evoked, conjured up, initiated; something was released or cast away. The person was transformed, a communion vital to man and precious to God established.

In the sacrifice of homage, God was a participant; in the sacrifice of expiation, God was a recipient. The sacrificial act was a form of personal association with God, a way of entering into communion with Him. In offering an animal, a person was offering himself vicariously. It had the power of atonement.[3]

How supremely certain ancient man was that sacrifice was what the gods most desired may be deduced from the fact that fathers did not hesitate to slaughter their own children on the altar. When Mesha, the king of the Moabites, was hard-pressed in war, he sacrificed his own son, who would have reigned as his successor, for a burnt offering upon the wall (II Kings 3:27).[4]

---

[2] For a long time the polemic of the prophets was taken to mean a radical rejection of the cult. In more recent studies it is maintained that the prophets merely criticized the abuse and absolutization of the cult. See the literature cited in R. Hentschke, *Die Stellung der vorexilischen Schriftpropheten zum Kultus* (Berlin, 1957), p. 1, n. 6.

[3] The original meaning of sacrifice is obscure; see R. de Vaux, *Ancient Israel* (New York, 1961), pp. 447 f., and the literature cited on pp. 548 f.

[4] The sacrificial cult was endowed with supreme "political" significance. It was the chief requirement for the security of the land and may be regarded as analogous to the cult of military defense in our own day. Both have their roots in the concern for security. Cease

To add paradox to sacrilege: all this grandeur and solemnity are declared to be second rate, of minor importance, if not hateful to God, while deeds of kindness, worrying about the material needs of widows and orphans, commonplace things, platitudinous affairs, are exactly what the Lord of heaven and earth demands! To give up a thousand fertile vineyards for an acre of barren ground? To find the presence of God in the shape of righteousness?

What they attacked was, I repeat, supremely venerable: a sphere unmistakably holy; a spirituality that had both form and substance, that was concrete and inspiring, an atmosphere overwhelming the believer—pageantry, scenery, mystery, spectacle, fragrance, song, and exaltation. In the experience of such captivating sanctity, who could question the presence of God in the shape of a temple?

> Let us go to His dwelling place;
> Let us worship at His footstool!
> Arise, O Lord, and go to Thy resting place,
> Thou and the ark of Thy might.
> Let Thy priests be clothed with righteousness,
> And let Thy saints shout for joy. . . .
> For the Lord has chosen Zion;
> He has desired it for His habitation:
> This is My resting place forever;
> Here I will dwell, for I have desired it.
>
> Psalm 132:7-9, 13-14

It is hard for us to imagine what entering a sanctuary or offering a sacrifice meant to ancient man. The sanctuary was holiness in perpetuity, a miracle in continuity; the divine was mirrored in the air, sowing blessing, closing gaps between the here and the beyond. In offering a sacrifice, man mingled with mystery, reached the summit of significance: sin was consumed, self abandoned, satisfaction was bestowed upon divinity. Is it possible for us today to conceive of the solemn joy of those whose offering was placed on the altar?

> Then I will go to the altar of God,
> To God my exceeding joy;

---

to appease the gods with offerings on the altars, and their anger will strike you down. Sacrifice is a way of preventing the attack. Even as late as the third century of our era "one of the commonest motives for the popular hatred felt toward Christians was the belief that, neglecting the sacrifices themselves and encouraging others to do likewise, they had aroused the fury of the gods against the Empire. In 410, after the capture of Rome by Alaric and his Goths, this prejudice had such power that Augustinus was compelled to answer it; in the first ten books of the *City of God*, he is engaged in showing that the Christians were not responsible for Rome's misfortunes." (A. M. J. Festugière, *Epicurus and His Gods* [Oxford, 1955], p. 54.)

> *I will praise Thee with the lyre,*
> *O God, my God.*
> > *Psalm 43:4; cf. Deut. 12:18-19;*
> > *31:11; Exod. 34:23 f.; Isa. 1:12*

GOD IS AT STAKE

Why should religion, the essence of which is worship of God, put such stress on justice for man? Does not the preoccupation with morality tend to divest religion of immediate devotion to God? Why should a worldly virtue like justice be so important to the Holy One of Israel? Did not the prophets overrate the worth of justice?

Perhaps the answer lies here: righteousness is not just a value; it is God's part of human life, *God's stake in human history.* Perhaps it is because the suffering of man is a blot upon God's conscience; because it is in relations between man and man that God is at stake. Or is it simply because the infamy of a wicked act is infinitely greater than we are able to imagine? People act as they please, doing what is vile, abusing the weak, not realizing that they are fighting God, affronting the divine, or that the oppression of man is a humiliation of God.

> *He who oppresses a poor man insults his Maker,*
> *He who is kind to the needy honors Him.*
> > *Proverbs 14:31; cf. 17:5*

The universe is done. The greater masterpiece still undone, still in the process of being created, is history. For accomplishing His grand design, God needs the help of man. Man is and has the instrument of God, which he may or may not use in consonance with the grand design. Life is clay, and righteousness the mold in which God wants history to be shaped. But human beings, instead of fashioning the clay, deform the shape.

The world is full of iniquity, of injustice and idolatry. The people offer animals; the priests offer incense. But God needs mercy, righteousness; His needs cannot be satisfied in the temples, in space, but only in history, in time. It is within the realm of history that man is charged with God's mission.

Justice is not an ancient custom, a human convention, a value, but a transcendent demand, freighted with divine concern. It is not only a relationship between man and man, it is an *act* involving God, a divine need. Justice is His line, righteousness His plummet (Isa. 28:17). It is not one of His ways, but in all His ways. Its validity is not only universal, but also eternal, independent of will and experience.

People think that to be just is a virtue, deserving honor and rewards; that in doing righteousness one confers a favor on society. No one expects to receive a reward for the habit of breathing. Justice is as much a necessity as breathing is, and a constant occupation.

THE A PRIORI

Power, omniscience, wisdom, infinitude, are the attributes that man associates with the Supreme Being. Justice is not necessarily regarded as an essential attribute of God, nor is charity considered in all religions an essential part of piety. The holy men of India, for example, stand aloof from moral issues, and the highest goal of Indian philosophy and piety is to shed the fetters of action by overcoming the inclination to be active. Indeed, books on religion in which no reference is made to morality are as common as books on morality in which no reference is made to religion.

Greek religion did not stress the connection between religion and morality.[5] It offered no precepts for the regulation of human conduct. Each god had his appointed sphere within which he exercised control. The gods were jealous to avenge any infringement of their privileges. But the sinner was punished, not as a moral offender, but as a trespasser against a divine power. In the tragedies the gods were considered guarantors of human justice, which consisted primarily of submission to destiny; but the gods in turn were not required to observe justice in their conduct toward mortals.

Occasionally we find the belief that certain gods who were the sources of the skills and wisdom of man had also given laws to him. In popular Greek religion there was a belief that specific laws were revealed by a god; among Cretans it was said to have been Zeus, and in Lacedaemon, Apollo. According to Homer, Minos, the Cretan lawgiver, "went every ninth year to converse with his Olympian sire"; his laws were derived from Zeus.[6] The difference, however, is that the laws, like the skills, are not regarded as being an expression of the personal will of the god; they are something that the gods have dealt out rather than something to which they remain personally committed.

There are few thoughts as deeply ingrained in the mind of biblical man as the thought of God's justice and righteousness. It is not an inference, but an *a priori* of biblical faith, self-evident; not an added attribute to His

---

[5] In Homer, "cruelty, provided again it be not too petty, is thought little of, either in the dealings of one of the kings with the people under his sway or in the behaviour of the gods towards their subjects, mankind as a whole." (W. K. C. Guthrie, *The Greeks and Their Gods* [London, 1950], p. 119).

[6] Plato, *Laws*, 624, 630, 632 (see p. 464 of the present volume).

essence, but given with the very thought of God. It is inherent in His essence and identified with His ways.[7]

> *The rock, His work is perfect;*
> *For all His ways are justice.*
> *O God of faithfulness and without iniquity,*
> *Just and right is He.*
>
> Deuteronomy 32:4
>
> *Righteous art Thou, O Lord,*
> *And right are Thy judgments.*
>
> Psalm 119:137

God is the source of right (Deut. 1:17), judge of all the earth. It is inconceivable that He shall not do the right (Gen. 18:25), that He shall pervert justice (Job 8:3), or do wickedly (Job 34:12). "For the Lord is a God of justice" (Isa. 30:18). "The Lord is righteous, He loves righteousness" (Ps. 11:7). That "God is a righteous judge" is the incontestable premise of Jeremiah's question, "Why does the way of the wicked prosper?" (Jer. 12:1.)

MISHPAT AND TSEDAKAH

The two key terms are *tsedakah* (*tsedek*) and *mishpat*. The word *mishpat* means the judgment given by the *shofet* (judge); hence the word can mean justice, norm, ordinance, legal right, law. The word *tsedakah* may be rendered by "righteousness." While legality and righteousness are not identical, they must always coincide, the second being reflected in the first.[8]

It is exceedingly difficult to establish the exact difference in meaning of the biblical terms *mishpat*, justice, and *tsedakah*, righteousness (which in

---

[7] On the problem raised in Plato's *Euthyphro* and its relation to biblical thinking, see A. J. Heschel, *God in Search of Man* (New York, 1959), p. 17. The concern of the Deity in the administration of justice to the poor is found in other religions as well. Amon Re, the Egyptian god, is addressed as he "who comes at the voice of the poor man. If I call to thee when I am distressed, thou comest and thou rescuest me. Thou givest breath [to] him who is weak; thou rescuest him who is imprisoned." (*ANET*, p. 380.) A moving prayer for a helpless client in the court of law who is bewildered by the demands of the administrators of justice has come down from Egypt: "O Amon, give thy ear to one who is alone in the court of justice, who is poor. . . . The court cheats him of silver and gold for the scribes of the mat as well as of clothing for the attendants. May it be found that Amon assumes his form as the vizier, in order to permit the poor man to get off. May it be found that the poor man is vindicated. May the poor man surpass the rich." (*ANET*, p. 380.) In a Babylonian hymn, Shamash the sun god is praised for punishing the unrighteous judge, the receiver of a bribe who perverts justice, and for being pleased with him who "intercedes for the weak." (G. R. Driver, in D. C. Simpson, ed., *The Psalmists* [London, 1926], p. 169.) See also J. Ferguson, *Moral Values in the Ancient World* (New York, 1959).

[8] The word *mishpat* seems to imply *the ability to discern between good and evil*. Thus prayed King Solomon: "Give Thy servant an understanding heart to judge Thy people: to discern between good and evil" (I Kings 3:9; cf. 3:11).

parallelism are often used as variants). However, it seems that justice is a mode of action, righteousness a quality of the person. Significantly, the noun derived from *shafat* (to judge) is *shofet,* which came to mean a judge or arbitrator; while the noun from *tsadak* (to be just) is *tsaddik,* a righteous man.

Righteousness goes beyond justice. Justice is strict and exact, giving each person his due. Righteousness implies benevolence, kindness, generosity. Justice is form, a state of equilibrium; righteousness has a substantive associated meaning. Justice may be legal; righteousness is associated with a burning compassion for the oppressed. When you extend a loan to a poor man, "you shall not sleep in his pledge; when the sun goes down, you shall restore to him the pledge, that he may sleep in his cloak and bless you; and it shall be righteousness to you before the Lord your God" (Deut. 24: 10-13).[9]

It would be wrong to assume that there was a dichotomy of *mishpat* and kindness; "Justice was not equal justice but a bias in favor of the poor. Justice always leaned toward mercy for the widows and the orphans."[10] Divine justice involves His being merciful, compassionate.

> *Therefore the Lord is waiting to be gracious to you;*
> *Therefore He exalts Himself to show mercy to you.*
> *For the Lord is a God of justice;*
> *Blessed are all those who wait for Him.*
>
> Isaiah 30:18

Justice dies when dehumanized, no matter how exactly it may be exercised. Justice dies when deified, for beyond all justice is God's compassion. The logic of justice may seem impersonal, yet the concern for justice is an act of love.

INSPIRATION AS A MORAL ACT

If intense regard and concern for man is the mark of a moral act, then inspiration of the prophets in which God's regard and concern for man are

---

[9] "Hear my prayer, O Lord. . . . Answer me in Thy *tsedakah*. Enter not into judgment (*mishpat*) with Thy servant; for no man living is righteous before Thee. For Thy name's sake, O Lord, preserve my life! In Thy *tsedakah* bring me out of trouble" (Ps. 143:1-2, 11). "He will judge the world with righteousness" (Ps. 98:9), namely, with kindness. "They ask of Me righteous judgments" (Isa. 58:2) rather than strict justice. "They shall judge the people with righteous judgment" (Deut. 16:18) is hardly a tautology. "O Lord, according to all thy righteousness [or righteous acts], let Thy anger and Thy wrath turn away from Thy city Jerusalem" (Dan. 9:16). The word *tsedakah* has often been rendered as *Strafgerechtigkeit,* though nowhere in the Bible is it used in this sense; see D. P. Volz, *Prophetengestalten* (Stuttgart, 1949), p. 188, n. 1.

[10] R. Niebuhr, *Pious and Secular America* (New York, 1958), p. 92. It is significant that particularly in later Hebrew the word *tsedakah* is linked with *hesed,* Jer. 9:29; Ps. 36:11; 40:11; 143:11 f.; see also Ps. 85:11.

disclosed and in which the prophet is entrusted with a mission to help the people, must be viewed as an eminently moral act. The moral aspect sets the prophetic act apart from intellectual, artistic, and mystical experiences.

In archaic religions the relationship between man and his gods and the relationship between man and his fellowmen represented two areas unrelated to each other. Man owed certain duties toward the gods—he must offer prayer and sacrifice, the neglect of which is sin—but these duties did not concern his relations to his fellow men. In performing the rites, in his search to share sanctity or to attain salvation, the religious man might experience the power and grandeur of the divine, the bestowal of grace, or the assumption of insight, but not the concern of the god for someone else.

Religious experience, in most cases, is a private affair in which a person becomes alive to what transpires between God and himself, not to what transpires between God and someone else; contact between God and man comes about, it is believed, for the benefit of the particular man. In contrast, prophetic inspiration is for the sake, for benefit, of a third party. It is not a private affair between prophet and God; its purpose is the illumination of the people rather than the illumination of the prophet. (See p. 362.)

The phenomenon of prophecy is predicated upon the assumption that man is both in need of, and entitled to, divine guidance. For God to reveal His word through the prophet to His people is an act of justice or an act of seeking to do justice. The purpose of prophecy is to maintain the covenant, to establish the right relationship between God and man.

PERVERSION OF JUSTICE

The fact that filled the prophets with dismay was not the absence of adequate laws, but the absence of righteousness. Judges were active in the land, but their judgments were devoid of righteousness. The prophets were shocked not only by acts of injustice on the part of scoundrels but also by the perversion of justice on the part of the notables. When warped and garbled, justice yields strife and distrust.

> Do horses run upon rock?
> Does one plow the sea with oxen?
> But you have turned justice into poison,
> The fruit of righteousness into wormwood. . . .
> O you who turn justice to wormwood,
> And cast down righteousness to the earth!
>
> Amos 6:12; 5:7;
> cf. Deuteronomy 29:17;
> Jeremiah 8:14; 9:14; 23:15;
> Lamentations 3:15, 19;
> Proverbs 5:4

They utter mere words;
With empty oaths they make covenants;
So judgment springs up like poisonous weeds
In the furrows of the field.

Hosea 10:4

Israel was the vineyard that the Lord had planted. He looked for it to yield grapes, but it yielded wild grapes. He looked for it to yield justice, but it yielded perversion of justice; for righteousness, but it yielded outrage (Isa. 5:2).

The prophets consistently singled out the leaders, the kings, the princes, the false prophets, and the priests as the ones responsible for the sins of the community. (See Hos. 4:6, 8 f.; 7:3, 16; 9:15; Jer. 2:26.)

Hear this, O priest!
Give heed, O house of Israel!
Hearken, O house of the king!
For the judgment pertains to you.

Hosea 5:1

The Lord enters into judgment
With the elders and princes of his people:
It is you who have devoured the vineyard,
The spoil of the poor is in your houses.
What do you mean by crushing the people,
By grinding the face of the poor?
Says the Lord of hosts.

Isaiah 3:14-15

After declaring that no one in the streets of Jerusalem did justice or sought truth, Jeremiah added:

Then I said, These are only the poor,
They have no sense;
For they do not know the way of the Lord,
The Torah of their God.
I will go to the great,
And will speak to them;
For they know the way of the Lord,
The Torah of their God.
But they all alike had broken the yoke,
They had burst the bonds.

Jeremiah 5:4-5

"The shepherds are stupid" (Jer. 10:21). "Thus says the Lord God: Behold, I am against the shepherds; I will require My sheep at their hand" (Ezek. 34:10).

THE SENSE OF INJUSTICE

The prophets' preoccupation with justice and righteousness has its roots in a powerful awareness of injustice. That justice is a good thing, a fine goal, even a supreme ideal, is commonly accepted. What is lacking is a sense of the monstrosity of injustice. Moralists of all ages have been eloquent in singing the praises of virtue. The distinction of the prophets was in their remorseless unveiling of injustice and oppression, in their comprehension of social, political, and religious evils. They were not concerned with the definition, but with the predicament, of justice, with the fact that those called upon to apply it defied it.

Justice may be properly described as "the active process of remedying or preventing what should arouse the sense of injustice." What is uppermost in the prophets' mind is not justice, "an ideal relation or static condition or set of perceptual standards,"[11] but the presence of oppression and corruption. The urgency of justice was an urgency of aiding and saving the victims of oppression. In the words of the psalmist:

> From the heavens Thou didst utter judgment
> The earth feared and was still,
> When God arose to establish judgment
> To save all the oppressed of the earth.
> > Psalm 76:9-10

NONSPECIALIZATION OF JUSTICE

Justice is scarce, injustice exceedingly common. The concern for justice is delegated to the judges, as if it were a matter for professionals or specialists. But to do justice is what God demands of every man: it is the supreme commandment, and one that cannot be fulfilled vicariously.

Righteousness must dwell not only in the places where justice is judicially administered. There are many ways of evading the law and escaping the arm of justice. Only a few acts of violence are brought to the attention of the courts. As a rule, those who know how to exploit are endowed with the skill to justify their acts, while those who are easily exploited possess no skill in pleading their own cause. Those who neither exploit nor are exploited are ready to fight when their own interests are harmed; they will not be involved when not personally affected. Who shall plead for the helpless? Who shall prevent the epidemic of injustice that no court of justice is capable of stopping?

In a sense, the calling of the prophet may be described as that of an

---

[11] E. N. Cahn, *The Sense of Injustice* (New York, 1949), pp. 13 f.

advocate or champion, speaking for those who are too weak to plead their own cause. Indeed, the major activity of the prophets was *interference,* remonstrating about wrongs inflicted on other people, meddling in affairs which were seemingly neither their concern nor their responsibility. A prudent man is he who minds his own business, staying away from questions which do not involve his own interests, particularly when not authorized to step in—and prophets were given no mandate by the widows and orphans to plead their cause. The prophet is a person who is not tolerant of wrongs done to others, who resents other people's injuries. He even calls upon others to be the champions of the poor. It is to every member of Israel, not alone to the judges, that Isaiah directs his plea:

> *Seek justice,*
> *Undo oppression;*
> *Defend the fatherless,*
> *Plead for the widow.*
> *Isaiah 1:17*

To the king as well as to the people, the prophet proclaims: "Thus says the Lord: Do justice and righteousness, and deliver from the hand of the oppressor him who has been robbed. Do no wrong or violence to the alien, the fatherless, and the widow, nor shed innocent blood in this place" (Jer. 22:3). "Amend your ways and your doings; . . . execute justice one with another; . . . do not oppress the alien, the fatherless, or the widow" (Jer. 7:5 f.).

In the *Iliad* gods as well as men are indifferent to wrongs inflicted, not upon themselves, but on others.[12] Quite a number of homicides are mentioned. However, "outside the circle of the dead man's kinsmen and friends, there is no indication of any popular sentiment against ordinary homicide. Odysseus, in his character of Cretan refugee, had told a tale to Eumaeus in which he represented himself as the slayer of the son of Idomeneus. It would be hard to imagine a more cowardly murder than this. And yet Eumaeus receives the supposed murderer with all the respect due to a stranger in accordance with the prevailing customs. Several murderers are mentioned as living as honored members of communities to which they had come as exiles."[13]

---

[12] S. Ranulf, *The Jealousy of the Gods and Criminal Law at Athens,* I (Copenhagen and London, 1933-1934), 20 f.

[13] R. J. Bonner and G. Smith, *The Administration of Justice from Homer to Aristotle* (Chicago, 1930), I, 16; II, 39 ff.: "Advocates were generally drawn from the litigant's friends and relatives. In the course of time they tended to become professional, and the practice of paying advocates arose. Yet there was a law which forbade the paying of advocates in private suits. Although the law could not be enforced, it nevertheless embarrassed the ad-

It was long after the time of the early prophets of Israel that a law of Solon's (d. 559 B.C.E.) was promulgated in Athens which presupposed the readiness of the citizens to interfere when wrongs were inflicted on others. Solon "believed that the best-governing state was that in which those who had suffered no wrong were as diligent in prosecuting and punishing the wrongdoers as those who had suffered wrong."[14] The first appearance of "advocates" was at a trial in 489 B.C.E. It was in Rome that the advocate, more through his oratorical art than through his knowledge of law, achieved outstanding eminence.[15]

An act of interfering in a case in which a wrong was inflicted upon someone else is reported from the time of David. After King David's sin with Bathsheba, the wife of Uriah, the prophet Nathan went to David and told him a parable.

> *There were two men in a certain city, the one rich and the other poor. The rich man had very many flocks and herds; but the poor man had nothing but one little ewe lamb, which he had bought. And he brought it up, and it grew up with him and with his children; it used to eat of his morsel, and drink from his cup, and lie in his bosom, and it was like a daughter to him. Now there came a traveler to the rich man, and he was unwilling to take one of his own flock or herd to prepare for the wayfarer who had come to him, but he took the poor man's lamb, and prepared it for the man who had come to him. Then David's anger was greatly kindled against the man; and he said to Nathan, As the Lord lives, the man who has done this deserves to die; and he shall restore the lamb fourfold, because he did this thing, and because he had no pity. Thereupon Nathan said to David: You are the man.*
>
> *II Samuel 12:1-6*

Ahab, the king of Israel (875-853 B.C.E.), insisted upon securing the property of Naboth of Jezreel. When the latter refused to sell it, he was put to death on false accusation. For this outrage, Elijah the prophet said to Ahab: "Have you killed, and also taken possession? . . . Thus says the Lord: In the

---

vocate who could not claim relationship or close association with the litigant." About the abuse of such persecutions, the so-called sycophants ("a happy compound of the common barretor, informer, pettifogger, busybody, rogue, liar, and slanderer"), see pp. 42 ff. Cf. R. J. Bonner, *Lawyers and Litigants in Ancient Athens* (Chicago, 1927), pp. 59 ff.; R. Pound, *The Lawyer from Antiquity to Modern Times* (St. Paul, 1953), p. 29.

[14] R. J. Bonner and G. Smith, *op. cit.*, I, 170.

[15] The institution of the advocate, of a person who pleads the cause of someone else, was one of the great revolutions in the history of legal theory and practice. The Egyptians believed that speeches of advocates would cloud the issues. In the words of the Greek historian-traveler Diodorus: "The cleverness of the speakers, the spell of their delivery, the tears of the accused, influence many persons to ignore the strict rules of law and the standards of truth." (Quoted by J. H. Wigmore, *A Panorama of the World's Legal Systems* [St. Paul, 1928], p. 31; on China and Japan, see pp. 178 and 485.) In Nuzi documents there seems to be provision for the appearance at the court of a representative or attorney or substitute with the right of arguing the case of another person. See E. A. Speiser in *AASOR*, X (1928-29), 63.

place where the dogs licked up the blood of Naboth shall dogs lick your own blood" (I Kings 21:1-19).

THE LOVE OF KINDNESS

The demand is not only to respect justice in the sense of abstaining from doing injustice, but also to strive for it, to pursue it.

> Seek *the Lord, all you humble of the land,*
> *Who do His commands;*
> Seek *righteousness,* seek *humility;*
> *Perhaps you may be hidden*
> *On the day of the anger of the Lord.*
> *Zephaniah 2:3*

"Righteousness, and only righteousness you shall pursue" (Deut. 16:20). The term "pursue" carries strong connotations of effort, eagerness, persistence, inflexibility of purpose. This implies more than merely respecting or following justice, walking in the way of righteousness; righteousness may be hard to attain; it may escape us if we do not pursue it. (See Isa. 16:5.)

> *Hearken to me, you who pursue righteousness,*
> *You who seek the Lord.*
> *Isaiah 51:1*

"You who pursue righteousness, you who seek the Lord"—what greater praise is possible than is given by the juxtaposition of these phrases?

The imperative includes more than doing; it asks for love;[16] beyond justice, it refers to good and evil. "Seek good and not evil. . . . Hate evil and love good and establish justice in the gate" (Amos 5:14, 15).

"It has been told you, O man, what is good, and what does the Lord require of you but *to do justice,* and *to love kindness* (ḥesed), and *to walk humbly with your God*" (Mic. 6:8) —*doing* justice as well as *loving* kindness. The prophets tried to excite fervor, to make ḥesed an object of love.

What the Lord requires of man is more than fulfilling one's duty. To love implies an insatiable thirst, a passionate craving. To love means to transfer the center of one's inner life from the ego to the object of one's love.

THE INNER MAN

Is this all the prophet came to teach us—social justice? Are there no other demands to be satisfied, no other goals to be attained?

God not only asks for justice; He demands of man "to regard the deeds

---

[16] "For I the Lord love justice; I hate robbery and wrong" (Isa. 61:8; cf. Ps. 37:28). "He loves righteousness and justice" (Ps. 33:5). "For the Lord is righteous, He loves righteous deeds" (Ps. 11:7). "You love righteousness and hate wickedness" (Ps. 45:7). The Lord is called "lover of justice" (Ps. 99:4).

of the Lord, to see the work of His hands" (Isa. 5:12; cf. 22:11), "to walk in His paths" (Isa. 2:3).[17] "If you will not believe, you will not abide" (Isa. 7:11).

> Give thanks to the Lord,
> Call upon His name,
> Make known His deeds among the nations,
> Proclaim that His name is exalted.
> Sing praises to the Lord, . . .
> Shout, sing for joy, . . .
> For great in your midst is the Holy One of Israel.
>   Isaiah 12:3-6

It is not only action that God demands, it is not only disobedience to the law that the prophet decries.

> They do not cry to Me from the heart.
>   Hosea 7:14

> This people draw near with their mouths
> And honor Me with their lips,
> While their hearts are far from Me;
> Their fear of Me is a commandment of men learned by rote.
>   Isaiah 29:13

The fault is in the hearts, not alone in the deeds.

> Their heart is false;
> Now they must bear their guilt.
>   Hosea 10:2

> Thou art near in their mouth,
> And far from their heart. . . .
> Break up your fallow ground,
> Sow not among thorns.
> Circumcise yourselves to the Lord,
> Remove the foreskin of your hearts,
> O men of Judah and inhabitants of Jerusalem.
>   Jeremiah 4:3-4

Amos condemns the rich who revel in luxuries for not being pained or grieved over the afflictions of the people (6:6).

> For the fool speaks folly,
> And his mind plots iniquity;
> To practice ungodliness,
> To utter error concerning the Lord,

---

[17] On Hosea's demand for *daath elohim*, see pp. 57 ff.

To leave the craving of the hungry unsatisfied,
And to deprive the thirsty of drink.

Isaiah 32:6

The Lord alone is holy; "let Him be your fear, let Him be your dread" (Isa. 8:13). To fear God is to be unafraid of man. For God alone is king, power, and promise. "Yet even now, says the Lord, return to Me with all your heart, with fasting, with weeping, and with mourning, and rend your hearts and not your garments" (Joel 2:13).

Thus says the Lord:
Cursed is the man who trusts in man and makes flesh his arm,
Whose heart turns away from the Lord.
He is like a shrub in the desert,
And shall not see any good come.
He shall dwell in the parched places of the wilderness,
In an uninhabited salt land.
Blessed is the man who trusts in the Lord,
Whose trust is the Lord.
He is like a tree planted by water,
That sends out its roots by the stream,
And does not fear when heat comes,
For its leaves remain green,
And is not anxious in the year of drought,
For it does not cease to bear fruit.

Jeremiah 17:5-8

AN INTERPERSONAL RELATIONSHIP

If justice be the mere relationship of a person to what he deserves,[18] then why should it take precedence over the relationship of a person to what he desires? Obviously the situation of one who deserves contains an element not present in the situation of one who desires, namely, having a claim, being entitled to something. An individual's desire is his private affair, an individual's claim involves other selves. The claim of one person to attain justice is contingent upon the assumption that there is another person who has the responsibility to answer it. Justice, then, is an interpersonal relationship, implying both a claim and a responsibility.

Justice bespeaks a situation that transcends the individual, demanding from everyone a certain abnegation of self, defiance of self-interest, disregard of self-respect. The necessity of submitting to a law is derived from the

---

[18] "Justice is the firm and continuous desire to render to everyone that which is due" *(Iustitia est constans et perpetua voluntas ius suum cuique tribuens)* is the opening statement in Justinian's *Institutiones.*

necessity of identifying oneself with what concerns other individuals or the whole community of men. Justice is valid because of the community that unites all individuals. The sense of justice is outgoing, transitive, inclusive.

There is an interpersonal correlation of claim and responsibility, but there is also an inner personal correlation of right and duty. Ancient Israel "does not distinguish between right and duty," and *mishpat,* the word for justice, denotes what a person may claim as well as what he is bound to do to others. In other words, it signifies, both *right and duty.*[19]

Justice as an interpersonal relationship, involving a claim and a responsibility, a right and a duty, applies, according to the Bible, to both God and man. In its fundamental meaning, *mishpat* refers to all actions which contribute to maintaining the covenant, namely, the true relation between man and man, and between God and man.

Thus, justice in the Bible must not be taken in a legal sense as the administration of law according to the rules of law by a judge. "One constantly 'judges' in the daily life, because one must constantly act so as to uphold the covenant, i.e., the whole of the common life of the community. Everything in which this kind of judging manifests itself is called *mishpat.*"[20]

A GRAMMAR OF EXPERIENCE

Why and for what purpose was Abraham chosen to become a great and mighty nation, and to be a blessing to all the nations of the earth? Not because he knew how to build pyramids, altars, and temples, but "in order that he may charge his children and his household after him to keep the way of the Lord by doing righteousness and justice" (Gen. 18:18-19). Righteousness is foremost among the things God asks of man. "Thus says the Lord: Let not the wise man glory in his wisdom, let not the mighty man glory in his might, let not the rich man glory in his riches; but let him who glories, glory in this: that *he understands and knows Me, that I am the Lord Who does kindness, justice, and righteousness in the earth;* for in these things I delight, says the Lord" (Jer. 9:23-24).

---

[19] "He establishes the right of the fatherless or the widow" (Deut. 9:18); "the right of redemption by purchase is yours" (Jer. 32:7). "Thou hast maintained my right and my judgment" (Ps. 9:5). "Why do you say, O Jacob . . . my right is disregarded by my God?" (Isa. 40:27). A special *mishpat* obtains between parents and children (Exod. 21:9), between neighbors (Exod. 21:31), between rich and poor (Exod. 23:6), between Israel and God (Jer. 5:4-5).

[20] J. Pedersen, *Israel,* I-II (London and Copenhagen, 1926), pp. 348 ff.; K. H. Fahlgren, *Sedaka* (Uppsala, 1932), pp. 120 ff.; N. H. Snaith, *The Distinctive Ideas of the Old Testament* (London, 1944), p. 76. In the book of Judges no mention is made of any judicial activity of Othniel, Gideon or Jephtah. They maintained the covenant by serving at critical moments as leaders of the people, and assuring their victory and independence.

This is sublime knowledge, sublime understanding, a new grammar of experience. What we encounter in the world is not neutral, impersonal being, things, forces, forms, colors. What we encounter is full of God's kindness, justice, and righteousness. "The earth is full of the kindness (*hesed*) of the Lord" (Ps. 33:5). "He is the Lord our God; His judgments are in all the earth" (Ps. 105:7). "The heavens declare His righteousness . . . and all the people behold His glory" (Pss. 50:6; 97:6). "Thy love, O Lord, extends to the heavens, Thy faithfulness to the clouds" (Ps. 36:6).

God's love and kindness indicate a road. It is a road not limited to a particular area in space nor to exceptional miraculous happenings. It is everywhere, at all times.

Kindness, justice, and righteousness are heaven's part in life. Its perception is the prophet's daily experience and the spring of joy. And this is why celebration is man's first response to life and being. Beauty and grandeur are not anonymous; they are outbursts of God's kindness.

In the passage quoted above (Jer. 9:23-24), knowledge of God is knowledge of what He does: kindness, justice, righteousness. In another passage, knowledge of God is equated with what man does: justice, righteousness. In exhorting King Jehoiakim, Jeremiah contrasts him with his father:

> *Did not your father eat and drink*
> *And do justice and righteousness?*
> *Then it was well with him.*
> *He judged the cause of the poor and needy;*
> *Then it was well.*
> *Is not this to know Me?*
> *Says the Lord.*
>
> *Jeremiah 22:15-16*

Here knowledge is not the same as thought, comprehension, gnosis or mystical participation in the ultimate essence. Knowledge of God is action toward man, sharing His concern for justice; sympathy in action.

Inner identification with God's will and concern is the goal of the new covenant:

> *I will put My Torah within them,*
> *And write it on their hearts;*
> *And I will be a God to them,*
> *And they to Me a people.*
>
> *Jeremiah 31:32*

The world is overwhelmingly rich; the human mind is incapable of paying attention to all its aspects. The painter sees the world in color, the sculptor in form; the musician perceives the world in sounds, and the economist in commodities. The prophet is a man who sees the world with the eyes of God, and in the sight of God even things of beauty or acts of ritual are an abomination when associated with injustice.

The world is overwhelmingly rich, but the prophet perceives the whole world in terms of justice or injustice. (See p. 7.)

AS A MIGHTY STREAM

Justice is usually defined as giving every person his due.[21] It connotes a conformity, a congruence, a proportion of some kind. This is reflected in the numerical symbols employed by the Greeks to express as the essence of justice the relation of parity between two contraposited terms: the *dyad*, also the number 8, which has 2 for its root, because of its peculiar divisibility. The idea of a balancing of two sides against one another is expressed in the most common symbol of justice, namely, the *scales*.[22] When the *sword* is added to the scales, it is a symbol not only of power, but also of precision; it seeks not so much to strike as to cut clearly the matter of controversy into two equal parts.[23]

In sharp contrast to these symbols, expressing calmness, congruence, and precision, stands the prophetic image:

> *Let justice roll down like waters,*
> *And righteousness like a mighty stream.*[24]
> *Amos 5:24*

One is uncertain of the exact meaning of this bold image. It seems to combine several ideas: a surging movement, a life-bringing substance, a dominant power.

A mighty stream, expressive of the vehemence of a never-ending, surging, fighting movement—as if obstacles had to be washed away for justice to be done. No rock is so hard that water cannot pierce it. "The mountain falls and crumbles away, the rock is removed from its place—the waters wear away the stones" (Job 14:18 f.). Justice is not a mere norm, but a fighting challenge, a restless drive.

Balancing is possible when the scales are unimpaired, and the judge's eyes sound. When the eyes are dim and the scales unsure, what is required is

---

[21] See Simonides in *Republic*, I, 331e, and Plato's refutation.
[22] Cf. Deut. 25:13 f.; 24:17: "You shall not pervert [or: incline] the justice due to the sojourner or to the fatherless." See also Prov. 16:11.
[23] G. Del Vecchio, *Justice* (New York, 1953), pp. 169 ff.; cf. I Kings 3:24.
[24] R. S. Cripps: "as a never failing stream." Cf. "Then your peace would have been like a river, and your righteousness like the waves of the sea" (Isa. 48:18).

a power that will strike and change, heal and restore, like a mighty stream bringing life to the parched land. There is a thirst for righteousness that only a mighty stream can quench.

Righteousness as a mere tributary, feeding the immense stream of human interests, is easily exhausted and more easily abused. But righteousness is not a trickle; it is God's power in the world, a torrent, an impetuous drive, full of grandeur and majesty. The surge is choked, the sweep is blocked. Yet the mighty stream will break all dikes.

Justice, people seem to agree, is a principle, a norm, an ideal of the highest importance. We all insist that it ought to be—but it may not be. In the eyes of the prophets, justice is more than an idea or a norm: justice is charged with the omnipotence of God. What ought to be, shall be!

Righteousness is a vast and mighty stream because God is its unfailing source.

EXALTATION IN JUSTICE

> *But the Lord of hosts shall be exalted in justice,*
> *The Holy One of Israel sanctified in righteousness.*
> *Isaiah 5:16*

This is a staggering assertion. Why should His justice be the supreme manifestation of God? Is not wisdom or omnipotence a mode of manifestation more magnificent and more indicative of what we associate with the divine? It would have been more plausible to declare: The Lord of hosts is exalted in majesty, the Holy One of Israel is sanctified in omnipotence. Omnipotence is an attribute which no mortal shares with God, while justice is a quality to which human beings, too, lay claim; It is a quality devoid of sublimity and mystery, elementary and undistinguished.

Isaiah's declaration is humble compared with the words the Lord spoke to Job out of the whirlwind. How trite and prosaic are justice and righteousness when matched against the transcendent majesty and the crushing mystery of the Creator of the universe; a still, small voice compared with a thunderbolt. Job's answer to the words spoken out of the whirlwind was:

> *I had heard of Thee by the hearing of the ear,*
> *But now my eye sees Thee;*
> *Therefore I despise myself*
> *And repent in dust and ashes.*
> *Job 42:6*

In contrast, Isaiah was able to exclaim:

O house of Jacob,
Come, let us walk
In the light of the Lord.
                    Isaiah 2:5

Perhaps this is the deeper meaning of the words, "The Holy One of
Israel is sanctified in righteousness." The holy is all mystery, inscrutable,
dwelling in "thick darkness." Yet beyond the darkness is righteousness.
Mystery is not the ultimate. Mystery is surpassed by meaning.

Cloud and deep darkness are round about Him;
Righteousness and justice are the foundations of His throne.
                    Psalm 97:2

History, what happens here and now, is the decisive stage for God's
manifestation. His glorious disclosure is not in a display of miracles, evoking
fascination, but in establishing righteousness, evoking appreciation.

Exalted[25] is the Lord,
He who dwells on high,
He has filled Zion with justice and righteousness.
He will be the permanence of your times,
Abundance of salvation, wisdom, and knowledge.
The fear of the Lord is His treasure.
                    Isaiah 33:5-6

The grandeur and majesty of God do not come to expression in the
display of ultimate sovereignty and power, but rather in rendering righteousness and mercy. "He exalts Himself to show mercy to you" (Isa. 30:18).

For Thou hast been a stronghold to the poor,
A stronghold to the needy in his distress.
                    Isaiah 25:4

Isaiah's declaration does not speak about values, and its intention is not to
assert that holiness and justice are very much alike, or that justice is holy,
or that holiness is just.[26] Isaiah speaks about God, and his intention is to
say that the Lord of heaven and earth, of nature and history, finds His true
exaltation in justice. Isaiah does not pronounce a theory, he proclaims what
is to come. He does not teach what ought to be, he predicts what shall be.

The importance of moral ideas was known to people everywhere. Yet
linked with the awareness of their importance was an awareness of their
impotence. The prophets proclaimed that justice is omnipotent, that right
and wrong are dimensions of world history, not merely modes of conduct.

25 Heb.: *nisgav;* cf. Isa. 2:11.   26 See Plato, *Protagoras,* 331

The existence of the world is contingent upon right and wrong, and its secret is God's involvement in history.

History is a turmoil. Survival and perdition are equally possible. But justice will decide; righteousness will redeem.

> Zion shall be redeemed by justice,
> And those in her who repent, by righteousness.
>
> Isaiah 1:27

Justice will not fail. Addressing himself to Assyria while she is at the height of her power, the prophet exclaims:

> Woe to you, destroyer,
> Who yourself have not been destroyed;
> You treacherous one,
> With whom none has dealt treacherously!
> You will be destroyed.
> When you have made an end of dealing treacherously,
> You will be dealt with treacherously.
>
> Isaiah 33:1

If justice is but a category, a conformity, then injustice must be regarded as an irregularity, a deviation from a norm. But justice is like a mighty stream, and to defy it is to block God's almighty surge. The moralists discuss, suggest, counsel; the prophets proclaim, demand, insist.

To sum up, the image of scales conveys the idea of form, standard, balance, measure, stillness. The image of a mighty stream expresses content, substance, power, movement, vitality.

Justice represented as a blindfolded virgin, while conveying the essential thought of the rightful caution of the mind against illusions and partiality of the heart, conceives of the process of justice as a mechanical process, as if the life of man were devoid of individuality and uniqueness and could be adequately understood in terms of inexorable generalizations. There is a point at which strict justice is unjust.

Immutable justice—the principle *fiat justitia, pereat mundus*—raises justice to a position of supremacy, denying to any other principle the power to temper it, regarding it as an absolute; the world exists for the sake of maintaining justice rather than justice for the sake of maintaining the world. Carried to the extreme, the principle sets up a false dichotomy of world and justice, betraying the truth that the survival of the world is itself a requirement of justice.[27]

---

[27] The maxim is said to have been the motto of Emperor Ferdinand I (1503-1564) (T. H. Harbottle, *Dictionary of Quotations* [London, 1906], p. 70). According to B. Stevenson (*The Home Book of Quotations* [New York, 1944], p. 1030), the maxim *fiat justitia et ruant coeli*

God's concern for justice grows out of His compassion for man. The prophets do not speak of a divine relationship to an absolute principle or idea, called justice. They are intoxicated with the awareness of God's relationship to His people and to all men.

Justice is not important for its own sake; the validity of justice and the motivation for its exercise lie in the blessings it brings to man. For justice, as stated above, is not an abstraction, a value. Justice exists in relation to a person, and is something done by a person. An act of injustice is condemned, not because the law is broken, but because a person has been hurt. What is the image of a person? A person is a being whose anguish may reach the heart of God. "You shall not afflict any widow or orphan. If you do afflict them, and they cry out to Me, I will surely hear their cry. . . . if he cries to Me, I will hear, for I am compassionate" (Exod. 22:22-23, 27).

When Cain murdered his brother Abel, the words denouncing his crime did not proclaim: "You have broken the law." Instead we read: "And . . . the Lord said: What have you done? The voice of your brother's blood is crying to Me from the ground" (Gen. 4:10).

AUTONOMY OF THE MORAL LAW

For all the centrality of ethos in the prophetic understanding of God, it is incorrect to say, as is often done, that "justice to the Israelitish mind was such an indispensable thing in the universe that it sometimes seems to stand out as some irresistible power independent even of God, as something which God Himself needs obey."[28]

In an effort to prove the similarity of Judaism and Kantian ethics, it was often maintained that, according to Judaism, "the moral law is autonomous

(let justice be done, though the heavens fall), was used for the first time in English literature by William Watson in 1601. (See also Büchmann, Geflügelte Worte [27th ed.; Berlin, 1925], p. 527.) The origin of the maxim is obscure. G. Del Vecchio in his Justice (p. 175), quoting the opinion by Salvatorelli and Hühn (La Biblia [Milan, 1915], p. 151) that it goes back to the prophets, assumes that the substance if not the letter of the maxim is derived from the Hebrew Bible. G. F. Moore (Judaism in the First Centuries of the Christian Era, II, 196), cites the maxim as a parallel to the statement by Rabbi Eliezer, son of Rabbi Jose the Galilean of the second century, that it is forbidden to arbitrate in a settlement. "But let the law pierce the mountain (let the law take its course). And so Moses' motto was: Let the law pierce the mountain. Aaron, however [loved peace and pursued peace and] made peace between man and man" (Tosefta, Sanhedrin I, 3; the words in parenthesis, Bab. Sanhedrin, 6b; see also Yebamoth, 92a). There is some difference, however, between a mountain to be pierced and the world to be destroyed. God, not justice, is alone ultimate, and His rule follows mercy as well as justice. Akiba's principle, "No pity is to be shown in a matter of law" (Mishnah Kethuboth, IX, 2) merely implies that pity must not enter the judicial process; it follows Exodus 23:3 ("nor shall you be partial to a poor man in his suit") and Leviticus 19:15. Hegel rephrased the maxim into the very different fiat justitia ne pereat mundus.
28 M. Lazarus, The Ethics of Judaism, I (Philadelphia, 1900-1901), 135-36.

because it originates in the nature of the human mind alone. . . . That autonomy implies the absence of every extraneous will in the creation of morality, every external power. . . . This exalted purity and this dignity of the moral are independent of every sort of theistic notion, because they spring from the very nature of the human mind." "Ethical holiness may be thought of detached from religious holiness. It has value and dignity of its own, without reference to God, the ordainer of morality; that is, the moral idea has an existence independent of the recognition that it is actualized in God."[29]

The prophets did not conceive of the ethos as an autonomous idea, as a sovereign essence, higher in the scale of reality than God Himself, standing above him like a supreme force. God to them was more than a moral principle or a moral exemplar.

The central achievement of biblical religion was to remove the veil of anonymity from the workings of history. There are no ultimate laws, no eternal ideas. The Lord alone is ultimate and eternal. The laws are His creation, and the moral ideas are not entities apart from Him; they are His concern. Indeed, the personalization of the moral idea is the indispensable assumption of prophetic theology. Mercy, grace, repentance, forgiveness, all would be impossible if the moral principle were held to be superior to God. God's call to man, which resounds so frequently in the utterances of the prophets, presupposes an ethos based, not upon immutable principles, but rather upon His eternal concern. God's repenting a decision which was based on moral grounds clearly shows the supremacy of pathos.

Crime is not a violation of a law, but a sin against the living God. "Against Thee, Thee only have I sinned, and done that which is evil in Thy sight," confesses the psalmist (51:6). "If Thou, O Lord, shouldst mark iniquities, who could stand?" (Ps. 132:3.)

To identify God with the moral idea would be contrary to the very meaning of prophetic theology. God is not the mere guardian of the moral order. He is not an intermediary between a transcendental idea of the good and man. The prophet does not think of Him as a being whose function it is to supervise the moral order and to bring about the realization of an autonomous morality. As love cannot be identified with the values found in it, so the relation between God and man cannot be simply equated with the value of the moral idea. The pathos structure of divine ethos follows from the unlimited sovereignty of God. If the moral law were something absolute and final, it would represent a destiny to which God Himself would be

---

[29] *Ibid.*, II, 13.

subject. Far from being sovereign, God would then fall into dependence on rigid, objective norms.

THE PRIMACY OF GOD'S INVOLVEMENT IN HISTORY

For a long time the importance of the prophets was seen to lie in the fact that they raised the religion of cult to a religion of morality.[30] Ethical monotheism was "their contribution to the spiritual growth of their race."[31] The religion introduced by the prophets was a sort of protestantism, directed against all sorts of "paganism" and ritualism, with the main emphasis placed upon faith. The image of the prophets was that of preachers of morals and spiritual religion as opposed to ceremonialism and ritual. This view has now been questioned. "The prophets have been isolated in too high a degree, and made makers of ideas which in reality were common Israelite stock, and modern scholars have in a one-sided way stressed certain ideas of the prophets which acquired importance for posterity, and to which there might be found a special connection in the nineteenth century."[32]

Ethical monotheism must not be regarded as the contribution of the classical prophets,[33] since it was known in Israel long before the time of Amos. Nor is "the primacy of morality" to be regarded as the chief characteristic of prophetic thought.

Divine ethos does not operate without pathos. Any thought of an objectivity, or a Platonic self-subsistence of ideas, be it the idea of beauty or of justice is alien to the prophets. God is all-personal, all-subject. His ethos and pathos are one.

The preoccupation with justice, the passion with which the prophets condemn injustice, is rooted in their sympathy with divine pathos. The chief characteristic of prophetic thought is the primacy of God's involvement in history. History is the domain with which the prophets' minds are

---

[30] G. Hölscher, *Die Profeten* (Leipzig, 1914), p. 188.

[31] A. Kuenen, *The Prophets and Prophecy in Israel* (London, 1877), p. 589.

[32] See J. Pedersen, "The Role Played by Inspired Persons among the Israelites and the Arabs," in H. H. Rowley, ed., *Studies in Old Testament Prophecy* (Edinburgh, 1950), pp. 127 ff.; "*Die Auffassung vom Alten Testament,*" *ZAW*, XLIX (1931), 161 ff.

[33] This view, based upon the theory that the early popular religion of Israel was polytheistic or monolatristic and that only under the influence of the literary prophets was monotheism established, has been challenged by scholars. If the term "monotheist means one who teaches the existence of only one God, the creator of everything, the source of justice, who is equally powerful in Egypt, in the desert, and in Palestine, who has no sexuality and no mythology," then Moses was a monotheist. (Cf. W. F. Albright, *From the Stone Age to Christianity* [Baltimore, 1940], p. 207). See also Y. Kaufmann, *The Religion of Israel* (Eng.; Chicago, 1960), pp. 221 f. On the much debated controversy whether monotheism goes back to Moses or to the prophets, see B. Balscheit, *Alter und Aufkommen des Monotheismus in der Israelitischen Religion* (Berlin, 1938).

occupied. They are moved by a responsibility for society, by a sensitivity to what the moment demands.

Since the prophets do not speak in the name of the moral law, it is inaccurate to characterize them as proclaimers of justice, or *mishpat*. It is more accurate to see them as proclaimers of God's pathos, speaking not for the idea of justice, but for the God of justice, for God's concern for justice. Divine concern remembered in sympathy is the stuff of which prophecy is made.

To the biblical mind the implication of goodness is mercy. Pathos, concern for the world, is the very ethos of God. This ethical sensitivity of God —not the ethical in and for itself—is reflected in the prophets' declarations. Prophetic morality rests upon both a divine command and a divine concern. Its ultimate appeal is not to the reasonableness of the moral law, but to the fact that God has demanded it and that its fulfillment is a realization of His concern.

INTIMATE RELATEDNESS

Is the prophetic message to be reduced to a simple, plausible prescription: *Do ut des*, "I give so that thou mayest give"? Be moral, and I shall make you happy, says the Lord.

What the prophets proclaim is God's intimate relatedness to man. It is this fact that puts all of life in a divine perspective, in which the rights of man become, as it were, divine prerogatives. Man stands under God's concern.

It is a thought staggering and hardly compatible with any rational approach to the understanding of God, that the Creator of heaven and earth should care about how an obscure individual man behaves toward poor widows and orphans. And if God is so powerful, and this concern so profound, why do the wicked prosper? (Cf. Jer. 12:1.)

Pathos is, indeed, *righteousness wrapped in mystery, togetherness in holy otherness*. Is the word of God irrational? But by what reason do we measure the word of God? By the reason expressed in our thoughts. But do we always understand our own thoughts? Can we always express what we mean? This, then, is our plight: What is most rational to the prophets seems irrational to us.

That incompatibility, however, is not ultimate. The goal is to establish compatibility, to refute idolatry and presumption that separate and antagonize man from what is supremely meaningful; to destroy illusions and to inspire realism.

God rules the world by justice and compassion, or love. These two ways are not divergent, but rather complementary, for it is out of compassion that justice is administered. But again and again His compassion, or love, is manifested in the world. Cain, slaying his brother, does not receive the punishment he deserves. Though justice would require that Abel's blood be avenged, Cain is granted divine pardon and protection.[34]

A father is disqualified to serve as a judge. Yet the judge of all men is also their Father. He would be unjust to His own nature were He to act in justice without being compassionate.

---

[34] Noticing that Gen., ch. 1, has *elohim* for God, not the Ineffable Name, while in ch. 2 both the Ineffable Name, the Tetragrammaton, and *elohim* occur, the rabbis remarked that in creating our world, God first intended to rule it according to the principle of strict justice (*middath ha-din*), but He realized that the world could not thus endure, so He associated mercy (*middath ha-rahamim*) with justice and made them to rule jointly. *Elohim* signifies strict justice; the Ineffable Name stands for mercy. It is maintained that when God acts according to mercy, the Ineffable Name is used, while *elohim* is used to signify His acting according to strict justice. Mercy has precedence over justice. Both justice and mercy as the main attributes of God's relation to man afford an insight into the polarity of God's dominion. Justice is a standard, mercy an attitude; justice is detachment, mercy attachment; justice is objective, mercy personal. God transcends both justice and mercy. See "*Yalkut Talmud Torah*" in J. Mann, *The Bible as Read and Preached in the Old Synagogue* (Heb.; Cincinnati, 1940), p. 271; Rashi, *Commentary* on Gen. 1:1; *Genesis Rabba*, 12, 15.

INDEX OF PASSAGES

I. HEBREW BIBLE

III. RABBINICAL WRITINGS

INDEX OF SUBJECTS AND NAMES